THE LITTLE RED READER

Notes of a Recovery Journey

Anonymous

Published by Toodle-Loo Productions

Copyright ©2020

FOREWORD

The way forward can sometime seem uncertain, even treacherous; and yet, with the help of others who truly care, I make progress; 'sometimes quickly, sometimes slowly'. The words and suggested thoughts of this daily reader are meant to be a reminder that there is, in fact, a way out of all the trouble. Take what you like and leave the rest.

The words of this reader hopefully represent the collective experience of many thousands, even millions, who have gone before; blazing the trail of recovery, beginning with Bill W, Dr. Bob, Lois W, and Tony A, right on down to the newcomer who attended their very first meeting today.
The journey of trudging <u>'the road of happy destiny'</u> continues.

'We arrive thus at a *morality of evolution*, in which the criterion for what we cultivate lies in the question: is a particular attitude or drive inducive or obstructive to my human growth? Self-knowledge, then, is *not* an aim in itself, but a means of liberating the forces of spontaneous growth.'

Karen Horney

'Indeed, mere intellectual insight is *not* sufficient; the therapeutically effective insight is *experiential* insight in which knowledge of oneself has not only an intellectual but also an affective quality. Such experiential insight itself depends on the strength of man's inherent striving for health and happiness.'

Eric Fromm

THE TOPICS
January

SUPPORTING MY SELF
STAYING IN TODAY
BEING PRESENT FOR MYSELF
SEEKING GUIDANCE
BECOMING AUTONOMOUS
PROJECTING GOOD OUTCOMES
REMAINING CENTERED
RETURNING TO SANITY
RESCUING, CARE-TAKING AND FIXING
TRUSTING THE PROCESS
FEELING SAFE
BEING RESPONSIBLE
TAKING STEP THREE
LOVING MYSELF
FOCUSING ON MYSELF
AWAKENING TO MY CORE SELF
PROCESSING EMOTIONS
CONTINUING THE JOURNEY
RESPONDING TO LIFE
ALLOWING TRANSFORMATION
CARING FOR SELF
ALLOWING OTHERS TO BE
BECOMING MYSELF
TAPPING INTO LOVE
KEEPING THE DOOR OPEN
KNOWING THE RIGHT TIME
CONTRIBUTING TO MY OWN WELL-BEING
SEEKING APPROVAL
EXPRESSING MY SELF
PRACTICING LOVE
BEING ONE'S SELF

February

ACTING FROM MY BASE
PRACTICNG RECOVERY
FACING MY TRUTH
ASKING FOR HELP
ADMITTING MY UNREALISTIC DEMANDS
ESTABLISHING BOUNDARIES
REMAINING OBJECTIVE
APPLYING STEP ELEVEN
IDENTIFYING OLD IDEAS
DECONSTRUCTING THE OLD BELIEF SYSTEM
LETTING GO OF OLD DEMANDS
MOVING TOWARD RECOVERY
TAKING THE NECESSARY STEPS
ACCEPTING MISTAKES
TAKING AN INVENTORY
SAYING NO TO UNSAFE PEOPLE
CONSIDERING THE STEPS
ASKING FOR WHAT I NEED
TAKING ACTION
LEARNING TO LAUGH
RECOVERING FROM BAD RELATIONSHIPS
FORGIVING
USING ADVERSITY TO GROW
GIVING BACK
MINDING MY OWN BUSINESS
RETURNING TO MY GENUINE SELF
PRACTICING THE "THREE R's"
TURNING TO SAFE PEOPLE
MAKING CHANGES

March

SIFTING THROUGH THE RUBBLE
ACCESSING RESOURCES
ALLOWING OTHERS THEIR JOURNEY
LISTENING TO OTHERS
RETURNING AND REST
BEGINNING ANEW
DEALING WITH LOSS
FEELING MY FEELINGS
SEARCHING FOR MYSELF
ENCOUNTERING EMOTIONS
ENJOYING CERTAIN MOMENTS
BECOMING SPONTANEOUS
TAKING STEP SIX
TAKING STEP SEVEN
BELONGING
GIVING VOICE TO MY THOUGHTS
PRIORITYZING EVENTS
CHOOSING MY REPONSE
EXPLORING MY PAST
LOOKING AT MY OLD IDEAS
LEARNING FROM MY MISTAKES
FAITHING MY WAY THROUGH
UTILYZING RECOVERY LITERATURE
KNOWING MY LIMITATIONS
CLEARING MY MIND
CHALLENGING MY PERCEPTION
PARTICIPATING IN MY OWN LIFE
RECOGNIZING MY OWN PROGRESS
TRUSTING A GREATER FORCE
RETURNING TO MY TRUE SELF
DEALING WITH ADVERSE FEELINGS

April

ACCEPTING OTHERS' BEHAVIOR
GIVING MYSELF A BREAK
PRACTICING THE PROGRAM
SENSING MY OWN VALUE
SOLVING PROBLEMS
BEING NICER TO MYSELF
KEEPING THE FOCUS ON MYSELF
TAKING RESPONSIBILITY FOR MY WELL BEING
CONSIDERING MY OPTIONS
HOPING FOR A MIRACLE
DETACHING WITH LOVE
CREATING A SAFE PLACE
BEING AWAKE
FEELING THE FEELINGS
ACCEPTING THE DISEASE CONCEPT
BEING FREE
DEALING WITH OLD WOUNDS
CONNECTING WITH MY GENUINE SELF
EXAGGERATING OLD DEMANDS
ATTENDING MEETINGS
SOLVING PROBLEMS
RESPECTING MYSELF AND OTHERS
PUSHING BACK ON OLD IDEAS
DEALING WITH COMPLICATIONS
LEARNING TO APPRECIATE MYSELF
BEING PART OF A GROUP
ABANDONING THE FALSE SELF
ADJUSTING MY EXPECTATIONS
CONFIDING IN SAFE PEOPLE
TOLERATING OTHERS

May

SEARCHING FOR EMOTION
ALLOWING MY EMOTIONS
KNOWING THE PLAY
ACTING WITH CONFIDENCE
TAKING WHAT I LIKE, LEAVING THE REST
CARING FOR MY TRUE SELF
SHARING AT MEETINGS
LOOKING AT MISTAKES
FACING A PROBLEM
CHANGING MY THINKING
FINDING SOLUTIONS
FEELING MY FEELINGS
RECOVERING MY TRUE SELF
BECOMING TEACHABLE
TAKING STEP FIVE
ACCEPTING THE DISEASE CONCEPT
ALLOWING REALITY TO BE MY FRIEND
LEARNING TO LIKE MYSELF
TAKING WHAT I LIKE, LEAVING THE REST
LEARNING TO ENJOY MY OWN COMPANY
LISTENING TO THE WORLD AROUND ME
ACTING WITH CONFIDENCE
ABSORBING THE PROGRAM
CREATING A SAFE PLACE
NURTURING ONE ANOTHER
LIVING THE DREAM
FIGHTING FAIR
STAYING IN PROCESS
EXERCISING THE POWER OF CHOICE
REQUESTING SUPPORT
OVERCOMING THE EFFECTS OF THIS DISEASE

June

TAKING RESPONSIBILITY
SEEKING GOD'S WILL
BEING HONEST
WELCOMING NEW IDEAS
ENJOYING LIFE
LETTING GO OF BEING THE VICTIM
GOING WITH THE FLOW
BEING HUMAN
FACING CHALLENGES IN RECOVERY
READING THE SIGNS
WEATHERING A CRISIS
JUSTIFYING MYSELF TO NO ONE
TAKING STEP TWO
TRUSTING OTHERS
OWNING MY BEHAVIOR
MAKING DECISIONS
TREATING OTHERS WITH RESPECT
REMAINING TEACHABLE
MAKING A LIST
TAKING STEP NINE
TAKING STEP TEN
TAKING STEP ELEVEN
SHARING MY EXPERIENCE
VENTING MY ANGER
KNOWING HOW TO HELP
CREATING NEW VALUES
WANTING WHAT I HAVE
RELATING TO HEALTHY PEOPLE
REMAINING CONSCIOUS
PRACTICING MEDITATION

July

STAYING FOCUSSED ON MY PROCESS
CULTIVATING SPIRITUAL GROWTH
CREATING NEW IDEAS
FREEING MYSELF OF DYSFUNCTIONAL BEHAVIOR
FORGIVING
CARRYING THE MESSAGE
RE-SETTING MY IDENTITY
ASSESSING OLD STRATEGIES
PRAYING
FEELING GOOD ABOUT MYSELF
MANAGING MY LIFE
HONORING THE JOURNEY
REMEMBERING THE PRIMARY PURPOSE
OWNING MY FREEDOM
BEING PRODUCTIVE
DEALING WITH INNER CONFLICT
EMBRACING THE PRESENT MOMENT
ANCHORING MYSELF
SORTING OUT THE TRUTH
RESPONDING TO EMOTION
CARING ABOUT OTHERS
CHOOSING MY OWN VALUES
PUTTING VALUES INTO ACTION
LENDING AN EAR
LEARNING TO RELAX
BUILDING A LIFE
TRUSTING THE RECOVERY JOURNEY
SETTING BOUNDARIES
EMBRACING CHANGE
ALLOWING LIFE TO UNFOLD
READYING MYSELF TO LEARN

August

RELEASING THE VICTIM STORY
UNDERSTANDING GOD
SAYING 'NO'
IDENTIFYING ILLUSION
SUPPORTING OTHERS
CONTINUING THE RECOVERY PROCESS
FEELING THE FREEDOM
HONORING MYSELF
TAKING THE DAY IN STAGES
RE-ESTABLISHING MY TRUE SELF
CHOOSING MY PATH
FACING THE PAST
RECOGNIZING MY REAL SELF
USING MY IMAGINATION
LOWERING MY UNREALISTIC DEMANDS
GROWING THROUGH DIFFICULT TIMES
MOVING TOWARD CHANGE
ACCEPTING OTHERS
CREATING RELATIONSHIP
CREATING DEEPER RELATIONSHIP
GRIEVING THE LOSS
RELYING ON THE PROGRAM
TRUSTING OTHERS WHO HAVE GONE BEFORE
WEIGHING MY OPTIONS
KNOWING THE DIFFERENCE
TAKING CARE OF THE BASICS
ACKNOWLEDGING MY OWN GROWTH
STAYING THE COURSE
TRUSTING THE TRUSTWORTHY
SUPPORTING MY SELF
SEARCHING FOR THE REAL ME

September

COMING TO BELIEVE
MOVING BEYOND THE 'MISTAKES'
EXPRESSING RAGE
APPRECIATING A FULL RANGE OF EMOTION
BREAKING DENIAL
ALLOWING GOD TO BE GOD
CRYING
RELINQUISHING THE BURDEN OF BLAME AND SHAME
BEING REAL
WANTING WHAT I HAVE
ATTENDING GROUP CONSCIENCE MEETINGS
GRIEVING
ACTING IN THE MOMENT
QUIETING THE MENTAL CHITTER CHATTER
CELEBRATIING MY REAL SELF
TALKING ABOUT WHAT MATTERS
ALLOWING FAILURE
TRUSTING OTHERS
GIVING VOICE TO MY CONCERNS
STEPPING AWAY
SURVIVING THE TERROR
DECIDING HOW TO RESPOND
STARTING FRESH
HOPING AGAIN
KNOWING MY LIMITATIONS
VISUALIZING THE NOW
CREATING MY OWN MORAL SYSTEM (part one)
CREATING MY OWN MORAL SYSTEM (part two)
LETTING GO OF DEMANDS

October

WALKING IN THE DARK
MAINTAINING A REASONABLY SAFE WORLD
TREATING OTHERS WITH RESPECT
GETTING OFF 'THE STORY'
BECOMING SPONTANEOUS
SORTING OUT EMOTIONS
RECOGNIZING RESOURCES
HAVING MY OWN PERCEPTION
DEALING WITH SEXUAL AND PHYSICAL ABUSE
DEALING WITH VERBAL ABUSE
BLASTING OFF
STRENGTHENING MY OWN RECOVERY SYSTEM
RECOGNIZING TWELFTH STEP OPPORTUNITIES
REMEMBERING MY PRIMARY PURPOSE
DISCOVERING NEW INTERESTS
GIVING MY SELF PERMISSION
WAITING FOR THE RIGHT TIME
CREATING SUPPORTIVE SETTINGS
LETTING DOWN MY GUARD
CREATING OPPORTUNITY
BREAKING FREE OF THE LIE
LIVING WITH THIS DISEASE
CALLING SOMEONE
CONTINUING TO TAKE A PERSONAL INVENTORY
STAYING IN FOCUS
NURTURING MYSELF
BELIEVING IN THE GROUP
HEALING IN THE LONG-TERM
MAINTAINING MY BALANCE
RE-ESTABLISHING MY SENSE OF CURIOSITY
HOLDING A CONVERSATION

November

BEING TRANSPARENT
MOVING BEYOND DOUBT
HEALING ORGANICALLY
MOVING BEYOND THE DISTRACTIONS
OWNING THE COLLATERAL DAMAGE
SAYING GOODBYE TO SELF DESTRUCTION
LEARNING FROM LIFE'S INTERACTIONS
PAYING ATTENTION TO MY INTUITIVE SELF
REUJUVINATING MY SOUL
STAYING WITH MY EMOTIONS
CHANGING OBSESSIVE THOUGHTS
RECEIVING THE ANSWER (part one)
RECEIVING THE ANSWER (part two)
MAINTAINING OPTIONS
TAKING THE ACTION; LETTING GO OF THE RESULTS
BECOMING MORE REALISTIC
RESPECTING THE DISEASE
CREATING HEALTHY BELIEFS
COLLECTING MY SUCCESSES
MAKING MY NEEDS KNOWN
BELIEVING IN 'MY WAY'
RENEWING MY INNER STRENGTH
GETTING THROUGH THE HOLIDAYS
KEEPING IT SIMPLE (part one)
KEEPING IT SIMPLE (part two)
FINDING NEW FRIENDS
TRUSTING THE TRUSTWORTHY
LOVING OTHERS
BEING LOVED
EMBRACING MY LOST SELF

December

REALIZING STEPS SIX AND SEVEN
KEEPING MY DREAMS ALIVE
RETAINING MY CAPACITY TO PROMISE
SITTING WITH MY CURIOUS SELF
SPOTTING 'IT'
LIVING LIFE FROM THE INSIDE OUT
RETURNING TO MY DEEP SOURCE (part one)
RETURNING TO MY DEEP SOURCE (part two)
OPENING MY MIND TO NEW BEGINNINGS
TRUTSTING A HIGHER FULFILLMENT
GROWING
NURTURING MY EMOTIONAL LIFE
BEING HAPPY
STAYING IN 'MY LANE'
ENGAGING MY OWN AUTONOMY
RELYING ON GOD
BATTLING FOR HIGHER GROUND
EXPERIENCING PLEASURE
LEARNING TO LOVE AGAIN
MEETING NEW OPPORTUNITIES FEARLESSLY
AWAKENING TO A LIFE BEYOND PLEASURE
DIGGING OUT
LETTING IT SNOW
RELEASING THE STRESS
TIDINGS OF COMFORT
REVIEWING ALL THE OPTIONS
CHOOSING MY CHOICES
VALIDATING THE AUTONOMY OF MYSELF AND OTHERS
TAKING IN THE BIG PICTURE
CHANGING LOCATION
GOING PLACES

JANUARY

January 1
SUPPORTING MY SELF

I spent a lot of time concentrating on the needs of others, especially the ones with most of the power. *My survival depended on how well I could read a situation, adjust accordingly and maintain my loyalty.*

I lost myself in the process. I overlooked my own needs in exchange for keeping others satisfied.

I showed up in recovery with few skills in supporting my genuine self. *In fact, my self-abuse had taken a variety of forms:* shutting down emotionally, eating to excess, drinking too much, inflicting inner verbal self-hate, withdrawing from others, working too much, spending too much time with toxic people, rescuing unavailable people and on and on and on.

I am attempting to feel my feelings. *<u>I am giving my genuine self plenty of time to emerge.</u>* Sometimes I can stay with my emotions longer than a few seconds.

Sometimes I can talk to a trusted friend who is available;
someone who can listen without fixing me;
someone who can respect my struggle for what it is:
my struggle.

My welfare takes priority. **MY interests** *come first.*

I act on behalf of myself. If something doesn't feel right, I leave it alone;
I go no further.

I can wait until I feel OK with what I am about to do.

I am awake to new approaches in self-care;
new approaches in being true to my genuine needs.

January 2
STAYING IN TODAY

Without really knowing it, I had developed a strategy to deal with my family dysfunction. This phantom strategy required an unending review and assessment of past events.

Upon determining that I had somehow failed to meet the expectations of myself and others, *__the logic proceeded that I would perform better next time in order to get my needs met.__*

This exercise proved to be the great obsession around which I would build most of my moral structure. Rather than engaging with my world spontaneously, I was constricted to a world of fear; the fear of being rejected over past and possible future offenses.

__I believed what I had to believe and did what I had to do in order to survive.__ The subtle requirement for 'peace of mind' was to perform perfectly all the time; a pretty tall order for a six-year-old.

I can still get easily distracted by allowing myself unscheduled trips to the past and the future. *I can reflect and I can plan, but morbid journeys into the __'should haves'__ of yesterday or the __'what ifs'__ of tomorrow no longer serve my best interest.* Yesterday is a canceled check. Tomorrow is a promissory note. Today is cash; I spend it wisely.

I remain present for myself. I linger in the moment. *__I stay awake to my thoughts and feelings.__* I act on taking good care of myself as best I can, *today*. I might go to a meeting. I might call someone I trust. I might enjoy the first sip of a fresh brewed cup of my favorite tea.
I might take a nap. I might pray. I might play tennis.

I am attentive to my own process.

I am alive.

January 3
BEING PRESENT FOR MYSELF

For years, I had abandoned myself in the false hope of becoming 'more than enough' to whomever I was connected; thus, always being assured of another's love and approval.

<u>When my efforts failed, I told myself that I needed no one.</u>
On occasion, I would withdraw entirely.

This kind of thinking; this morbid dependence set me up time and time again for disappointment, as people could sometimes love and support me; sometimes they couldn't. *I suffered from 'attention deficit disorder'. I needed attention and when there was a deficit, I felt disordered.*

I am easily triggered when it comes to feelings associated with abandonment or rejection. *Reviewing the old ideas which drive my thinking in the Fourth and Fifth Step, I am discovering new ways in which I can appreciate and love myself.*

Sometimes it's as simple as being awake to how I feel or knowing what I really want to do on a free day; and then doing it.

When I connect with my core self and act on how I truly think and feel, I usually stay in a pretty good frame of mind. *<u>I remain present for myself.</u>* Problematic disappointments of relationships don't seem as large.
I am learning how to stand alone.

No longer totally dependent on the approval of a few, I am free to be myself in the presence of many.

January 4
SEEKING GUIDANCE

When asking for help from others, I felt extremely apprehensive. Could they help, would they help? ***Many of my ideas regarding 'help' had been formed on experiences with people who were unavailable and sometimes toxic.*** For the most part, I had built a solid wall around myself by the time I found recovery. I felt closed off.

If asking for help meant going to God, I often took a pass. Who was God anyway? Did He even exist? Where was God when my father was kicking down our front door; threatening my mother with violence? Was He a 'she' or was She a 'he'? Or was It simply an 'it'? ***And why would an 'almighty' God concern himself with MY little problems?*** Peering at the stars, I would sometimes feel terrified at the vastness of a black abyss. At the end of the day, I felt separated and all alone.

I understand the Second Step to suggest that there can be a solid hope re-established in trusting a power greater than myself; a power, at the very least, represented by my home group.

Allowing genuine support from others is a great relief, as I find my way along the road to recovery. I am not alone in my mission to reconnect with my abandoned self.

There is a solid confidence growing. Meetings are available on a regular basis. ***I can express how I think and feel without the fear of being dismissed or discounted.*** I can take what I like and leave the rest as others share of their personal adventures on this journey.

I am keeping an open mind to what this 'higher power' could potentially mean. I grow stronger each day as 'I trudge the road of happy destiny.'

Now. Let me see. Where ***DID*** I put those hiking boots?

January 5
BECOMING AUTONOMOUS

The concept of being true to myself seemed strange. ***In fact, the idea of taking responsibility for myself and allowing others the same courtesy seemed wrong.*** Rescuing, fixing and caretaking had become a non-productive habit. My identity depended on it.

Furthermore, trying to control life had become a full-time distraction; a distraction that rarely left any time to relax. ***I berated myself when I failed to live up to my demands and expectations.*** I needed others to see me in a certain way. I acted as though my life depended on it.
The tyrant of 'perfection' barked its orders.

Today, I am moving toward my individuality by uncovering who I truly am in the Fourth and Fifth Step, eventually to discard who I am *not* in Steps Six and Seven. I am putting my needs first.

Sometimes I can help a situation; sometimes I can't; that's OK. ***I no longer desperately need 'others' approval.*** The phantom spectator in my head that judges my every move is being dismissed.

I am returning to a place where it is OK to simply be who I am. I am giving others total permission to be who they are, as well. My ongoing thoughts, feelings and actions are merely the moving parts of a larger process;
the process of 'becoming'. ***And I don't have to control the process.***
I hear the whispered words of wisdom…

Let it be, let it be, let it be, let it be
There will be an answer, let it be.

January 6
PROJECTING GOOD OUTCOMES

I spent a lot of time thinking about what could go wrong in the future, sometimes keeping myself paralyzed emotionally due to anxiety. *I disconnected most of the time from what I genuinely wanted.* I was laser-focused on gaining the approval of others.

This strategy seemed to assure my belonging in the family or the group. The reasoning was simple: If I am not rejected, I will survive.

Having taken the Fourth and Fifth Steps, I am moving toward my true self today. *I know, more and more, what I want; what is healthy for ME.* I am relying on a power greater than myself to provide what I need. No longer exclusively dependent on a few, I am free to explore my core self.

I am learning with each new endeavor to embrace the process of Steps Six and Seven. *I have become entirely ready to have all the elements of my 'black and white' thinking removed.* I do not demand perfection of myself or anyone else. I accept that I live in a limited world. Sometimes I get the outcome I hope for; sometimes I don't. That's OK. Taking risks is OK.

One thing I can be assured of: I always get the *experience* that goes with asserting myself; and in the immortal words of Edison, <u>*experience is everything*</u>.

As I approach Step Eleven, I project healthy living conditions in meditation. I imagine doing what I truly want to do in order to earn a living. I can creatively visualize what I *really* wish for instead of trying to conform to something I think I should always be.

The clearer I can be with myself, the more likely I can recognize God's providing exactly what I need, when I need it.

As they used to say, "Perfect timing!"

January 7
REMAINING CENTERED

Having lost myself in order to survive a dysfunctional world, I rarely stayed in contact with my genuine feelings. **_Sometimes, I denied my emotions altogether._** I would distract myself with an assortment of behaviors in order to avoid intrusive feelings like anger, fear and resentment.
Some of these behaviors grew into addiction.

As a result of these distractions, **_I usually felt pulled in several directions._** I was scattered, often unable to maintain the minimal effort required to see something through from beginning to end. I would involve myself in too much activity, become overwhelmed and drop out entirely for a while.
I was unavailable to myself and others.

The rooms encourage my reconnecting with emotions. It is OK to feel! Wow. In fact, being able to tap into how I feel is an absolute essential part of knowing *and* being who I am.

Before I 'think' anything, I will usually feel something first.

It is my thinking, however, that precedes the 'conscious registering' of emotion. I blend these two aspects of my human condition. I remain awake.

By 'owning' my process of recovery, I can **_'sit with what is going on'_** longer; talk about it more in depth; stay with the feeling.

Sometimes resolution comes; sometimes it doesn't.
What matters is that I am staying focused on the journey; **_my journey_**.

I am, with God's help, **_remaining available to my genuine self_**.

I am present. I am sober.

January 8
RETURNING TO SANITY

I remember when new events in the environment would sometimes trigger old emotions. My 'not- enough' story was reinforced. I felt embarrassed and humiliated. *My dysfunctional old ideas with their unique demands on myself and others would careen out of control, unchecked.*

I should have done this; I'm no damn good! They should have done that. What the hell were they thinking?!

My reactions often set up *even more events* that would further weave a tangled web of confusion and damage; and on and on it would go. At one point, there was no turning back. Without really knowing it, I was stuck with the 'story'. *My identity demanded that I maintain certain conditions in order to advance my victim narrative.* The sad truth? I *WAS* a victim.

Today, having reviewed my old ideas and demands, I can check my emotional reactions most of the time. *I am no longer a pawn tossed about as the hapless victim on a sea of unconscious pain and hurt.* I can 'push back' with my thinking when triggered. I make choices that benefit me. I act in my own best interest.

I am letting go of the demands on how I should always perform. Sometimes I can perform as I should; sometimes I can't.
I am lowering my expectations on others.

Sometimes others can perform as I think they should; sometimes they can't. This realistic approach to the human condition is paving the way to my being restored to sanity.

I am meeting life on life's terms.

January 9
RESCUING, CARE-TAKING AND FIXING

I developed a fine art of helping in order to survive the conditions of my dysfunctional family. Whether I took charge of a situation or merely assisted 'off-stage', I fixed situations. Naturally, or so it seemed,
I believed that I had a moral responsibility to help others.
I demanded it.

The old idea seemed to go something like this: *I should always be able to ensure a good outcome for the sake of those who are counting on me.* Sometimes that meant giving great advice, putting people in their place, going the extra mile, taking up the slack, pitching in to help,
and sacrificing for the good of the team.

I still believe that I can help others and yet, I understand that each person I meet, family included, is on their *own* journey. *I allow others their own experience in learning what they are to learn on the road to becoming who they are.* I avoid meddling. I am content with keeping the focus on myself.

I can give the greatest gift one human being can provide another:
I can carefully *listen*.

I can respect another's struggle by being available, by being present.

I can honor their capacity to come up with their own solutions.
I don't have to tell them what they should do.

I can detach with love.

January 10
TRUSTING THE PROCESS

I could hardly trust the process in the early days of recovery. *I had spent a lifetime avoiding my process and why not?* After all, my best effort had led me to the admission that my world was not working; that my life, emotionally and otherwise, had become unmanageable.

I discover that trust takes time.
I need to confirm to my inner most being that the meetings are safe;
that the meetings for the most part are absent of chaos;
that I can talk about my stuff without being shut down;
that the meetings are predictably available;
that the meetings respect my anonymity.

I rely on the permanence of the meetings. I am beginning to develop friendships with others; people who are, for the most part *safe, available and supportive*. I grow more and more comfortable with turning a deaf ear to my old neurotic self, my false critical self.

My real self, my true supportive self, embarks on a new journey;
the journey of discovery in the Fourth and Fifth Step.

Each time I show up at a meeting, I am moving toward recovery. Each time I listen to another's telling of their experience, strength and hope,
I am making progress. Each time I feel my feelings,
I am growing in leaps and bounds.

'*Now faith is the substance of things hoped for, the evidence of things unseen.*'

Although I cannot always see my progress, *I am coming to trust my process;* the process of recovery.

January 11
FEELING SAFE

I was a person who rarely allowed others into my inner world. I even kept *myself* out of my inner world, shutting down unwanted emotions, endlessly distracting myself. *I had, in fact, created a false self that was highly critical not only of myself, but of those around me, as well.*

I was anxious most of the time, always on; always afraid.
There seemed to be no place to hide.

In many ways, I hated myself for not being able to perform as well as I thought I should. I felt isolated from others.

Today, I know that I am first and foremost, a human *being*; not a human doing. *Sometimes I get the recipe just right; sometimes I don't. It's OK.*
I am not going to get kicked off the planet for making a mistake.
I am part of a bigger picture called the 'human race'.
And I belong here.

My safety comes first. I begin by turning down the volume in *my own head* around the unrelenting "shoulds" from the past. I no longer 'beat myself up'. *To those who would continue their clamoring for a perfect performance, I can say, "Mind your own process."*

Keeping myself safe, *inside and out*, is my number one priority.

January 12
BEING RESPONSIBLE

Before I found the rooms of recovery, **_I was entirely disconnected from my genuine interests._** Whether events concerned myself or others, I was mostly on autopilot, ricocheting from one crisis to another. I was driven, trying to live up to my old survival demands; checked out emotionally and unavailable to those closest to me.

Thanks to the Steps, I am connected now. I respond to my genuine self in such a way that I keep my best interests in mind. I take time to further know myself through practicing Steps Ten and Eleven.

I truly care for my own well-being and I act accordingly.
I *know* what interests me *most* of the time.

I listen to friends and family tell their stories. I appreciate their sovereign journey through old and new conflicts. I care about their history. I can *respond* to others because I take time to genuinely know them. Those with whom I freely *choose* to spend time are interesting to me.

WHAT I DON'T DO: rescue, caretake and fix. I allow others their own struggle out of respect; respect for their unique process in becoming who they are. I honor their autonomy.

I am first responsible FOR myself and TO myself. My choices to support others are thoughtful responses, not habitual reactions. Today, I act in a healthy way to meet my needs and the requests of others.

January 13
TAKING STEP THREE

I used to have fixed ideas about God. I had fixed ideas about certain religions associated with God. In short, I didn't really trust God.

Getting over the hump of Step Three was practically insurmountable. Early on, someone suggested that simply going to meetings on a regular basis represented a kind of practice of the first three steps.

For the hour duration of the meeting, I had admitted on some level that I had a problem (Step One); that perhaps the group had some solutions (Step Two); and that I could turn my will and life over to the care of the group at least for that one hour (Step Three). I liked the simplicity.

I didn't have to have my "as we understood Him" totally understood in order to take this step.

I came to believe that the Third Step could be a mere steppingstone to the next step, Step Four, where my old ideas *could be* reviewed; where my belief system *could be* re-evaluated considering my cultural history and personal events. **_By taking Step Three, I made a decision to move on; to take Step Four_**; to trust the rest of the process lest I get stuck in my grief.

The God I brought to the party is not the God I took home.

January 14
LOVING MYSELF

I didn't know it, but on a very deep level, I was riddled with self-hate. I had spent many years trying to live up to being what I thought I **had to be** in order to survive physically and emotionally. *I had become highly skilled at numbing down and shutting off my feelings lest I feel the grief of not being enough.*

When I fell short of my "shoulds", tyranny set it. Self-beratement was the order of the day. I would abuse myself with all kinds of distractions: food, sex, media, alcohol…relationships. In short, I felt ashamed of myself. *It seemed that I could never measure up to my unrelenting expectations.* There was no 'off' switch.

I am letting up on myself now. At the very least, *I am turning down the volume on the old tunes.* Some of the songs: 'Perfectly Yours, Perfectly Perfect, Perfection Always with Love, Perfectly Perfecting Perfection' and my all-time favorite, 'It's Hard to be Humble When Your Perfect in Every Way'.

Sometimes I perform as well as I think I should, *sometimes I don't.* And that is OK! *Minute by minute, I embrace the human in 'human being'.* When I endeavor to act according to my genuine thoughts and feelings (my true self), I am being productive, regardless of the fulfilment an anticipated 'outcome'. It is enough that I am acting as I am.
It is enough, that *I am*.

I move deeper into my own history of events; my own defining moments on this sovereign journey. Steps Four through Seven allow my *total* acceptance of all that I am in the big picture. *I move in unison with my complete self.* I embrace my true energy source; the real me.

I express who I am by whatever means possible. I celebrate my being in the world.

January 15
FOCUSING ON MYSELF

Other people's behavior caused me a lot of grief. After I hit the rooms, *I came to see that MY THINKING about other people's behavior caused me a lot of grief;* what they should always do, how they should always think. I set myself up for disappointment much of the time.

Except for catastrophic loss, if I am disturbed longer than an hour about a current event, the emotion is NOT exclusively about what just happened. *It's about my thinking related to past events that felt like what just happened.* When offenses come and I am triggered emotionally, I am ultimately responsible for the 'reset'.

I allow myself to stay awake to MY process. It is OK. I feel the feelings. I can be on my journey! *<u>I can allow others the dignity of their journey</u> without blaming them, resenting them or justifying my own abusive behavior toward them.* I am under no obligation to immediately 'forgive and forget' either.

I can negotiate the terms of a relationship going forward. I treat myself with respect.

The process by which I am becoming my true self often leads to events of the past re-enacted in the present; events laced with strong emotion. *When I overreact, I can always turn my attention the Tenth Step in order to isolate the old ideas that keep setting me up for trouble.* The lower my demands for myself and others, the greater my serenity.

A demand on another, simply put, is a premeditated resentment.

January 16
AWAKENING TO MY CORE SELF

I was covered up with 'shoulds' placed on myself and 'claims' placed on others. Demands so fierce, in fact, that I could not be my real self, hear my true voice, or feel my genuine emotions.

When I wasn't distracting myself with something or someone new, I usually felt alone, ashamed, embarrassed or humiliated.
I was never enough. They were never enough.
Or so it seemed.

I have inventoried my moral system. I have lowered the expectations attached to my beliefs. ***No longer tyrannized by the ideal of perfection foisted on myself and others, I am awakening to my genuine interests.*** The pressure is off. I am who I am.

I can hear new ideas and I am connecting with my core self. ***My emotional life has a greater variety of content.*** I am becoming more and more spontaneous; less and less rigid. I am free to move toward safe situations that awaken my true self even further.

I move beyond the emotional and physical circumstances that keep me 'comfortably' chained. I hold the key.

I review old ideas, admitting freely the unrealistic nature of demanding perfection from myself and others. I move on. I am entirely ready to be released from my old disordered views which lead to old defective ways of acting.

I ask God to set me free; ***and I am free***.

January 17
PROCESSING EMOTIONS

I spent a lot of my time denying how I felt, distracting myself in order to avoid my 'stuff'; my 'baggage'. I had essentially flat-lined. **<u>My range of emotion was extremely limited.</u>**

I am literally coming to my senses today. I am giving myself permission to feel. With the help of others in the meeting, I am talking about how I feel, as well. ***Nobody is discounting my perception, dismissing my concerns, shaming my decisions or otherwise invalidating my process.***

I am unconditionally accepted for who I am and where I am on my journey to recover my lost self.

Reliable friends simply sit with me and listen to my sharing of certain struggles along the way; no giving of advice, no fixing, no moralizing; just listening. ***In this way, I know they have heard my struggle; they support where I am emotionally.***

As a result, I am arriving at my own solutions.
I am returning to a sense of autonomy.
I am interpreting my own reality.

Sometimes I process a condition quickly; sometimes slowly.
The solution eventually presents itself.

<u>I am restored to a sense of being the captain of my own ship, capable of making decisions that truly work instead of conforming to old ideas that don't.</u> My genuine feelings help set a course toward trusting ***my own*** perception.

Now. Where the dickens *did* I put that compass?

January 18
CONTINUING THE JOURNEY

My existence before recovery was rife with all kinds of dysfunctional relationships, friends and family alike. Growing up with alcoholism had affected every fiber of my being. By the time I found the rooms, my thinking had become distorted. As a result of this thinking, my actions had become rigid; my ways inflexible. My life had become one big habit of misadventure. **Disentangling myself was no easy task.**

Due in large part to my taking Steps Four and Five, I soon found a freedom from the attachments of the past. *I began viewing myself and others in a more realistic way.* I could lower the demands on myself, set clear boundaries with others and re-connect with my true feelings.

'Our adventures before and after, make clear three pertinent ideas.' *My life was a mess. No human power alone could help. That God could and would if He were sought.* Steps Ten, Eleven and Twelve provide the support for my ongoing 'adventures'.

I still go to meetings. I meet new people and create new situations that are healthy for me. I enjoy being alive most of the time.

I have losses; but when I get knocked down, I get up again. The journey towards my true self continues! I am awakening to new possibilities.

I meet others along the way who are teaching me in their own way what I need to learn in order to move forward.

Some of these 'teachers' are complete strangers;
some are my very own family members; some are old friends.

If I remain open to learning, almost *anyone* can be a teacher as I trudge this road of 'happy destiny'.

January 19
RESPONDING TO LIFE

Living with self-centered, narcissistic people, I learned from an early age that plans could change suddenly; that rules applied on a Wednesday may have nothing to do with circumstances on a Saturday.

Afraid of being left behind, I reacted quickly, desperately trying to keep up; modifying and adjusting; always vigilant, always on alert.

The rooms have set a very predictable pace. I can count on consistency for the most part. I can respond in my own way, in my own time. I can speak my mind. I can talk about my feelings without fear.

I am not locked into any one plan. I realize that sometimes things work out; sometimes they don't. **<u>I am no longer terrified of being abandoned.</u>**

I *can* adjust my expectations. I *can* modify my thinking. I *can* make new choices based on what is healthy…for me. I *can* remain relaxed in the face of change. I *can* stay present for myself, knowing that I have everything I need right now to genuinely be who I am.

I am growing more and more comfortable with 'boring'. No longer addicted to excitement, I am responding to life rather than reacting.

When the only tool I have is a hammer,
everything in life begins to look like a nail.

I have more tools today; more finesse, less pounding. ☐

January 20
ALLOWING TRANSFORMATION

I have certainly stalled out from time to time in my effort to recover from the effects of growing up in a dysfunctional world. Following a great deal of time invested, regarding the Fourth and Fifth Step, I was entirely ready to let go of my old dysfunctional ideas; and yet, I was worried about exactly *how* and *when* these intrusive demands on myself and others would be removed.

<u>*I have regressed at times.*</u>

The universe is a big place. The possibilities are endless. Someone once said, 'God works through other people.' ***Whatever presents itself today has the potential of being my classroom; whoever I meet, my teacher.***
I see reality as my friend to be embraced, not avoided.
I can learn from the most treacherous of events.

My transformation is usually something that happens to me while I am planning something else. Who am I supposed to meet this day?
What am I to learn? ***I am thoroughly prepared to learn what I need to learn in order to break free from old behavior patterns that have ceased to work.*** I am staying awake for the entire show!
I *am* changing.

I am 'going with the flow' of events which are naturally unfolding.
I am wading the waters of the stream, allowing the river to carry me; trusting the journey, hoping for a good outcome.

Every day that I remain above the water line is a good day.
Some days are more perilous than others. That is why I pray.
I need all the help I can get.

Those fellow travelers I meet along the way serve as my guides. I am beginning to trust the process of my own journey; the ***greatest*** adventure of all, ***my life!***

January 21
CARING FOR SELF

I used to push myself way beyond the point of frustration and exhaustion. This resulted in unbearable anxiety; push, push, push…collapse; pull, pull, pull…cave-in. The pattern seemed to never end.

The unrelenting pursuit of how I thought I should always be and the never ceasing claim on what others should always do dogged my every step. Even when I was supposed to be having fun,
my mind was somewhere else.

I am 'lightening up' to some degree. ***The slogan, 'Easy Does It,' reminds me to lower my expectations on myself and others.*** Situations sometimes turn out just the way I hope and sometimes they don't.

I am taking full advantage of any comfort I find in my world: a good cup of tea, a hot bath, a good meal, a night out, a weekend away. If an activity is fun and healthy, I do it! Even if it's just for practice.

I treat myself with the same respect that I would show someone else who survives a harrowing ordeal and lives to tell about it. ***Growing up in a distorted world, the world of addiction, leaves a huge 'mark' on the soul.*** Healing the pain and grief takes time. Time takes time.

With each passing day, ***<u>I participate in my own recovery.</u>***

I take care of me.

January 22
ALLOWING OTHERS TO BE

In the past, my happiness sometimes depended on how others lived up to my expectations. Whether it was at work or home; school or parties, *I was extremely vulnerable to conditions in the world outside myself.* I could be easily triggered emotionally.

Having taken all the Steps, I know myself reasonably well. I know my interests. *I am forming my core values, regarding a variety of areas: politics, religion, sex relations, work ethics, family connections, relationships with friends, money issues, etc.*
I have a sense of self. I have boundaries.

I know where my world stops, and other people's world begins. I can, in most situations, decide whether I want to move toward or away from a condition. I can even stand up, use my voice and hold my ground. Regardless of my position, I can give others the permission *and the dignity* to be exactly who they are.

Their beliefs, their emotions, their actions are not my responsibility.
I am on my journey; awake and alive!

I can view others from afar, knowing that their travels are leading them in a direction that is intended for their ultimate higher good. *I rarely intervene; give directions or otherwise, presume to know what is best for another.*
I leave that to the individual and their God.

And, by the way, I sleep a whole lot better.

January 23
BECOMING MYSELF

So often in the past, I could not simply be myself. All the unrealistic, old ideas attached to who I should be clouded the open, blue skies of who I might be. *__My genuine interests were put aside.__*

Often, I would lose my way in determining what I truly wanted, preferring other's expectations ahead of my own heart-felt desires. **What's more, my own raging demands from my false self often muted the voice of my true self.** Somewhere along the way, I lost myself.

With the help of safe people in the rooms, I am now able to search out who I am; my interests, my values, my desires. The blues skies of potential ignite the fires of joy; the joy in becoming who I am.

__I am beginning to connect with my core self, my healthy self.__

I can dream again. **Regardless of any expected outcome I might have for the future,** I remind myself of the old song:

*You don't always get what you want. You don't always get what you want.
But if you try some time, you just might find…
You get what you need.*

At this moment, *__I have everything I NEED in order to be who I am.__*

January 24
TAPPING INTO LOVE

I was not sold on the concept of love. My cynicism had reached new heights just before I found the rooms of recovery. The Darwinian principle of 'survival of the fittest' had become the order of the day; and I was *barely* surviving. <u>**Trust had reached an all-time low.**</u>

Someone once said, *'To know someone is to respect someone; to respect someone is to care; to care for someone is to genuinely respond and, in that response, I am able to love.'* I am remaining long enough in recovery to begin my return to love. Why? The rooms listen.
The rooms respect my struggle.

The rooms care. *And so, I believe that a power greater than myself can help me.* I trust the process. I am beginning to let my guard down.

I recognize love today; and *naturally*, I move toward that love. I am hearing my own voice in a new way. My self-hatred is diminishing. I am listening to my own story and feeling what I need to feel; the grief.

I respect my own struggle, seeing it for what it truly is; an indisputably courageous effort to really live again. I genuinely care for myself. I respond to who I am and what I need in order to grow.

I am sold on the concept of love.

January 25
KEEPING THE DOOR OPEN

Before I ever showed up in the recovery rooms, somebody had remained long enough to keep the door open for me. This door would lead to my lost, abandoned self; my true self. ***This door would lead me to freedom.***

This door would lead me to others, struggling to stay on the path; struggling to remain awake; struggling to come to terms with the hurt, disappointment, shame and humiliation that goes with active dysfunctional behavior in parents and others. ***I would become part of a greater process;*** a process of healing.

I am keeping the door open now. ***I am no longer all alone.*** I rest assured, knowing I will always have a safe place to go; a safe place to talk; a safe place to feel; a safe place to fearlessly pursue my own spiritual progress.

By suiting up and showing up at my home group, whether I feel like it or not, I guarantee my own growth and the chance for others to find a new freedom and a new happiness.

I am convinced that Step Twelve is as much a part of my recovery process as any other Step. The choice to 'carry the message' is all mine.

And when my journey on earth is complete, I know there will be others yet to come…

keeping the door open.

January 26
KNOWING THE RIGHT TIME

I was on auto pilot for a long time, reacting to life from old chronic emotions attached to past events; events, the substance of which, I was mostly unaware. I functioned as an automaton. **_I was 'sleep-walking'._**

I have looked at the major events that played a part in creating most of the old emotions; old emotions upon which I built a survival/defense system called my 'moral values'. **_I have inventoried my beliefs;_** some I have kept; some I have turned over to Steps Six and Seven.

I am connecting with my core interests. I am becoming who I am minus some of the extra baggage.

The events of any given day can teach me something of myself which I didn't know before. I am awake to new ideas. I am open to new experiences. I am creating new values.

More and more, **_I act according to how I genuinely think and feel_**. I am true to myself most of the time. If something doesn't feel right, I don't have to go ahead and do it any way. I can pause and ask for the next appropriate thought or action. I intuitively know when the time is right for me to respond.

A new day is dawning; a new world is unfolding; and for me...

timing is everything.

January 27
CONTRIBUTING TO MY OWN WELL-BEING

I wasted a lot of time doing things that I didn't want to do with people I didn't want to be with. Given some of the unreal expectations I would bring to these events, I often felt disappointed and uncomfortable. My story of being a victim continued. *I felt compelled to participate out of loyalty, often neglecting my own welfare.*

I have difficulty relaxing and having fun;
and so, I practice enjoying myself.

One of the new ideas I have created in the Eleventh Step, following my Fourth and Fifth Step process:

It's OK to place my well-being first in my life, for my life.

Some days are better than others and yet, I think I am getting the hang of it. I am happy to simply make a cup of tea, take a walk, talk to a friend, read a book, watch a good movie, go for a run, take a drive, take a nap.

I am moving toward people who are *safe and available*; people who can simply *let me be*. *I allow spontaneity to return.*
I lose myself in genuine curiosities.
I explore the world around me.

I protect my sense of well-being, setting boundaries that are right for me. I am beginning to discover what the old-timers meant:
this is a selfish program.

My well-being *IS* my number one priority.

January 28
SEEKING APPROVAL

It seemed that I was very different from most other people and yet, I *needed* to belong. ***Even though I tried to look the part, I rarely felt the part; forever the outsider, looking in.*** Something was never quite right.

I guarded secrets. I created entire belief systems around how I should always act when around others. I stretched the truth. I sometimes lied. I outperformed others but seldom felt included. I withdrew. <u>*I felt alone.*</u> I would try again…and again…and again to belong.

The social techniques that I developed as a child, techniques that I would carry into adulthood, were no longer serving me very well. By reviewing my old ideas through the Fourth and Fifth Step, ***I began to grow beyond the survival/dependency days.***

With God's help, through Steps Six and Seven, I am lowering the exhaustive demands on myself and others. <u>***Ordinary is OK.***</u>

I still seek approval. Sometimes I get the outcome I want, sometimes I don't; the difference today? <u>***I do not desperately need or demand approval.***</u>

I have begun to connect with my authentic self. I am no longer compelled to take a vote of those in the room in order to determine ***what is right for me or whether I belong here***.

I am free to be me and being me is what I do best.

January 29
EXPRESSING MY SELF

I spent an inordinate amount of time moving toward people who, for whatever reason, were unavailable, unappreciative and sometimes down right mean. *I felt discouraged a lot of the time due to my choices in relationship whether it was with individuals, groups or institutions.*
I felt limited in freely expressing myself.

There were moments when approval would come, but I rarely trusted the whole process. *I am discovering the events of the past that shaped my old beliefs; beliefs that I co-created; beliefs that no longer work.*
I am turning down the volume on how I always 'should' be.
I am letting go of unrealistic 'claims' on others, as well.
Total approval is less important than before.

Taking the Fourth and Fifth frees up a lot of 'anxious' space in my head. No longer plagued with an incessant drum beat of perfection, I am relaxing into my life. Genuine interests are emerging, as I am growing more and more confident about who I am.

When I talk to someone today, I am aware that sometimes people are available, sometimes they aren't. That's OK. I can adjust my conversation and expectations accordingly. *Displaying my interests, either verbally or otherwise, can take on a variety of forms of expression.*
I am returning to an earlier interest in art and music.

It is enough that I am available today…*for myself*. The journey ahead seems hopeful. I am coming to see that all of life's expression is merely a course of practice.

When I express myself in a way that is true to how I think and feel, I am usually happy; regardless of the outcome.

January 30
PRACTICING LOVE

I used to do a lot for others. I secretly prided myself for that trait. *I sometimes resented others when I didn't get the recognition that I thought I deserved.* The old idea seemed to dictate that I should always do for others so that I would be considered 'valuable'. I would never be banished. More importantly, I would *never* have to be alone.

By nature, I am a narcissist. I think about my concerns most of my waking hours. I don't apologize for that. In fact, if I am truly honest about it, my needs and desires for myself and those closest to me are priority one; always have been, always will be.

With the help of the program, I am standing on my own. I am allowing others to stand on their own, as well. I don't have to control every living thing that moves. *I can allow others to truly be who they are and where they are on their unique journey.*

I can sometimes support them by listening, by validating, and by being available. *I am respecting each person's autonomy;* each person's *freedom*; each person's *dignity* to make their own choices.

Am I still by nature 'self' centered? Probably. *At the end of the day, is it still all about me? More or less.* Am I learning how to support another human being in a healthy way? Absolutely.

I grow more and more confident as I practice the 'art' of loving.

January 31
BEING ONE'S SELF

I was driven to compare myself with others whether it was in the classroom, at work, with my family or simply watching a television show; always comparing my 'insides' to other people's 'outsides'. I had no identity of my own. ***I often felt 'apart from' rather than 'apart of'.***

I have begun to attend meetings regularly and as a result, I get to see real people up close and personal. ***I am privileged to be in the presence of others who are struggling with painful personal events and the emotions attached to those events.***

I am realizing that I am not alone;
that others have intense feelings just as I do,
regardless of how they may appear.

Allowing myself to speak freely in the company of strangers is still a challenge; the safer the room, the more comfortable I feel. ***Often, I simply hold my own space, giving myself permission to simply be present; content with merely observing.*** Sometimes I can just listen. There is no pressure to speak. I am growing more at ease with my story; my highs and lows.

I can pick and choose those with whom I *want* to reveal myself; those with whom I feel safe.

Little by little, I am emerging from the shadows of secrecy and shame. ***I am becoming transparent with those whom I trust.***

I fully embrace who I am.

FEBRUARY

February 1
ACTING FROM MY BASE

I spent a lot of time 'acting out' old ideas created during my childhood; ideas designed to keep me alive; ideas created to counter-act the fear of abandonment. I was distracted from discovering my genuine interests and natural curiosities. Rather than trust my own emerging perceptions, I had to rely on other's approval. *I grew more and more dependent on their total favor* in order to feel included. The overwhelming need to survive dictated that I remain true to my various 'strategies' connected to how I 'should' be, all the time.

I was rigid with my standards of perfection. I was consumed with trying to perform according to my dictates. When I failed to live up to these standards, **I literally hated myself.**

Today, as I move through the day, I have my being based on a spontaneous true self; not a false, driven self.

I have a better idea of what I am genuinely thinking and feeling most of the time.

Through the Eleventh Step, *I am creating a core of new ideas* designed to keep me safe and healthy. When I respond to life accordingly, I am naturally more confident in my action.

Human nature being what it is, sometimes I react to life; sometimes I respond. I am trusting the bigger process. **I am entirely content with partial progress rather than total perfection.**

I make it a practice to remain conscious of what I genuinely want, moment by moment. *I trust that the resources I need will appear at the time that I need them*. I am remaining true to my emerging healthy self. I am confident in my response to daily events and challenges.

Now. Let's see. I want to do the dishes, but I have no soap. *What to do?* ☹ Ah! Off to the store I go. Splendid plan! ☐ (I am so *SMART*!)

February 2
PRACTICNG RECOVERY

I rarely sought, through an applied discipline, to promote my own psychological, emotional or spiritual well-being. *I was usually too busy, running from various emotional calamities to be consciously involved with my genuine welfare.* I was on autopilot most of the time; checked out and distracted.

Today, I am taking the Steps; *and I am taking as much time as I need.* I trust the process. I attend meetings regularly. *I share how I feel at meetings.* I am remembering events that have contributed to my belief system; my moral structure. I inventory those beliefs in a Fourth Step.

I am searching for my core dysfunction, the exact nature of my distorted thinking; distorted thinking, stemming from unworkable expectations on myself and other people. Unrealistic ideas regarding how *I should always be* or how *others should always be* are under review.

In this Fifth Step process, *the unrelenting need for perfection* seems to weave a common thread throughout the tapestry of my old dysfunctional behavior. *I readily admit it.*

With the help of God and others, I am facing difficult situations; both past and present. I am 'processing' troublesome emotions and allowing my disordered thinking to be removed through the Sixth and Seventh Step. *Facing life honestly, I am naturally willing to mend any damage brought on myself as a result my old behavior.* When appropriate, I make amends to others, as well.

I promptly let go of dysfunctional old ideas and the accompanying distorted thinking that goes with those old ideas; in other words, *the over demanding 'shoulds'*.

With God's help, I am awakening to new relationships and I am revising old relationships that never worked. *I am carrying the message of hope*; the hope of recovering my true self.

February 3
FACING MY TRUTH

To a large extent, I denied my past; that unapproachable place where reality was **not** my friend. I was afraid to look, unwilling to go back, fearing what I might find. ***Ironically, my dysfunctional belief system, co-created in a distorted world and designed to assure my survival, KEPT me chained to the past.*** I was unaware of my genuine needs and wants; shut down to my own interests and feelings.

Numbed out and distracted, I was sleep-walking through my life, thinking that I was simply 'being me'. In fact, it was my false self, calling the shots most of the time. I created an entire 'pride system' around how I thought myself and others should always be. I was easily disturbed from my slumber when 'things' went wrong.

I want to wake up. ***I want to know the truth of my past.*** Through those distant episodes, I have a chance to reconnect emotionally with the self I had to leave behind; my true self; my abandoned self.

The Fourth Step is difficult. Looking at the past is painful. Grief is a big part of the recovery process and yet, ***I know the grief will pass.*** I see the 'grief phases' at work which eventually bring me closer and closer to a genuine state of acceptance, regarding *whatever* has happened. However, some events I may never be able to *fully* accept.

Sometimes, I can identify an old idea immediately by looking to the origin; the event that created the belief. ***My emotions serve as guideposts.*** I can uncover the source of my dysfunctional thoughts. I can expose the thoughts for what they are: habitual, non-productive, distorted and unworkable.

These unrealistic demands on myself and others don't have to keep setting me up for hurt, disappointment and shame. ***Today, reality is my friend.***

The truth is setting me free.

February 4
ASKING FOR HELP

I rarely asked for help because I had grown to believe, in a twisted way, that: I should always be able to 'figure it out'; I should always be independent; **_I should always be self-reliant;_** I should never be a bother; I should never appear 'stupid', and my personal favorite of all (not!)… I should *always* look good!

Today I realize that *sometimes* I can be all these things; *sometimes* I can't. It's OK. **_Perfection is HIGHLY over-rated._** Even when I can sustain for some length of time what I think I should be, something comes along to mess it all up.

I have officially joined the human race, flawed as it is. Reasonably healthy families are *inter-dependent*. Moderately functional companies, making millions of dollars, are *inter-dependent*. Successful sports organizations that win a lot of games are *inter-dependent*.
I can be *inter-dependent*, as well.
No shame! No blame!

Yes, I am limited. Yes, I need the support of others. Yes, I like to be right.

No, I don't have all the answers.

Thank God for the internet!

Thank God for the program!

February 5
ADMITTING MY UNREALISTIC DEMANDS

I was plagued with an internal barometer that gauged not only how I should always perform, but how others should always perform, as well. **<u>My standard was nothing short of perfection.</u>**

I was disappointed most of the time, consumed with self-hate and resentment. Every time I would fail, or they would fail, it seemed to re-open old wounds; core wounds.

Having taken the Fifth Step, I am better able to recognize the unrelenting 'shoulds' on myself and my unreasonable 'claims' on others; **the exact nature of this disease**.

Through a Tenth Step process, I am remaining aware of this inner tyranny; a disorder which begins with my thinking and extends to some form of unhealthy behavior: **drinking in excess, working too much, obsessing with social media, over-eating, using drugs abusively, being too dependent on a relationship, etc.**

With the help of my group, God and the Steps; I am, for the most part, awake today. **At the very least, <u>I am conscious of my old ideas.</u>** I am aware of the attached demands to those old ideas.

I feel the emotions that emerge when myself and others fail to live up to those old demands. **<u>I can admit my error</u>** and move on to Step Eleven, praying only for the knowledge of His will for my life and the power to carry it out.

I can reset.

February 6
ESTABLISHING BOUNDARIES

I was a person who either had the walls so high that few dared to approach; or the gate was forever wide open, allowing all kinds of unacceptable varmints to invade the castle. *I rarely had the confidence to simply stand up for myself, use my voice and ask for what I needed.* Truth be told, I was scared. I feared being rejected by those upon whom I depended.

The program has given me a chance to review some of my old ideas. I depend on the program. I am ultimately responsible for my thinking and if I am ultimately responsible for my thinking, I am ultimately responsible for my acting, as well. *I act in such a way, for the most part, that serves my best interest now.* I don't apologize for that.

When I am true to my core self; when my actions agree with how I genuinely think and feel, I am usually more confident. *It is OK to set limits, not only on others' behavior; but on my own behavior, too.* For example, I cannot be all things to all people all the time.
I can realistically assess my situation and act accordingly.
I treat myself with care and respect.
I am complete.

When I find myself in relationship with others, *I can voice my concerns and request my preference around certain behavior.* For example, if a friend is chronically late and I am bothered, I can use my voice: 'This is what's going on; this is how I feel; this is what I need going forward…please.'

I have a self today. I respect that self; enough to ask for what I need.

I have limits on what I allow from others. I have constraints on what I demand from myself.

February 7
REMAINING OBJECTIVE

Before the program, I was ricocheting from one event to the other with little or no thought. ***I was on autopilot; usually 'numbed down' or characteristically distracted, unable to remain available to my own feelings.*** Avoidance ruled the day; whatever it took: food, booze, relationships, work, social media.

The journey toward becoming more objective about myself, my surroundings and my circumstances began the moment I walked through the door of my first meeting. On some micro-cosmic level, I admitted that I had a problem. Just how unmanageable my life had become would later be revealed over the course of attending more meetings.

I now realize, usually sooner than later, when *I am* bothered; when *I am* avoiding my emotions; when *I am* distracting myself from being 'present'. With the help of others, I can look at my process regardless of the intensity. I can unravel, in time, the tangled mass of thoughts, feelings and actions which, when taken altogether, are my life. I move forward with confidence into the Fourth Step, knowing I am not alone.

I stand at a turning point. ***I want to see the big picture. I want to own my truth.*** I want to be free of the myths and superstitions of my old ideas.

I want to recover my true self.

February 8
APPLYING STEP ELEVEN

I was in the business of taking the shot before I knew the play. Often, I would fall short. Often, I would beat myself up. Often, I would blame others. I was frustrated and felt insignificant. My preferred outcome seemed illusive, often changing in midcourse; the answer to my dilemma, blowing in the wind.

Nothing seemed workable. **The only voice I could hear was that of my false self** with its unyielding assessment of my 'performance'; my ability to act as I 'should'. With each passing day, I lost a little more of my authentic self to these nonsensical, incessant demands. I was exhausted and afraid.

I am in the business today of being myself; my genuine self. I have spent a lot of time in the Fourth and Fifth Step. I have been willing to 'become teachable' in the Sixth and Seventh Step. I have owned my behavior toward myself and others in the Eighth and Ninth Step. I continue to place myself in a learning position in the Tenth Step.

<u>I am awakening to my genuine desires; my real hopes and dreams.</u>

With God's help, I am trying to remain awake to what I *truly* want rather than what I *'should'* become. I am asking for guidance from those who are experienced. In meditation, I am creatively visualizing events that will assure my welfare. I am keeping an open mind. I now know that God sometimes works through other people. I can receive clear direction on this spiritual journey. And I can act.

When I know the play, I take the shot. **<u>Sometimes I get what I want, sometimes I don't.</u>** One thing is for sure, I always learn. I always have a chance for a 'do-over'.

Practice, practice, practice…

February 9
IDENTIFYING OLD IDEAS

I spent a lot of time *reacting* to most of the events in my life; forming and reforming ideas about how I should always be and how others should always be. **Most of this activity was unconscious.**

However, these notions that would become my moral system were, in fact, my own creation. What I eventually allowed or disallowed in myself and others was my sole responsibility.

I am taking a Fourth and Fifth Step. I am reviewing my old ideas in order to determine what makes me who I am. I am still forming and reforming ideas and yet, I am more conscious of the old ideas that are working and the ones that aren't. The tyranny of the 'shoulds' I have dismissed altogether: 'I should always do this; they should always do that.'

This demand for perfection, by its very constitution, is the exact nature of all my difficulties.

The notion that anyone can perform perfectly all the time has been smashed. This unrealistic claim around perfection has proven to be the *fundamental core* of my distorted thinking.

This erroneous declaration for perfection in myself and others *IS*…the exact nature of my wrongs.

Steps Six is my way out.

February 10
DECONSTRUCTING THE OLD BELIEF SYSTEM

My moral structure was locked in place. The problem? I didn't know what it was most of the time, nor did I truly know from whence it had come. I had become an automaton for the most part, trying my best to fulfill my chosen role; a role I had co-created to fit my unique needs around survival.

I am taking the time to review my old ideas. I realize that relationships lead to events; events lead to emotions; and ***emotions re-enforce old beliefs***. I know that some of the major relationships that shaped my moral structure started not only with family, but with others outside the family, as well; even the media had its effect.

I deconstruct my value system initially through the Fourth and Fifth Step process; and now, through the Tenth Step. I remain open-minded to letting go of the old ideas that no longer serve my best interest. ***I exchange these old ideas for new ideas*** that do, in fact, contribute to my well-being.

Old ideas that don't work anymore are usually laced with absolute 'shoulds'. My new ideas are taking on a more 'easy does it' aspect. If some demand on myself or others isn't working anymore; if it is only creating more grief and shame, I let it go.

I am entirely ready to have ***God remove*** my exaggerated demands that keep setting me up for disappointment and resentment.

I take Step Six.

February 11
LETTING GO OF OLD DEMANDS

I spent an inordinate amount of time feeling ashamed of myself; and when I wasn't shaming myself, I was blaming others, either directly or behind their backs. ***I was driven to perform well, if not perfectly.***

I was haunted by my own conflicting standards centered around independence, love and control. I seemed to go from one extreme to the other. Nothing was ever quite right; something was always missing.

I am learning of my exaggerated expectations. I know when the volume is way up. I can usually adjust my over-reactions to events in my life by accepting ***'life on life's terms'.*** For example, I am highly motivated toward being independent: 'I should manage my affairs as to never be bothered by anyone or anything'. The truth: sometimes I am bothered; sometimes I'm not.

I am coming to terms with reality; ***my reality***: Life is like a mixed bag of assorted nuts. Sometimes I get what I want; sometimes I don't.

I am awakening to a new value system. I am not as driven as I used to be. I still over-react; and yes, with God's help, I can usually ***lower my old demands*** sooner rather than later (before all hell breaks loose), or I can even let go of them entirely. (Step Seven)

The lower my demands, the greater my serenity; ***<u>or so it seems.</u>***

Hell breaking loose is not pretty. Now, where ***DID*** I put that fire extinguisher?

February 12
MOVING TOWARD RECOVERY

Long before I thought about approaching the rooms of recovery, I was seeking a solution to my problem. I didn't know it, but looking back, events had naturally aligned, bringing me to a solid turning point; a crossroads: stay in the problem or get into the solution. When the program presented itself, I was ready to try anything.

Today, I am consciously heading in, what I trust is, the right direction. <u>**And I am not alone**</u>. I have a plan; the Steps. I don't expect miracles overnight and yet, *I am changing*.

<u>**Emotions pushed down for years are surfacing. The grief is very real.**</u>

I am confident that the Steps are not going away, nor is the program. I can get through the various phases of my recovery. Come what may, I have discovered a way out of the mess.

With the help of God and the support of others who are looking at their issues, I have no doubt that I can continue to *participate in my own recovery*; that I can get to the other side of any obstruction; that I can continue the journey in search of my lost self.

I can make it.

February 13
TAKING THE NECESSARY STEPS

I spent an unnecessary amount of time, venturing forth into the world without the confidence of even knowing that I was headed in the right direction. **What's more, I really didn't know where I WANTED to go.** Much of my thinking was based on the past; a past that kept me in survival mode most of the time. I had disconnected from my genuine self.

I am reconnecting with my true self and others. I am feeling my feelings. I am talking with people whom I trust. <u>**I am 're-membering' the past; connecting the dots; putting the pieces together.**</u>
I am allowing my buried grief to surface.

I am told that the Steps were initially written by a recovering alcoholic; a former disrupter by his own admission. His intent with the Steps? To return to a healthy relationship with himself, with others and with a God of his understanding; and so, remain sober.

I do not understand the Steps and yet, I am *willing* to move in the right direction: go to meetings; stay awake emotionally; read diverse offerings of recovery literature; take action on the Steps; talk to others who have gone before me.

I can take what I like and leave the rest. My journey is unlike anyone else's. I am unique. The Steps are mere suggestions.

I relax, resting assured in this proven process; knowing that God is doing for me what I cannot or will not do for myself.

February 14
ACCEPTING MISTAKES

At the first sign of a mistake, I was unrelenting in criticizing myself and others. According to my thinking, I had to always perform in such a way that assured an absolute result attached to my demands.
Others had to perform perfectly, as well.

For example, I was to never allow myself to be cheated. On one occasion, when I had been short-changed at a store, I was livid when I later discovered the error. 'How could I have been so stupid!'

With a mistake comes a sense of loss, naturally. Grief takes on many forms. Initial anger lets me know that something is not right in my world; something has gone wrong. There are minor losses and there are huge losses. My emotional barometer sometimes
doesn't know the difference.

In time, thanks to the 'grief process', I come to accept both the great and small mistakes of myself and others.

I still over-react from time to time over relatively small setbacks; when I don't live up to my demands or when others don't meet my expectations. ***I have the Tenth Step.*** I promptly look at the old idea that is setting me up and with God's help, I adjust the volume. I lower my demands.

I am meeting life on life's terms. ***Sometimes I get the outcome I want; sometimes I don't.***

And as the old song says, that's life.

February 15
TAKING AN INVENTORY

I was seldom aware of what I was telling myself, following a disappointment or hurt. I knew that I felt "bad" and would use any means necessary to distract my attention from what was really going on. I had been practicing this method since the age of three.
I would do this for the next 27 years.

I was stuck, enmeshed with ***all kinds*** of mood-altering distractions: relationships, food, work, school, travel, entertainment, sex…

Although I didn't know it at the time, I began my spiritual awakening the first time I set foot in a meeting where people were talking about what was truly going on. Soon thereafter, I would begin meeting one on one to gain clarity about situations, past and present; situations in which I had over-reacted emotionally.

Usually, the person would simply allow my telling of the event, my venting of emotion, my resolution of the problem; a kind of mini Fourth and Fifth Step. I could talk things out with a validating person; someone who allowed me to be me without advising, criticizing or otherwise, rescuing me.
I owned my process.

The Fourth and Fifth Step, the first Steps that suggest measurable action, set me on a solid path of awakening; ***a path of awakening to the process of my real self.***

Oh, I still have 'distractions' to be sure. ***I am not perfect.***
I don't even want to be.

Thank God for the Sixth and Seventh Step.

February 16
SAYING NO TO UNSAFE PEOPLE

I used to crave the approval of those who thought the least of me. I considered it a challenge. It wasn't enough to simply be included by most. I wanted to be *seen by all* and eventually, *loved by all*.

I would work double-time in my head, plotting and scheming in order to win over the last man sitting. I wanted everyone on their feet, applauding. Then I could be happy. Having failed with this strategy many times, I eventually withdrew from others altogether; Sour Grapes Syndrome (SGS).

I am aware now that I can't possibly please everyone all the time; and, what's more, I don't have to. I am no longer compelled to be all things to all people. I have a self! *I can be me*. If folks move away from me or even against me for some reason, I can allow it. Perhaps their behavior has nothing to do with me.

*I choose to move toward safe people: Available, Awake and Attentive; **the three A's**.*

*I move away from unsafe people: UN-available, UN-awake and UN-attentive; **the three UN's**.*

I am growing more and more able to stand *for myself, by myself*. I am sometimes alone, but I am not lonely. I am available to myself. I need not be seen by all and loved by all in order to appreciate who I am.

I am no longer dependent on unavailable, toxic people.

February 17
CONSIDERING THE STEPS

I was accustomed to launching into new territory, not having taken the appropriate steps necessary to complete the imagined journey. *I often found myself asking for directions from people ill-equipped to show me the way.* Some even went so far as to insist, 'Ya can't get there from here; you'll never make it; turn back now!'

Really?! Please.

The program assures my safe travels. There are those who have gone before me; those who have experience taking the steps; those who can validate, nurture and support; those who can allow me to have my struggles without rescuing, caretaking and fixing.

My limited experience with the Steps has shown me that most people take the Steps *at their own pace, in their own way, in their own time.* I see the Steps as reliable suggestions. I have seen people come and go; the Steps are always there, always the same.

I contemplate my progress in the Steps. I give myself permission to proceed in my own time, in my own way. *No two people take the Steps in the same way.* What helps me might hold another back. What holds another back may help me. The Steps are mere guidelines to progress.

I am free to choose what works best for me.

February 18
ASKING FOR WHAT I NEED

I had over the course of my life created a belief system that, by design, kept people at a distance. *__I trusted only a few.__* When it came time to ask for help, I did so reluctantly. Much of my life had been spent in frustration, looking for support and approval in all the wrongs places; kind of like going to a hardware store to buy a loaf of bread; not happening.

Now, I am moving toward people who are available most of the time, emotionally and otherwise. I have a broad base of friends. I have done some of the work to recover my lost self and I am discovering that I have genuine interests; interests that sometime require help from others.
I can use my voice.

When I am clear about what I need in order to get to where I want to go, I move with confidence in that general direction. The risk of disappointment, having asked for help and been denied, is still very real.
Sometimes certain people can help; sometimes they can't.

It's OK. I move on; make another call; search another web site. Sometimes, with God's help, I come up with the answer on my own.

I go to hardware stores for hammers; I go to bakeries for bread. Imagine that. I am requesting what I need from the people most likely to have the answers.

Now, let me see. What to do about that clogged drain?

February 19
TAKING ACTION

There were moments when knowing what to do was an impossibility. Conflicting demands kept me frozen. And when I did finally make a move, I felt scared most of the time; rarely confident.

Often, I would take the shot, before I knew the play; ***I reacted to life most of the time.***

In the rooms, I have found a safe place where I can explore my emerging true self. I talk about my struggles; my ups, my downs. ***I speak of my successes and I can speak of my failures, as well.*** Just because I fail at something does not make *me* a failure. It simply means that I did not get the outcome I was hoping for; it has absolutely ***nothing*** to do with my worth as a human being.

In professional baseball, if a batter hits the ball just one out of three times at bat, he is going to the Hall of Fame. Baseball doesn't demand that I get a hit ***EVERY*** time. ***There is room for error.***

When I act on my core interests (my genuine thoughts and feelings), I am happy most of the time.

I remain true to myself.

Win or lose, I'm OK.

February 20
LEARNING TO LAUGH

Laughing did not come easy. Life itself was coming at me like the iceberg on collision course with the Titanic. Or was it the Titanic on collision course with the iceberg? Hey! I just made a joke! LOL

Maybe I *should* quit my day job!

Here's the point: It was extremely difficult to be light-hearted when each passing day seemed to bring a new chapter of unresolved anger, resentment and grief. It was kind of like trying to play tennis in a snowstorm with my mother as the line judge; not fun. (No ill intended toward my mother; she just so happens to hate tennis and snowstorms; loves to judge, though)

As time progressed in the program, the stress of life seemed to dissipate. I grew less and less distracted with others' 'needs' and more available for myself. ***Self-care had ceased being a strange concept***. In fact, I began doing things that I knew would be reasonably fun:
going to the movies, taking a bike ride, going for a canoe trip,
hiking in the woods, playing tennis (not in the snow),
going to a comedy club.

I lighten up. ***When I laugh now, I laugh.***

So…a Bassett Hound walks into a bar and the bartender says, 'Hey, why the long face?'

On second thought, maybe I *shouldn't* quit my day job.

February 21
RECOVERING FROM BAD RELATIONSHIPS

Before the program, I was clueless when it came to assessing relationships. ***What's more, when I could sense that 'things' were not OK, I had no idea how to change.***

I usually tried to 'leave' the situation only to find another circumstance, waiting right around the corner like the one I had just left.

I realize today that everyone in my life has the potential to teach me something. ***<u>I am keeping an open mind.</u>***

Most mysteriously, I believe God, through Steps Six and Seven, can use all kinds of situations to assist in removing the defects of my *thinking* (old ideas that have ceased to work) which used to set me up for grief.

Unless conditions are abusive, I allow all sorts of relationships today, knowing that ***my higher power will change the circumstance when I have learned what I need to learn***.

I no longer volunteer to be a victim. I spend my free time with people that I *want* to be with. All the others, I tolerate. Through other people, I believe that God is doing for me what I could not or would not do for myself.

Amazingly, when I learn what I need to learn, the relationships seem to disappear of their own accord, or they get stronger and stronger; sometimes even lasting a lifetime.

February 22
FORGIVING

In times past, I held my feet very close to the fire when it came to always performing the way I thought I should. Whether it was in the classroom, at home, or on the dance floor, I set the standard very high. I hated myself most of the time. In turn, I held others in contempt, as well.

What I couldn't blame away, I tried to justify; what I couldn't justify, I would rationalize; what I couldn't rationalize, I would resent. I was at the top of the list when it came time to take Step Eight. I had abused myself without really knowing it. I had harmed others, too.

The tyranny of my 'shoulds' ***is and was*** the 'exact nature' of all my wrongs; harmful actions, based on unrealistic thinking, directed not only toward myself, but toward others, as well. ***Perfectionistic standards are at the core of my harmful behavior.***

Regardless of my moral standards for myself and others, the truth seems to be simply this: Sometimes I do what I should and sometimes I don't; sometimes others do what I think they should and sometimes they don't.

I am one of seventy billion other struggling mortals on the planet; a human being.

Leaving my wallet at home; forgivable. A professional football player who makes millions of dollars, dropping a winning touchdown pass in the end zone; **UNPARDONABLE!**

Oooooops…there I go again.

February 23
USING ADVERSITY TO GROW

I was accustomed to things not going well. After all, I was raised in a dysfunctional home. ***Adversity was a way of life; crisis upon crisis upon crisis.*** I was exhausted.

Solving problems is a big part of my program. Whatever my problem, when I come up with a workable solution, the problem goes away. With God's help, I stay out of the problem and into the solution.

Having surrounded myself with people who respect my process; people who allow me to *have* my process, I can work through my problems at my own pace. *I can come up with my own solutions; solutions that work for me.*

Sometimes I get the outcome I want; sometimes I don't.
I can always go back to the drawing board.

With each problem solved, my confidence grows more and more.

With each problem solved,
I embrace my own autonomy.

February 24
GIVING BACK

My earliest attempt at solving conflicts in my dysfunctional home seemed like a very good idea at the time: ***please everybody***; give, give, give. At the age of four, the belief went something like, 'If I am a good boy, I won't be abandoned; therefore, I should always be a good boy.'

I chased that solution for about ten more years. The behaviors at home grew worse. The dysfunction hung on. ***My anxiety doubled over the years; even tripled.*** Eventually, I changed the solution. I simply disappeared. I vanished with a little help from, none other than, my worst enemy; booze.

I am grateful for Alcoholics Anonymous, Al-Anon, Adult Children of Alcoholics and the countless thousands who have gone before, blazing the trail of recovery. I take all the Steps and do all that I do for one reason: to aid, assist and further my recovery, especially the Twelfth Step. They say this is a selfish program.

Some have said that these programs are for people who want it, not necessarily for the people who need it. *I don't* chase practicing drunks. I *don't* chase those for whom the Twelve Steps don't appeal. I *do* give freely of what I have found.

'I have to give it away in order to keep it.'

In the process of giving it away, I get to keep it; a selfish program? Perhaps.

It works for me.

I am who I am, 'trudging the road of happy destiny'.

February 25
MINDING MY OWN BUSINESS

I spent a lot of time criticizing others in my head. I sometimes felt outrage at other's behavior without really knowing it. **There seemed to be this program of hate constantly running in the background.** Anyone and any event could trigger some very strong emotions just under the surface. Idiots, I would mumble under my breath; what a nut case; what a whack job; what a dumb ass.

My own self-hate had grown exponentially over the years, as well. By the time I found the rooms, my true self had 'left the building'. **The critical false self had completely taken over, inventorying every indiscretion;** commenting and criticizing; sometimes barking: you're so stupid, you're so selfish, you're such an idiot, get a grip, straighten up! On and on it would go.

I was overwhelmed. I shut down emotionally; and yet, my self-hate could 'safely' come out in the form of blaming others. I could take their inventory and avoid looking at my own inadequacies. My 'victim volume' was blaring and I couldn't even hear it.

Today, my true self is regaining its rightful place. The false self with its old ideas is being removed courtesy of the Sixth and Seventh Step. **<u>As a result, I see myself with more compassion.</u>**

I can place the focus on my own struggles and allow others the dignity to do the same. The slogan, 'Live and Let Live', is making sense.

I stay in my lane.

February 26
RETURNING TO MY GENUINE SELF

Looking back, I realize that I *absolutely* had to abandon myself in order to survive. *I survived, but I paid a great price;* the leaving behind of my authentic self, my best friend.

Simply put, *that self* did not belong in a war zone. The self that wanted to simply trust, to laugh freely, to love and be loved, to explore life unafraid, to try new things, to be included; that real self could not function. **<u>Being on guard was the order of the day.</u>**

My Post Traumatic Stress Disorder began at the age of four.
Each passing year brought increased intensity.
By age seventeen, my anxiety level was through the roof!

For my true self to return, I am responsible for creating safe conditions; not only in my immediate environment, but in my mind, as well.
The Eleventh Step allows me a certain freedom to explore silence.
I can create moments where I pause, even amidst twenty-first century distraction. I have the power to turn down the volume on the world's incessant clamor.

A good cup of tea, some headphones and a few minutes are all it takes sometimes to reset emotionally. I have a neighbor who allows my visits to her garden at sunset. *I spend time alone with my best friend.*

Me.

February 27
PRACTICING THE "THREE R's"

So much of my conflict at an early age looked like having no safe place to go. **When times grew unbearable with the alcoholic, all I could do was 'duck and cover'.** Like a mule in a hailstorm, I would simply hunker down and take it. I would find distractions designed to hide my emotions: TV, food, the radio, books, magazines, even homework. Eventually, I would sneak away, only to come back to the same chaos.

When I find myself in times of trouble, I can retreat from the scene, regroup my thinking and then, return if I so choose; the three R's:
Retreat
 Regroup
  Return.

Whether I am at work, at home, a party, a family function; anywhere I am, I have the option of getting away long enough to regroup. <u>**Sometimes I find a private spot and call a trusted friend.**</u>

Sometimes I leave long enough to do something along the lines of self-care. Sometimes I pray. Sometimes I go to a meeting.

When and if I choose to return, I am more mindful of my personal boundaries.

Perhaps, I lower my expectations for what a group of people, or an individual, can reasonably deliver.

I am free to choose.

February 28
TURNING TO SAFE PEOPLE

In years past, I seemed to pick people who were naturally unable to 'be there'; and when they were there, often they would criticize, moralize, warn, direct, advise and even lecture. *Sometimes they would ask question after question that seemed invasive or off point entirely.* Often, they would attempt to minimize my situation or worse, divert my attention
by talking about their problems non-stop.

I am growing more and more aware of people capable of practicing the gifts of the program: the gift of allowing others their grief, their anger,
their struggle; in short, the gift of allowing others their *entire process.*
I move toward people who are safe. I move away from people who are not.

I am becoming available to myself, as well. I can listen to my own voice.
I can simply sit and listen to others. I allow others to 'talk out' their situation without intervening by rescuing, care taking and fixing. I can support others right where they are, validating how they feel unconditionally.

I have several people on whom I can depend most of the time; people who are awake and present; people who allow my work in recovery, support my journey, acknowledge my progress, and encourage my autonomy.

They give me the room to come up with my own solutions,
in my own good time.

Available people are available.

February 29
MAKING CHANGES

There was a time when I had big dreams of what my life would look like, 'eventually'. ***The plan seemed to go something like this: I will escape my current dysfunctional conditions, I will apply my skills, I will get the outcome I want, and I will be happy.***

I had overlooked one thing; reality. I had high hopes, but a very low tolerance to frustration. I lacked follow through.
I lacked genuine confidence.
I gave up easily.

The program has re-introduced me to my genuine self; the self I had to abandon in order to survive. As a result, I have core interests as opposed to fleeting fantasies designed to escape my pain.

In order to arrive at a certain outcome, I want to know what the outcome will *possibly* look like. Next, I become willing to apply my effort. ***Then, I get ready.*** I surround myself with people who are supportive.

I research what others have done who have gone before me. Whatever it takes to bolster my confidence, I do it. ***Next, I come up with a plan of action.*** Finally, I put the plan *into* action.

I know the play; I take the shot. Sometimes I get the result I want, sometimes I don't. I always get a chance for a do-over.
I can always "take it from the top".

I can *always* begin again.

MARCH

March 1
SIFTING THROUGH THE RUBBLE

There was never a time when I stopped and asked myself:
'Why am I doing what I am doing and is it, in fact, working?' I lived life on 'auto-pilot'. I did what I did because that's the way I had always done what I had done. **_Period._** The possibility never occurred to me that my error in thinking; my error in judgement could be setting up the very situations that caused me the most pain.

These situations, brought on by behaviors associated with my incorrect thinking, seemed endless as I moved from one frustration to another.

One crisis sometimes followed another with little or no break in between.
What common factor was present in all the chaos?
What strange characteristic was present in all the frustration?
What was 'at the bottom' of all this pain?

Enter the Fifth Step. I am admitting to God, myself and another human being the *exact nature* of my wrongs. In other words, I am looking at the thinking that drives the behavior; the behavior that continues to set me up for contempt toward myself and others; my resentment.

Someone reported in a meeting one night a new realization; that before she could react to any situation, she had to *think* something first; *that her thoughts ALWAYS preceded her harmful actions; her 'wrongs' toward herself and others;* that her excessive demands on *herself and others* usually gave birth to her impending responses.

I am a person habitually drawn to the notion that I *should always* behave in a certain way; furthermore, I am inclined to unrealistically require others to behave in a certain way, as well. And so, it would seem, that the exact nature of my dilemma lies between my own ears; in my own brain.
Steps Six and Seven offer me the opportunity to 'turn down the volume' on the 'shoulds'. When I try to hold onto my old ideas,
the result is usually nil; or worse.

As I move forward, **_LIFE ON LIFE'S TERMS,_** serves to remind me of a great truth: **_NOBODY_** performs perfectly **_ALL_** the time.

March 2
ACCESSING RESOURCES

I was convinced that nothing was going to work out for me. And indeed, that seemed to be the case. I lacked confidence.

I rarely knew what I wanted. Having been driven by a system of tyrannical 'shoulds' for years, it didn't seem to matter what I truly wanted anyway.

Measuring up to my unrealistic demands was my obsession; and, I never seemed to measure up. Without really knowing it, I lacked the resources necessary for healthy development.

I had abandoned the idea of asking for what I needed, as I seldom believed I would get it.

I like sports and in sports, even the most talented player allows a coach to help along the way. I am moving closer and closer to my genuine core interests. I have a deeper sense of who I am; that is, what I *used* to believe about myself, my world and what I believe *now*.

When I ***KNOW*** what I want, I am more likely to find it.
I can ask for directions. I can request clarification.
I can admit when I am stuck. I can fail.

I can make mistakes. ***I can learn.*** I can search for the resources I need in order to get the outcome I truly hope for. My outer effort matches my inner passion.

I am moving toward my genuine self; my greatest resource.
I am asking for help when I need it.

March 3
ALLOWING OTHERS THEIR JOURNEY

I spent a lot of my time looking at others, comparing their situation with mine. I criticized them and sometimes blamed them. I guessed at what 'normal' looked like. *I felt threatened when others seemed to be 'winning'.*

I was triggered emotionally by others, as well. What emotions I could not own, I placed on others. I hated myself.

My pride system kept me in denial about my own true process. I was obsessed with living up to the unreasonable standards I had set.
The tyrannical 'shoulds' kept me in shackles.

I am walking away from my false self, the author of my tyrannical shoulds. I am turning down the volume on demands to perform perfectly *all the time.* As a result, I am letting up on others, too. Even when other's problems don't seem apparent, I can recognize that *we all struggle* in one way or another.

And when others are obviously struggling, I don't have to take on their feelings.

I don't have to abandon myself in order to rescue them. I can give them the dignity to work out their own situation, usually just by listening.
I stay in my own lane.

I keep the focus on my own process.

March 4
LISTENING TO OTHERS

I spent a lot of time 'talking at' others, trying to get a word in 'edge-wise', preparing my thoughts as others spoke, searching my brain for the perfect response, sometimes interrupting them in mid-sentence; anxious about what to say. *I was very uncomfortable in most social settings.*

I am stepping into a new practice; the art of listening. I am relieved to be 'off the hook' in trying to find just the right words to say to others. As a result, I am more present. I am more available. *I am naturally more comfortable in social settings, as I let others do most of the talking.*

I listen in order to get to know someone and in knowing, I am more likely to respect their journey in a *genuine* way.

Most of the time, I can use simple ques in order to let people know that I have just heard what they have shared: 'Hmmm. Oh? I see. You don't say? Wow!' Sometimes I can just be silent, maybe nodding my head to let them know that I have heard them.

For me, *listening is the greatest gift I can give another human being;* free passage to express thoughts and feelings. In listening, I am really saying, 'I care'.

When I am heard, I feel validated; and when I feel validated, I move closer and closer to my genuine self. The journey of recovery toward my lost self is underway.

March 5
RETURNING AND REST

As much as I hate to admit it, I thrived on chaos; or so I thought. <u>***Chaos was, in fact, slowly killing me.***</u>

Running from one crisis to the next was somewhat exciting, but it proved exhausting. Even more so, as I grew older. When I found the rooms of recovery, I was twenty-nine years old. I felt more like seventy. **My anxiety level was off the charts.** It felt normal.

The concept of 'One Day at a Time' was foreign to me in the beginning of recovery. I preferred projecting into the future, far away from the 'here and now'. Someone suggested that I create a safe place for myself where I could go throughout the day in order to regroup; to gather my thoughts; to allow myself some 'down-time'.
(Yeah, right. Like that's going to happen.)

Years later, I discovered the absolute joy of being able to return home after being out for the day. I have a spot; ***my spot*** where I have ***my thoughts, my feelings, my cup of tea, my favorite book, my favorite music.***

My two daily high points, now; highpoints that I can ***always*** count on: returning to my spot and getting a good night's sleep. ***And that, coming from a former adrenaline junky!***

Wonders never cease!

March 6
BEGINNING ANEW

By the time I showed up in the rooms, I had given up. I had reached the end of my rope. All the things I had tried were no longer working. I was stuck. The more I showed up for the weekly meetings, the greater traction I seemed to be getting in my recovery and yet, there were setbacks and with the setbacks came feelings of disappointment, even anger and frustration. Some days I wanted to quit.

I am seeing segments of time differently, realizing that 'time takes time'. I am viewing setbacks not as signs of failure, but as opportunities to start again. ***I can take my time on the journey.*** I expect delays.

I am training for the marathon, not the fifty-yard dash.

I remember the first moon-shot in the late sixties. America's very ambitious dream began with a single vision: to land a man on the moon and return him safely home. **YEARS** would follow before we would hear that lone voice from the surface of the moon, 'Houston. The eagle has landed'. Along the way, there had been many setbacks and many do-overs; many 'Houston, we have a problem' moments.

With each passing day, I have a solid shot at recovering my lost self; a solid shot at putting into practice the new skills I have learned in order **TO** recover my lost self. If something isn't working, I can come up with a new plan. ***I take each failure, each mistake in stride; all part of the training.***

I can see each day as a new beginning.

March 7
DEALING WITH LOSS

I lost many 'things': myself, relationships, careers, opportunities; so much, in fact, that I doubted the day would ever come when I might feel consistently happy. Grief seemed to envelop all that I had become.

I remain vulnerable to loss and yet, I have a process upon which I can entirely rely; the 'grief process'.

This process assures my eventual acceptance of a situation, regardless of the event. My grief process has a course all its own; nevertheless, it **has** a course.

The five stages of grief are: denial, anger, bargaining, sadness, and acceptance. Given enough time, I can integrate losses, emerge to the other side, and eventually return to a reasonably comfortable state of mind.

When perceived losses come in waves, I have learned to simply ride out the losses, making sure that I am not creating any more crises than I have already endured. ***I don't give up five minutes before the miracle of acceptance.***

In the meantime, I get back to the basics: regular meetings, the Steps and safe people. I stay awake.

I trust the process.

March 8
FEELING MY FEELINGS

I had grown accustomed to shutting down my emotions lest I be distracted from my primary task; living up to the demands I had created for myself in order to 'survive'. ***Stressful conditions prevented my spontaneity.***

Feelings seemed to get in the way. And besides, my anxiety level disallowed most emotion outside of fear, anger and excitement.

I return to my feelings as I awaken to the journey within. My emotion is the guidepost; the sign pointing me in the right direction as I search for my real self.

Talking about how I feel with a safe person opens the region of buried memories and I am better able to sort through the rubble in search of my true self. I can distinguish between ancient emotions attached to my old self with its unrelenting demands for perfection and the natural feelings associated with past grief and loss. ***I am getting a clearer picture of my emotional landscape.***

Sad, mad and glad; these are the essentials. Often, current events will trigger old emotions attached to memories of the past. This is important in my search for who I am. ***I WANT to know what happened.***

I want to feel the feelings that I could not feel, during the time I endured 'the war zone'. I am awake when I can recognize how I am feeling; at the time I am feeling it; about what I am feeling it about.

I feel what I feel and I'm keeping it real.

March 9
SEARCHING FOR MYSELF

I had no interest in putting the puzzle pieces of my life together before I found the rooms of recovery. *Indeed, the less I could remember of the years gone by the better.* I was 'forward thinking'.

The events of the past came with emotions and most of the emotions were not 'warm and fuzzy. They were emotions of grief, anger, rage; even terror.

I am willing to look at my past in order to fully embrace the future. *I inventory old beliefs at the core of my moral system that keep setting me up for hurt and abuse.* I am ready to take the necessary step in the journey toward recovering my abandoned self. I am making a searching and fearless moral inventory of myself. I am taking Step Four.

On this journey, I am encountering emotions attached to events I had long forgotten. I want to literally re-member the shattered pieces of my past. I am thorough.

I want to know as much as I can about myself and the history that is me. I am taking the time I need, but I am making the completion of my moral inventory a very high priority, one day at a time. I am creating a sense of urgency in a way. Why?

My journey forward *absolutely* requires my knowing from whence I come. This is my history. ***This is my life.*** This is my self.

The closer I get to the past, the brighter my future appears.

March 10
ENCOUNTERING EMOTIONS

I was rarely aware of what I felt at any given time. I was semi-conscious most of the time. ***I resisted unwanted feelings by distracting myself:*** sabotaging relationships, moving to a new town, taking a new job, buying new things, taking up a new hobby; and on and on it went.

I look for feelings now. I am growing more and more conscious of my inner life. ***I am discovering feelings still attached to old ideas;*** excessive over-reactions to unrealistic expectations placed on myself and others:
rage, shame, blame, humiliation, depression, anxiety.
These emotions come from my old false self.
I process these emotions with a safe friend.

I am aware of other feelings, as well; feelings of assurance and peace of mind. My true self is emerging and with its surfacing, I am creating new ideas; new ideas that are friendly to myself and others. With the advent of the new ideas comes a sense of relief as I lower my demands.
I can practice, *'Easy Does It,'* and really enjoy certain
moments of serenity, even joy.

I can own my disappointment, my anger, even my hurt over current events, without feeling ashamed of who I am. ***Reality is my friend.***
It's OK for me to feel what I am feeling.

It's OK to talk things over with a friend. It's OK to be who I am.

March 11
ENJOYING CERTAIN MOMENTS

Part of the problem, having been emotionally numb for most of my life, was the utter lack of appreciation for moments when 'things' were going well. ***My hyper-vigilant anxiety refused any reprieve from the constant onslaught of demands;*** the 'tyranny of the shoulds'.
I was rarely 'in the moment'.

I am awake to the moments of my day when 'things' are going well. ***I pause, allowing the emotion of well-being to register consciously.*** Even if it only lasts for a few seconds, I allow the feeling of serenity to wash over me. When I am lucky enough to realize these moments, I try to extend my awareness, registering the happy memory; savoring the joy.

With the help of God, I am freeing myself of the pernicious claims about how I ought to be and how others ought to be. I am becoming more and more spontaneous as **<u>I embrace the liberty of letting go</u>** of the 'police state' in my head.

I am aware of my interests. I enjoy certain 'things': classic folk rock, a factual news item, a relaxing shower, a walk in the park with my dog, my cat curling up on my lap, a good pizza, my wife's arrival home, my wife's departure ***(just kidding!)***. ☐

I relish the moments of simple satisfaction.

March 12
BECOMING SPONTANEOUS

Due to the intense design of my strategy around survival, I was on high alert most of the time. I believed I had to perform in a certain way all the time in order to not be rejected. ***I walked a tight-rope.*** Some would say I was obsessed, always insisting on a preconceived outcome.

Having finished my Fourth and Fifth Step, I am ready to be free of the unrelenting mandates that drive my behavior. ***The Sixth Step invites me to consider a new way to live.*** I am entirely ready to have God remove all the defects of my thinking that sets up my old dysfunctional behavior.

I am finding situations unfolding that help in removing my rigidity of thought. When I find myself in times of trouble I can pause, feel the feeling, identify the old idea and let go of the exaggerated demand either on myself or another human being. ***It's a God thing.***

I am lightening up as I choose to be around people who are mostly available, nurturing and fun. I can laugh. ***I can think of something I would like to do and do it.*** I can think of something I want to say and say it. I can move from one feeling to the next without getting forever bogged down and if I do get stuck, I can talk about it.

If something isn't working, I can change it; go to plan "B".
I discover a new freedom; a new happiness.

March 13
TAKING STEP SIX

Before I found the rooms, changing anything was a big deal. ***'My way' had become a safety barrier between me and the rest of the world.*** The upside to this approach was that it did keep me reasonably 'safe' some of the time; the downside? It kept me stuck and isolated most of the time.

I stand at a turning point, following the completion of Steps Four and Five. I want to change the thinking that has set up my dysfunctional behavior. I am *entirely ready* to have God remove the old demands on myself and others that keep me upset.

The key for me is a simple willingness to allow ***God*** to remove the defects of my thinking; to allow ***God*** to arrange conditions upon which change can happen; to allow ***God*** to bring people into my life from whom I may learn; in other words, to allow ***God to be God***.

<u>Everyone has the potential of becoming my teacher; every circumstance, my classroom.</u>

With any event, I can feel the feeling, identify the old idea and with God's help, become willing to let go of my chronic toxic demands on life.

I trust the process. I stay awake. I remain connected to others on the path. I talk about what is going on. God is doing for me what I could not or would not do for myself. Step Six requests my willingness; Step Seven invites my action ***to join God*** in removing my dysfunctional behavior…
by asking for help. ***<u>I can't. He can. I think I'll let Him.</u>***

Easy peezy.

March 14
TAKING STEP SEVEN

Asking for help was like volunteering for a front row seat at an execution; with my being on the receiving end of the main event. My unrelenting demands around how I should always perform made it almost impossible to admit that I needed help. It was a pride thing.

Just the mere thought of being dependent on others would send me into a fit of shame and embarrassment. Even worse, when I would ask for help and not get my expected result, I felt disappointed and humiliated.
A strong dose of resentment usually followed.

I am asking God, "Who am I supposed to meet and what am I supposed to learn?" Old events are re-presented in real time so that I can awaken to my dysfunctional process; so that I can ask God for help in removing my unproductive behavior, my 'shortcomings'.

I am teachable. I embrace the help of the universe.

Someone once said, 'God works through other people.' I am open to that process. I am learning from a variety of circumstances and individuals. I am receptive to the idea that my Higher Power can arrange conditions whereby my disorders; my 'defects of character' are being removed by virtue of exposure. Like a thief in the light of day, a troubling old idea can be identified and dealt with through the power of Step Seven.

I trust God to help. I trust the process of the Steps.

March 15
BELONGING

There were times when I felt so out of place that a gentle breeze could have knocked me over. *I seldom identified with others as I was obsessed with masking who I was and how I felt.* People pleasing seemed to be my greatest skill in alleviating the tension and yet, I rarely felt connected regardless of how well I played my part.

I am trusting myself more and more. I am comfortable with the details of my story. I can take my place in a group of people as 'one among many'.
The meetings are teaching me how to interact.

I go early enough that I can purposely engage with people, learning as I go.
I stay after the meeting so I can practice connecting with others.

When I find myself in unfamiliar settings, *<u>I can rely on simply being me</u>*.
I am no longer a stranger to myself; no longer hiding from myself.
I am comfortable in my own skin.

At the end of the day, I know that I have a solid group of people in recovery who support me right where I am. *The rooms give me the place to practice being who I truly am.* I am settling into my unique self; the self that separates me from the rest of the crowd and allows me the confidence to hold my own in a room full of strangers.

I am connecting with myself; I am connecting with others.
I belong.

March 16
GIVING VOICE TO MY THOUGHTS

I kept most everything inside; my thoughts, my feelings, my perceptions. *It seemed I was an island unto myself; a rock. Don't talk, don't trust, don't feel.* This strategy served me well in my dysfunctional world; however, this approach in real time had stopped working altogether. The gears had locked up.

I have a new approach. I discover those in my group who *are available, nurturing and supportive*; usually people *who can simply listen* without rescuing or otherwise, fixing me.

As best I can, I talk about what is going on. When I honestly address my thoughts and feelings with someone else, something amazing happens. The stress, the pressure, the anxiety either diminishes or goes away entirely.

I trust a conversation only to the extent that I perceive the other person is honestly listening without prejudice. If a person repeatedly makes suggestions or asks prodding questions, I realize their distraction with caretaking has taken over and I change the topic. It happens.

Sometimes even available people can be side-tracked with old behavior. *I find another person who is available to simply listen.*

When I hear my own thoughts and feelings reflected in the voice of another person, I have a chance to change. I become a little more objective in knowing my own process. I make better choices.

I discover solutions that are right for me.
My autonomy is preserved.
My dignity is restored.

March 17
PRIORITYZING EVENTS

I played a lot of roles: good employee, loyal son, faithful friend, smart student. When it came time to choose how to spend my time, **the decision was usually based on what I "should" always do, rather than on what I genuinely wanted to do**. This, in turn, led to a lot of dead ends with little or no pay off.

I am discovering a new moral structure, having completed the first nine Steps. This belief system is emerging from a healthy sense of self; a self that is becoming more and more connected with genuine interests, honest thoughts and true feelings.

New ideas are overtaking the old demands. I am functioning from a relatively new place; emotionally, spiritually, intellectually, even physically.

I still have deep, heartfelt beliefs; but I don't allow the "shoulds" to drive **ME**.

With God's guidance, I am steering the bus today. *I choose* how to arrange my events. *I choose* with whom to spend my time. *I choose* my own interests. *I choose* everything.

I am ultimately responsible for my own well-being. I am the ***only one responsible*** for remaining true to my genuine self. When I stay true to myself, I usually feel productive and happy at the end of the day...

win, lose, or draw.

March 18
CHOOSING MY REPONSE

Reacting to life seemed to be my only option. *I remained dazed and confused a lot of the time, going from crisis to crisis, trying to return to some sense of normalcy.* I had tired many approaches to alleviate my stress, most of which had ceased working by the time I found the rooms of recovery.

I am more centered. Crises come and go. I am learning the fine art of responding rather than reacting to events, especially events that involve other people's attitudes and moods. Even when I am triggered emotionally by some situation that is reminiscent of a previous traumatic episode, I can retreat, regroup and return if I so choose. **_I have options._**

When it comes to knowing what to do next in response to life's requirements, I throw myself into Step Eleven. Sometimes, "the knowledge of His will for my life" comes in the twinkling of an eye; a new idea, a simple suggestion from a favorite book, someone's sharing in a meeting, a stranger mentioning a possible resource.

I take the time to "know the play". Then I take the shot. Sometimes I win, sometimes I lose. Responding, rather than reacting buys me some time to make decisions that are right for me; healthy decisions.

March 19
EXPLORING MY PAST

Before the program, I had absolutely no desire to look back. ***Why would I willingly subject myself to memories littered with pain and grief?***

Hmmmm, let's see. I can go out, have dinner and go to the ball game or stay at home and write my memoir. I went for the ball game and dinner every time.

<u>I am searching for my true self</u>. I am on a quest. I am looking at the past through Step Four in order to create a new future. This is my life; one day at a time, one event at a time, one feeling at a time, one moment at a time.

I don't have to go there alone. I enlist the help of others in the program to support my efforts.

In remembering situations of the past, I sometimes need to talk about the emotions that surface. I do this sooner than later. I don't have to wait until I do a Fifth Step.

The command center of my dysfunction is headquartered in the past. Old ideas that keep setting me up for disappointment are there. The mission? ***<u>Keep the ideas that are working and with God's help get rid of the ones that ain't.</u>***

I set sail for my journey into the future,
knowing that ***I must go back in order to go forward.***

March 20
DEALING WITH OLD WOUNDS

When feelings of shame, humiliation, anger and resentment would come up, *I usually denied what was truly happening and moved on to my next distraction*, making certain to avoid such situations in the future.

By seventeen, I was drinking every day, trying to avoid my mother altogether as she acted out her addiction to love and romance. I had mastered the art of shutting down my feelings.

In recovery, I become willing to deal with life; life on life's terms. Past emotion is triggered by current events. This is a good thing. *With the help of others who are facing their own fear, I can talk about the past, identify old events, examine the details, and feel the feelings;* feelings I could not or would not allow. Powerful old events, laced with strong emotions, set the stage for my ensuing life. My old ideas; my 'moral' structure was formed on those events. Old emotions shored up my 'value' system.

<u>Grief is part of my recovery and pain is part of my process.</u>
Old emotions are stuffed feelings.

I accept it. The way to get past my hurt is to go *through* the hurt. I can identify old dictates on myself and others; harsh 'orders' coming from my old belief system; and with the help of God in Steps Six and Seven, I can let them go.

When old wounds are re-opened, I have a way to recover…

I FEEL TO HEAL

March 21
LEARNING FROM MY MISTAKES

I used to view my making mistakes as an indication of who I was, fundamentally. As a result, when I made a mistake, the first emotion that usually surfaced was anger (sometimes rage) and then the onslaught of shame. *<u>I came to believe that I was somewhat of a loser</u>*; doomed for failure; that I belonged in the land of the 'mis-fit' toys.

I realize that I was *AND AM* a perfectly functioning human being who merely got the wrong owner's manual. I have changed manuals and with the help of others, I am going places.

<u>I am learning all kinds of 'new' things:</u> feeling my feelings, talking about what is going on, trusting my own perception, acting from my true interests, remaining genuine to me, moving toward safe people, not rescuing others. Amazing stuff!

Occasionally, I make mistakes along the way. I still feel angry, sometimes even guilty; but I am done with shame. *<u>Shame says, 'You are a mistake.' Guilt says, 'I made a mistake.'</u>*

My life and my actions *associated* with my life sometimes turn out the way I want, sometimes they don't. When they don't, I can always try again.

Correcting mistakes is a way of life for me today. *I expect delays and detours on my journey toward becoming fully human.*

It's all part of the process.

March 22
FAITHING MY WAY THROUGH

I had very little confidence in people, especially myself. I had grown to mistrust almost everything.

What could go wrong, would go wrong; and often, it did. **When things went wrong, I would blame myself and others.** In my world, I had long accepted that God was the original source of all my discomfort in life; trusting a loving God? Forget about it!

I have reviewed some of my hard-core beliefs in Steps Four and Five. I have come to believe that, in fact, ***I have the capacity not only to care for myself, but to allow available others to care for me, as well.*** And yes, God is in the picture too; only now, there is a strategic component that had been missing: ***my own connection with a genuine self.***

When I know what I want, I have a better chance of finding it. The tyranny of the "shoulds" has diminished and so, ***<u>I have a greater capacity for knowing my genuine interests.</u>***

I am having moments where I am receiving what I need in order to create what I truly want. ***When this happens, I move a little closer to the <u>God of my understanding.</u>***

Someone much wiser than I once said, 'Now faith is the substance of things hoped for; the evidence of things unseen.'

I can dream again.

March 23
UTILYZING RECOVERY LITERATURE

I was aware of psychology even before finding the rooms of recovery. I read popular 'self-help' books.

Some of the theories made sense. *I hoped to find a magic formula that could help; with what, I really didn't know.* Inspirational books seemed to work for a time also.

I know that I had been on a quest even before showing up for my first meeting. Something was guiding my search for self. When I discovered others, who were on a similar journey, suddenly many options were available. Lucky for me, a lot of authors were writing about the effects of having been raised in a dysfunctional home. A favorite Al-Anon slogan rang true as it still does today: ***Take What You Like and Leave the Rest.***

I realize that certain information presents itself at a time when I can receive it. I usually get what I need, when I need it in order to further my course.

<u>*I keep an open mind*</u>. I view all sources as possibilities for learning. I am particularly awake to suggestions of others, regarding helpful books.

My spiritual travels are unlimited. In seeking to connect with my genuine self, *I find when the student is ready, the teacher will appear.*

March 24
KNOWING MY LIMITATIONS

Part of the problem, having been raised in a dysfunctional, upside down world, was my inability to conceptualize a little thing called 'reality'. **_'Normal' was not normal._** I relied on sources outside the family to define how 'things' should be: television programming, religious programming, educational programming. By the age of nine, I was programmed pretty good.

I was lured away with deceptive whispers of grandeur by my false self; 'you can become anything you set your mind to do'. Eventually, the whispers would become marching orders centered around how I should always be rather than my great potential. **_Mistakes became shame-based catastrophes._** I doubled down on perfection; no more mistakes! I lived with this demand for years.

I am introduced to a new concept: ***EASY DOES IT***. I find comfort in hearing other's stories and struggles around trying to live up to the perfection myth. I realize that I am not alone. Having recovered my real self, I connect with genuine interests.

I have looked at a large portion of my history through Step Four. I keep some of the old programming. **_I prepare to let go of the remaining ideas that are extinct._** And I readily admit, in Step Five, the 'exact nature' of the errors in my unrealistic demands; my relentless entitlements.

I prepare myself to have God remove these incessant, distorted ways of thinking; these exaggerated expectations of myself and others; these defects of thought, word and deed. I embrace my own innate vulnerability and the human frailty connected with the entire family of man. **_I am not perfect, nor is anyone else._** Far from it, I am and always will be challenged: emotionally, spiritually, intellectually and physically; as is every man, woman and child on the planet.

I walk. I stumble. I fall. *I get up.*
I walk. I stumble. I fall. *I get up again.*
I walk. I stumble. I fall. I get up again.
And I go get some new shoes!

March 25
CLEARING MY MIND

I had a lot of 'outstanding' problems; problems that seemed insurmountable; problems that had been problems for years; problems that, by their very nature, created more problems. ***I was overwhelmed***. The chattering in my head was distracting. The barking of self-criticism was deafening.
My resentment, under the surface, was raging.

I still have outstanding problems. If I can do something about them today, I do it. If I can't, I clear them from 'today's agenda'. I wait for opportunity to present itself. ***One of my most useful skills is the practice of staying in the day***.

I remain awake to the realities of the day: rent is due, car needs repair, children need clothes, deadlines need to be met, food needs to be purchased, interviews need attention; dog needs a bath; yard needs mowing; on and on and on. Life goes on.

At any time during the day, I give myself permission to **STOP**. I turn off the machines. *I take a break from the noise and clamor.* If the actual environment is too loud, I use ear plugs to bring silence to my world. I close my eyes and return to a time-honored slogan:

EASY DOES IT   *LIVE AND LET LIVE*

ONE DAY AT A TIME   *LET GO AND LET GOD*

JUST FOR TODAY   *DETACH WITH LOVE*

      TO THINE OWN SELF BE TRUE

And my favorite? When all else fails, ***READ THE INSTRUCTIONS***.

March 26
CHALLENGING MY PERCEPTION

I used to experience things that I believed to be true when, in fact, my perception had sometimes skewed the reality of the event altogether. **When in doubt, I rarely 'checked out' my conclusion with those involved.** I would read into conversations phantom inuendo. I would mis-interpret the intentions of others, sometimes shaping the narrative of what happened to 'fit' *MY* story. Previous events colored my assessment.

<u>This distortion of reality was not my friend.</u>

I am aware of my current daily events. I am aware of how those events can shape important relationships. *I have the capacity, through Step Ten, to challenge any process of any event at any time.* If something is bothering me, I can check it out with the source: what, in fact, happened?
Is this what you meant? Did you think I meant this? I can clarify my position; perhaps apologize if my thinking or the action attached to my thinking is wrong.

I am still triggered emotionally by experiences in today. I can honestly 'push back' with my own thoughts and feelings.

<u>*I am reasonably comfortable with knowing the truth*</u>. Sometimes I over-react. When I make a mistake in my thinking, I can admit it. With the help of God and others, I can get a 'reality check'. Sometimes my perception is spot on; sometimes it isn't. That's OK.

I am comfortable with simple progress, rather than absolute perfection.
I can own my stuff without losing my true self.

Reality is my friend.

March 27
PARTICIPATING IN MY OWN LIFE

I had grown terrified of life without really knowing it. Many of my old ideas and the coping strategies attached to those ideas had ceased to work.
A lot of the 'chosen' roads had led to ambush, betrayal and abandonment.
I was at a dead end when I found the rooms.

<u>The Fourth and Fifth Steps allow my freedom of choice to return,</u>
as I admit to God, myself and another human being the 'exact nature' of my errors *in thinking;* my fearful, unrelenting demand for perfection which lay at the core of all my 'wrongs'; wrongs committed toward myself and others.

I am slowly returning to my true self; my innocent self that lived and breathed *before* all the trouble began.

I let go of the behavior associated with these dysfunctional ideas in Steps Six and Seven, making space for new ideas and healthier behavior.

With God's help, I embrace life on new terms.
I am forgiven. To some extent, I am forgiving others, as well.

Even with all the risks, ***I step boldly into my new life; my healthy self.***
I am exploring genuine interests, returning to true curiosities,
allowing ***the day to be the day*** with all its ups and all its downs.

I have dreams for the future. Most of the time, I act according to my core self; what I genuinely think and feel. I hope for possible results.
<u>Sometimes I get the outcome I want, sometimes I don't.</u>

That's OK. I can trust the process. I can absorb the losses and celebrate the gains. Astonishing things are coming to pass because ***<u>I am free</u>***, once again, to simply…be me.

March 28
RECOGNIZING MY OWN PROGRESS

In times past, I was filled with self-hate. It seemed I was rarely able to measure up to the unrelenting demands attached to my old ideas; ideas about how I should always perform. Mistakes often triggered a sense of self-loathing.

I projected my sense of failure on to others, as well; pointing out their inability to always behave in a certain way. I was mercilessly focused on results. It was not about how I had played, but whether I had won or lost.

Subtle shifts in perception often change a lifetime of demands. Sometimes I win, sometimes I lose. I still acknowledge results and yet, I am usually the last to know of my own progress in the rooms.

Each day, with the help of God, I pick myself up, dust myself off and make my next move…hopefully, forward. I expect setbacks; one step forward, three steps back; it's part of the process.

I am growing free of the clinging vines of dysfunctional distractions: rescuing others, rehearsing old victim stories, blaming others, abusing myself with obsessive-compulsive thinking, harming myself with mood altering substances, and on and on and on. **_I recognize relapses sooner._**

Sometimes I hear my own story in the sharing of others. I am reminded of where I have been; what it was like before my recovery journey; what it is like today. *I take comfort in the words, 'we claim spiritual progress, rather than spiritual perfection'.*

I rejoice in my progress, great and small.

March 29
TRUSTING A GREATER FORCE

I counted myself a logical person. I took pride in devising a plan and sticking to it. Sometimes events would turn out just as I had hoped; however, even with all my 'talent', I was forever unable to guarantee with a hundred percent certainty that things, great and small, could always be managed.

<u>When I hit the rooms of recovery, I reluctantly admitted that I was, in fact, powerless;</u> that my life had become unmanageable.

With the help of a Higher Power, my life is now reasonably manageable. ***Things still go 'wrong' and when they do, I pause;*** sometimes just taking a deep breath, feeling the feeling, whispering a prayer.

Truth be told, ***anything I have ever truly 'let go' of***, usually has claw marks all over it. Roarrrrr!

I strongly believe that God is doing for me what I can't or won't do for myself. Circumstances beyond my control ***sometimes guide the outcome*** of my best laid plans. The results are often better than I could have imagined.

I GO WITH THE FLOW.

I am becoming more and more serendipitous; more spontaneous.
Step Eleven invites me to join forces with a power greater than myself; to align my will with the will of the Great Force.

A founding pioneer on recovery's path, Bill W., says that this, in fact, is the proper use of the will; the result being, a heightened state of humility; ***the inward desire to know and do God's will.***

Today, I combine the two: my way and the ***High Way.***

March 30
RETURNING TO MY TRUE SELF

In order to emotionally survive the chaotic world of dysfunctional behavior and its characteristic explosive contradictions, I shut down the process of my emerging young self. ***I ignored my feelings altogether.***
I denied my observations. I denied my own assessment of life.
Reality was not my friend.

In fear and confusion, ***I walked away from my genuine self***, my inner child who wanted to live simply: explore the woods in curiosity, worry when the family dog was lost, rejoice in helping with the dishes, celebrate the wonder of a blossoming flower, cry at the passing of a beloved pet,
laugh at the funny antics of a favorite uncle.

One of the greatest observations ever shared by
Al-Anon Family Groups is simply this:

'*Recovery does not mean that I have to become a different person.*
It means I need to start being myself again.'

I create safe places with safe people in order to return to love.

More and more, I feel what I am feeling today; at the time I am feeling it; about what I am feeling it about.
Reality is my friend.

The lessons I'm learning…are lessons I already know.
I just need to remember.

March 31
DEALING WITH ADVERSE FEELINGS

Emotions were a luxury that I could not afford. I was numb; locked down, shut up, closed off. They got in the way. They disturbed, they interrupted, they bothered. By closing off the unwanted feelings, I also hindered the desired feelings, as well.

I am awake now. I cry. I laugh. I get sad. I get angry. I get scared. I get disappointed. I get embarrassed.

Every emotion I can identify has the potential of unlocking doors leading to larger and larger spaces.

I am remembering more about my history than ever before and thus, I am getting to know my real self; that self that I had to leave behind in order to survive. I am feeling my pain; I am mourning my loss; and with God's help, I am moving on.

When deep emotions come up, I ask myself: ***What past event does this feel like?*** I can usually determine what belief came from the event and then, check my demands around the belief. Usually, my expectations are unrealistic. 'I should always do this; they should always do that.'

I can turn down the volume on these neurotic, dysfunctional dictates. ***Truth: sometimes I perform the way I should, sometimes I don't; sometimes others perform the way they should, sometimes they don't.***

Perfection, I have found, is terribly over-rated and ***WAY*** too difficult to maintain!

APRIL

April 1
ACCEPTING OTHER'S BEHAVIOR

When others offended, disappointed, lied, abused, cheated, manipulated or otherwise behaved in a way that I found unacceptable, *<u>I had three options: comply and deny; fight with fury; or leave.</u>* All three had their place in my overall coping strategy. Eventually, I would pick one as my primary means to cover up; to shut down; to protect myself from feelings of embarrassment, shame, hurt and anger.

Following a thorough Fourth and Fifth Step, I am emerging with a true self; my genuine self. I know what I will tolerate. I know what I will not tolerate. I have a grief process that allows my emotions to work for me, not against me. Reality is my friend.

I can respond to my environment in such a way that puts my welfare first.

I create relationship with myself, insuring as best I can, an atmosphere of health and safety. *I remind myself often, that others may not be altogether available; may not be altogether 'there'.*

When my safe space is breached; when conflict appears as it often does in an imperfect world, I sometimes compromise, allowing others the benefit of the doubt. Other times, I stand up for myself; enough is enough.

And, naturally, I *always* reserve the option to leave.

Regardless of what I choose to do, I talk to another safe person about what, in fact, is going on with my feelings. *Sometimes I comply, sometimes I fight, sometimes I exit the stage altogether.*
There is no shame in taking care of myself.
Whatever the outcome, I choose to…

LIVE AND LET LIVE.

April 2
GIVING MYSELF A BREAK

I labored with the notion that I could live up to all my beliefs, all the time. I required nothing short of perfection. **_When I failed, shame ensued._** These requirements on my thinking, feeling and acting had been created by me, for me.

This moral system with its incessant demands had kept me alive. I remained loyal to the pride system I had created. The problem? I was disintegrating. *My true self was dying due to the stress that came with never quite measuring up.* I was imploding with self-hate and humiliation.

My healthy established beliefs, the moral ideas that I want to keep, following my 'searching and fearless moral inventory', remain at the core of who I am. Sometimes I think, feel and act accordingly, sometimes I don't.

I do not claim anything close to perfect adherence to these principles. I am, after all, a mere mortal; only human, through and through.

I give myself credit. *I enter the day, knowing before-hand that there will be mistakes; errors consciously committed and best actions conveniently left undone.*

Steps Ten and Eleven invite me to embrace *all* that I am: fully human, fully lovable, fully flawed, fully capable and yes, fully forgiven.

April 3
PRACTICING THE PROGRAM

I was not aware of the concept called 'preparation'. In fact, I expected things to simply fall into place. People, places and things would magically work out; only they didn't. <u>**And as time went on, those upon whom I had counted grew more and more unavailable.**</u> The dysfunctional behavior in my family was weaving its tangled web. I was stuck; left to fend for myself.

Asking for help? **OUT OF THE QUESTION.**

I am a trip in progress. I have a road map in the Twelve Steps.
I know others who have travelled similar paths; others who ARE available; and still others who are searching for direction, just as I am.
I am not alone.

For me, *repetition strengthens and affirms habit; faith, then becomes natural*. Every meeting I attend, every person I encounter on this broad highway, every piece of recovery literature I read, every action I take toward applying the Twelve Steps; every time I talk about my feelings with a safe person; every time I simply listen without fixing; all these little repetitions add up.

Eventually, I am carrying the message. *I am practicing time-honored core principles in most of my affairs.*

By God's grace, I am living the Twelfth Step.

April 4
SENSING MY OWN VALUE

My self-confidence had plummeted to an all-time low. Nothing, it seemed, was working. I was hanging on by a thread. <u>**Without really knowing it, I had come to see myself as a loser;**</u> someone who was destined for failure; a freak. I was on the outside and most everyone else was on the 'inside'.

I am in recovery. I am capable, now. I have my correct owner's manual; the one that really fits the make and model of **my vehicle**, my true self. *My journey is slow and steady; some days, uphill; some days, downhill; some days, straight away.* With each day, I awaken to a genuine self; a self that has been with me since the day I was conceived.

When I act in accordance with how I really think and feel, I move closer and closer to my heart. I have interests. I have preferences. I have choices.

My value comes from my heart.
When I try something and it works, I feel happy.
I enjoy the process of being me most of the time.

Whether I am making myself a favorite cup of tea or designing a logo for my new company, I am awake to the process.

The 'inside', that I was always hoping for, is within my own heart; always has been.

Win or lose, I have a life!

And gosh-darnit, people like me!

April 5
SOLVING PROBLEMS

I avoided problems. Problems spelled trouble. And besides, I had problems stacked on top of problems.

These problems seemed to follow me, sometimes presenting themselves in different circumstances altogether; and yet, very familiar.
Instead of my 'seizing the day', the day had seized me.
I was overwhelmed, afraid and exhausted.

How does one eat an elephant? One bite at a time, or so the old joke goes. I still have problems, most of which are manageable. I believe there are only three kinds of problems: past, present and future.

If I can fix a problem right now, I fix it. If I cannot, I defer to a later time.

With God's help, I sometimes discover a solution in ways that I could not have designed alone. I avail myself of obvious resources: other people, instruction manuals, course descriptions, the evening news,
recovery meetings, lawyers, bankers, car dealers,
counselors, realtors, plumbers.

'Today's the day. Now is the time. This is it. Make no mistake, this is not a dress rehearsal'.

This is my life.

These are words of reminder. I can stay in the day, awakening to solutions as they present themselves. Once I find a solution, the problem magically goes away. I live in the solution…

ONE DAY AT A TIME

April 6
BEING NICER TO MYSELF

I was notoriously harsh with myself. *I had little tolerance for failure; failure to perform as I 'should'.* In fact, I despised myself when I failed.

The demands seemed to run the gamut; I should always: love others, go the extra mile, help family, be pleasant, take responsibility, look good, be a winner, stay in control, take command, meet deadlines, avoid trouble, be independent, dodge distractions, obey my moral code, stand up for myself, stay focused, be a good loser.
And be home by five o'clock.

Shame, embarrassment, disappointment and hurt seemed to be at the center of my false self's accusation and criticism. **Resentment fueled the fire; false pride kept the fire going.**

<u>**Self-hate was my master.**</u>

I am inventing ways to lower the volume on my unrealistic expectations. My favorite way? To remind myself often: sometimes I do what I should; sometimes I don't. The bottom line? I make mistakes.

To the degree I hear my own voice as compassionate is, in fact, the degree to which I hear the voice of God as compassionate.
I am a human being; not a human doing.

I am a worthwhile person and gosh-darn-it, people like me.

April 7
KEEPING THE FOCUS ON MYSELF

I was a people pleaser; a chameleon of sorts. Whether I admitted it or not, **_I spent a lot of time examining the behavior of others, comparing my 'insides' to their 'outsides'._**

I rarely measured up to those above me. And those below me rarely measured up to me. I was stranded in the middle, disconnected with myself and others; unaware of my process; asleep.

I am awakening to an inner life; my life. I am naturally curious to discover what, in fact, makes **ME** tick.

When I over-react to an event, I see my reaction as an opportunity; an opportunity to 'peel back another layer to the onion'; an opportunity to discover the center of the old demands of my false self, the old ideas that keep setting me up for disappointment, shame and humiliation.

I am 'staying in my lane'. My real self emerges each day with new interests. Old interests are revisited in new ways. I am awake to my emotional cosmos.

I pause when agitated. I return to a restful place. I allow my process. **_I give myself permission to be…fully human._**

What others think of me today is none of my business. I can…

LIVE AND LET LIVE.

April 8
TAKING RESPONSIBILITY FOR MY WELL BEING

I had a lot of beliefs about how life should be; how others should treat me. Most notably, **_I believed life should always be fair for everyone._**

'Everyone', including me! I had been thoroughly disappointed with some of the most important players in my life. Life had **_NOT_** always been fair; in fact, it seemed that I had been mysteriously disadvantaged.

The most available adult in my life today is ME. The well-being of my psychological, social and spiritual self is my number one priority. I am awake to my emotions and I take the time to process the major events of my life with someone I trust; someone who can listen without advising, judging or criticizing. I give myself the dignity that comes with freely expressing my thoughts without fear; the fear of being rejected.

Having completed a Fourth and Fifth Step, I know who I am.
I am seeing my actual self in a softer light.

I take the time to explore what I can realistically do **AND** can't do for myself and others. **_I have limits._** I set boundaries. Some situations are naturally safer than others. I gravitate toward the safer ones.

When I make mistakes, whether at home or work or play, I realize the value in learning from those mistakes. I use the 'maintenance' steps, Ten and Eleven, to reset my emotional/spiritual compass.

I surround myself with people who are emotionally available; people who are safe. I celebrate my interests. **_I treat myself well, as often as I can._**

I enjoy being who I am.

April 9
CONSIDERING MY OPTIONS

I had been locked into a course of action that was directing me further and further away from my true self. My own well-being seemed to not matter. **_A false self was in control, calling most of the shots._**
Old demands drove most of my behavior.

I felt compelled to act accordingly. And when I didn't, there was 'hell to pay'. **_Self-criticism and doubt dogged my every step._**
I felt exhausted most of the time.

With the help of the program, I am reconnecting with a self I had long abandoned. Beginning with Step One, I see where I *can* begin again. I am not stuck. **_There are options._** Others are returning to a healthier sense of self by practicing Step Two, 'Came to believe that a power greater than ourselves could restore us to sanity'.

I am challenging the old demands; pushing back with my 'all or nothing' mentality; **_LOWERING MY UNREALISTIC EXPECTATIONS._**
The old compulsions are slowly fading away.

I am letting go of old ideas that no longer work. My clinging entanglements still cling and yet, I have moments where I am breaking free. I am stepping into my genuine self; the self that wants to explore, wants to create, wants to grow.

ALL OPTIONS ARE ON THE TABLE.

April 10
HOPING FOR A MIRACLE

The days I spent living in a dysfunctional world left me to doubt the meaning of it all. Rarely did events come together in such a way that I could feel the trust of family and friends. ***The proverbial 'apple cart' was in constant need of being reset.*** Although crises were weathered, there never seemed to be an end to the 'excitement'.

As time went on, I felt alienated from myself, my conscious internal process; and I felt alienated from others. ***Whether I prided myself on my independence, my friendly nature or my ability to master things around me, I frequently felt lonely and afraid, regardless of the outcome of my actions.*** Distracted with looking for the next 'fix', I had no genuine interest in my life's trajectory. I merely coped.

Much like one who is in attendance for a favorite sporting event, I have front row seats for my life today. ***I suit up and show up in order to be a part of the game.*** I have a real interest in the outcome. Sometimes my team wins; sometimes it doesn't. I always hope it will.
<u>And sometimes it takes a 'miracle'.</u>

Step Eleven allows attendance to my own process. I have tickets to the game. I connect with my real self. ***I awaken. I come alive. I explore what I truly want.*** When I know what I need in order to get what I want, I am more likely to find it. And when I find it, I feel connected. Perhaps for just a moment, I trust the process. The moments add up. Trust builds.
I begin to expect a miracle as events unfold.

Knowing that I need a miracle and getting that miracle is the game changer. ***When I get what I need at the exact time I need it in order to be who I am, I am thrilled!*** Praying for the knowledge of His will for me, the power to carry it out; and then, doing it?

Well now! That ***IS*** a miracle.

April 11
DETACHING WITH LOVE

I am a person still struggling with an old idea that demands that I should always help another person when they are not doing well. In fact, I am *attracted* to people who seem to need my rescuing and caretaking skills. I love people. And yet, I can get lost. My true self is sacrificed.

On better days, I am reminding myself that love, in fact, is *a process*. I meet someone. I get to know them. In knowing, I naturally respect their human struggle. ***In respecting that struggle, I begin to care.*** In caring, I naturally respond;

I act in a loving way toward that individual whom I have grown to know over time.

I am letting go of the old idea that I should always help everyone who needs my help; that I should always be able to love everyone unconditionally; that I should always be able to fix troublesome situations; that I should always be able to control unmanageable situations.

In most relationships, friends and family alike, ***I know today that my 'love' can know limitations***. I can establish realistic boundaries that are right for me. Sometimes I can help someone and sometimes I can't.

And that is ENTIRELY OK.

April 12
CREATING A SAFE PLACE

I had a knack for moving toward people and places that were ***not*** in my best interest. Being addicted to excitement, I said things and did things that set up unsafe conditions. As a result, I remained upset a lot of the time. ***I moved from one distraction to the next, hoping for a daily reprieve from the anxiety that had become my way of life.***

I am aware that my true self needs 'safe' in order to thrive; and for that, I am responsible. The rooms of recovery are safe most of the time. I can express myself without fear of being advised, rebuffed, ridiculed or otherwise, excluded as one 'not belonging'. Short of behaving in an abusive way, ***I can stay as long as I like; no rules to obey; no bi-laws for membership; no secret handshakes; no demands.***

I am hearing my own voice with less criticism. I am lowering the volume on the dictates of my 'shoulds'. Sometimes I perform well; sometimes I don't.

I am nurturing my own true voice.

I am making better choices about how and with whom I spend my time. I surround myself with nurturing people. I can walk away from 'toxic'. ***I can ask for what I need in a conversation.***

I can request that one simply listen, allowing my expression of joy, frustration, anger, even rage. This is where my real self shines.
This is where my true self gets to finally talk.
This is where I am validated in my recovery work.

I am only as healthy as the safe place I create, inside and out.

April 13
BEING AWAKE

I was often distracted by the clamor of my false self. ***I invented distractions to avoid the accompanying discomfort of old demands; doing, doing, doing; going here, going there.***

I rarely stayed still long enough to simply rest. The idea seemed to be that if I kept moving, they couldn't hit a moving target. Who 'they' were, I didn't quite know; perhaps the judge and jury in my head.

<u>***I did what I had to do in order to avoid my grief.***</u>
The lights were on, but nobody was home.

<u>***I am connecting with how I feel.***</u> I have moments during the day when I can stop all the activity and be still. Even if I have only a few minutes, I can check in with what is going on. The world on the inside is just as important as the world on the outside. My feelings can be my guide.

I am intuitively knowing how to handle situations. I am growing confident in my own perception. ***I am hearing what I need to hear, at the time I need to hear it, in order to move closer to my true self.***

The lyrics of an old forgotten song sometime seem to be exactly what I need. The words in a sermon speak to my core self.
<u>***The voice of a trusted friend comforts me.***</u>

The process of my genuine self is *always* present; always has been.
I am growing more and more ***AWARE*** of the process today.

I am awakening to who I am.

April 14
FEELING THE FEELINGS

I was obsessed with avoiding people, places and things in order to feel normal. *Certain distractions 'helped': mood altering substances, work, sex, chores, hobbies, trips, sex, television, children, family, food, sex, social media, religion, school; on and on and on.*

<u>And my favorite avoidance strategy? Stay home.</u> I did just about anything to not feel. Having an emotion was not OK; becoming emotional, even worse.

I am becoming emotional. I am allowing what goes on in my heart to get into my head. With the help of the program, I am open to exploring past episodes of grief; those moments in my life that I buried.

I am embracing my pain, sitting with the sadness,
talking about the anger.

I am more spontaneous because I am feeling what I am feeling at the time I am feeling it. By being more spontaneous, I am making better choices about events which affect me now. I have an inward 'barometer' of sorts.
I am no longer unconsciously acting to avoid;
I am consciously acting to connect.

The lights are on and I am DEFINITELY home…wherever I am.

April 15
ACCEPTING THE DISEASE CONCEPT

I was convinced that I should be ashamed; ashamed of my father's drinking, my mother's drinking, my uncle's drinking and eventually, my own drinking. People were heard to say things like, 'He knows that it's bad, why doesn't he stop?'

I was convinced that the whole alcoholism thing was a matter of weak character; that somehow, with the right moral values,
a person could 'straighten up and fly right'.

I have a disease. ***I have a disease for which I am, according to leading studies, genetically predisposed.*** There is no known cure. It is progressive. It is fatal. I don't have cancer. I don't have muscular dystrophy. It's not my heart. It's alcoholism. The good news? I can live a normal life if I don't engage my addiction; simple enough.

There remains a social stigma attached to the disease of addiction. Most folks won't do a walk-a-thon to raise money to fund a cure for addiction; won't pledge money; won't help create foundations; won't lobby local, state and federal government. Most stories associated with this disease **DO NOT** end well.

I believe Dad's behavior was a ***direct*** result of this disease. I believe Mom's behavior was a ***direct*** result of this disease. I believe Uncle Mack's behavior was a ***direct*** result of this disease. I believe my behavior was a ***direct*** result of this disease.

THERE IS NO SHAME IN HAVING A DISEASE.

April 16
BEING FREE

I spent a lot of time trying to control circumstances in order to avoid certain emotions; emotions buried in the past; emotions laying just under the surface. *I had strategies designed to dissolve conflicts before they ever came up.* I worked very hard to maintain these strategies; who I should be all the time; what I should say; what I should always do.

It was like trying to play soccer in a straight-jacket and shackles.
Not entirely impossible, but it took all the fun out of the game.

I am reasonably free now. I am lowering the incessant demands that were designed to keep me safe; the 'shoulds'. What worked back then stopped working. I am tapping into my core interests; giving myself permission to explore and try new things.

With God's help, I am removing the filter of shame. *I don't have to 'hold it all together'*. I can lose it. I can take risks. I like an adventure, even if it's just to the grocery store. Sometimes I get the result I hope for; sometimes I don't.

(They were out of my favorite salsa yesterday. Ugh!)

Just because I make a mistake doesn't mean that I AM a mistake. I can pick myself up, dust myself off and try again; or not. I can move on to other interests. I am free to choose how I spend my time with any one person, place or thing.

I am letting go of the past and living in the moment; awake and alive.

April 17
LOOKING AT MY OLD IDEAS

The source of my old ideas (a.k.a., my moral system) had begun in childhood. These notions of my identity, having merged into my teenage years, had grown rock-solid by adulthood. By the time I hit the rooms of recovery, my identity was formed. ***My old belief system was not up for debate.*** I had grown very rigid in my personal development.

Many of the beliefs which had helped me survive were no longer working. ***I had ceased to grow.*** A false self had taken over completely. I had become a slave to antiquated demands without really knowing it.

I am convinced of the value in reviewing my old ideas via the Fourth Step. I look at the process of how a belief is formed: I have relationships; from those relationships come events; from the events emerge feelings that are immersed in my old beliefs. ***These beliefs are reinforced over the years and become 'second nature'.***

I am ultimately responsible for what I believe. I look at my old ideas in order to better respond to my genuine self today.

I am, at this moment, a composite of all that has gone before. ***With God's help, I can look at ideas formed in the past and review their functional value as it relates to the here and now.***

I keep the values that are working. ***I let go*** of the ones that aren't.

April 18
CONNECTING WITH MY GENUINE SELF

I was a very disconnected person; not only with myself, but with others, as well. I worried about not truly belonging; about being eventually abandoned. My false self's obsession robbed me of time better spent developing my own interests, forming my own ideas and experiencing my real self.

My false self was unrelenting with its demands. *I traded joy and laughter connected to celebrating my REAL self for anxiety and fear that came with the nagging sense of never being enough.*

My false self is no longer driving the bus. The Fourth and Fifth Step settled that issue a long time ago. With God's guidance, I am ultimately responsible for all my choices. I have the freedom to go where I want to go; do what I want to do.

Make no mistake, my false self is still *on the bus*; but it stays seated most of the time; a nervous Nelly, anxious that I will make a wrong turn, some days insisting to drive, waiting for the right moment to spring into action with old road maps, old directions, and old demands. Poor thing.

This is my bus! This is my adventure; it always was! I am reclaiming my process. Today's the day; now's the time and *my* journey *IS* the journey.

With each passing day, I am developing my own interests, forming my own ideas and experiencing my real self. *I have a new map.* I ask for help along the way from trusted sources. And if I make a wrong turn? Big deal. Do overs are part of the equation.

And besides, I am precisely *where I am* in order to fully be…*who I am.*

April 19
EXAGGERATING OLD DEMANDS

I lived life as one walking a high wire in a three-ring circus. I could see the clowns below; the lions, the tigers and bears (oh my!); the ringleader, the grand master, watching my every move. *All I had to do was stay on the wire and all would be 'fine'.* The exaggerated requirements of remaining in the circus kept me on the wire even after the crowd left, practicing and rehearsing. The show demanded it!

I judged myself harshly for the smallest mistakes. *I laid awake nights, rehearsing what I could have done better; what I would do next time; what I should do all the time.* The show must go on! My over-blown sense of responsibility kept me anxious and upset most of the time.

Without really knowing it, I quit the circus the night I walked into my first meeting. Hearing the reading of the Laundry List, I realized specific traits associated with being raised in a dysfunctional family. In other words, I realized who I had become. I knew that I was in the right place.

I still go to the circus… *as a spectator.* I watch the clowns; the lions, tigers and bears. And what of the ringleader, the grand master? He sees me in the crowd from time to time and yells, 'Get back in the show! Get back on the high wire! Your place is in the circus!'
Oh, yeah? I don't **THINK** so.

I don't sweat the small stuff. Oh, and by the way, it's all small stuff today. Someone told me once, 'When you go to the circus, you're *supposed* to laugh at the clowns.' My new motto?

EASY DOES IT

April 20
ATTENDING MEETINGS

With my family, I felt included in the beginning; even nurtured at times. And yet, as the environment grew more and more toxic, I had difficulty returning home; feeling safe. *I disconnected from myself and in the process, unconsciously abandoned all hope of truly connecting with anyone else, as well.*

I would try over and over to feel included through various activities. I dressed the part, looked the part, even talked the part; and yet, integrating with others on a genuine level seemed out of reach.

<u>Fear blocked the way.</u> I felt intolerably alone. Before finding the program, the one thing that entirely eluded my awareness was the extreme degree to which my real self, in fact, had utterly disintegrated.

I know today that moving toward others and feeling genuinely appreciated is a big deal. *I have a human need to feel nurtured and included.* I can move away from others in order to establish my independent self; and yet, <u>*being able to return to a safe, solid source of support is essential to my growth and well-being.*</u>

This is where meetings come in. *I join with others in a common mission.* I depart to find my own way on my own journey. And I return the following week to report of my adventures; the high points and the low points of my expedition into the great unknown.

Most meetings are safe. I can *talk* of my experience, *trust* that I am accepted and *feel* what I need to feel in order to be on my way once again. My travels are appreciated as I return 'home' each week, safe to reconnect with myself and others.

April 21
SOLVING PROBLEMS

I showed up in the rooms with problems stacked on top off problems. I had grown weary, indeed exhausted, trying to figure out what to do, when to do it and with whom to do it with. Sometimes my over-reaction to situations would create even greater trouble. I was overwhelmed a lot of the time; anxious, angry and afraid.

One of the great gifts of the program came to me in the reading of some recovery literature written by Bill Wilson, an early recovery pioneer and co-founder of Alcoholics Anonymous. The idea was simple enough:
my many problems were mere symptoms of a disease.
The disease seemed to be rooted in my thinking, not necessarily in my doing. My perception of myself and the world around me was misaligned.

The Fourth and Fifth Step are problem solvers. By identifying the beliefs in my old moral system, **I begin to understand the exact nature of my troubles;** that is, the exaggerated demands that hound me: I should always be nice; I should always be helpful; I should never allow myself to be fooled; I should always be in control; I should never allow myself to be bothered; they should always treat me fairly; they should always do what they say they will do; they should always be honest. The list goes on.

When a pipe bursts and water is flooding everything, I first find the main valve; then turn off the pressure. *Lowering the volume of the incessant demands attached to my old ideas is the 'game changer'.*

Sometimes I act according to my ideals; sometimes I don't.
Sometime others act according to my ideals; sometimes they don't.
With the help of the program, I am solving one problem at a time…

ONE DAY AT A TIME.

April 22
RESPECTING MYSELF AND OTHERS

I lived in a world where even the closest people to me had become objects; objects either to be avoided or manipulated. *__I hated myself a lot of the time,__* rarely living up to my idealized standards; standards that my false self had created; standards that had become the base for my moral system of survival.

I reviled my actual self. I harbored the false hope of one day, appeasing an idealized, tyrannical self; once and for all. ***The only requirement? Absolute perfection.*** My own contempt with failure often poured onto others; sometimes in silent rage, other times in verbal outbursts.

Through Steps Four and Five, I am making peace with my false self; the self that had to survive; the self that had to be on high alert, lest something terrible happen. I know the dark roads of my past.

I respect my human struggle in navigating those troublesome times. I care for the interests of my genuine self; the self that was abandoned for the sake of survival. *__I respond as nurturing as possible to my human condition;__* my flaws, my mistakes; my high crimes and misdemeanors.

I can do the same for others, as I am convinced that we are all part of a universal group of raw humanity; that of the 'silent walking wounded'. Everybody hurts. In hearing others' stories, I naturally respect their journey's hardship and I am more likely to *genuinely care* for their interests and concerns.

*At the very least, I can respond with courtesy, knowing that we are all merely **TRUDGING** the road of happy destiny…*

ONE STEP AT A TIME.

April 23
PUSHING BACK ON OLD IDEAS

I rarely had the presence of mind to challenge my value system before recovery. When I violated one of my moral demands, I usually felt embarrassed or ashamed. When others would transgress the line of my high standards, I felt humiliated, often blaming them for their 'poor conduct'. **_Most of my old ideas were set in stone._**

I realize today that a lot of the demands formed for myself and others had come from a moral system of dysfunction; thus, I was limited. *I was hamstrung by the very system I had created in order to survive.*

When I find myself in times of trouble; outraged, ashamed or generally 'bent out of shape' over something, I immediately pause and check my thinking. Step Ten saves me a lot of grief. Most of the time, I have revisited an old exaggerated order issued from 'high command'; I should always, they should always! **The tyranny of the 'shoulds'!**

The truth? **_Sometimes I do what I should; sometimes I don't._** And the same goes for others. After all, I am just one of billions; simply being human, warts and all. I am developing a heightened awareness of my thoughts. I notice the change in my demeanor when my thinking becomes distorted.

I can pray…for the knowledge of His will for me and the power to carry it out.

I can **_LET GO AND LET GOD._**

April 24
DEALING WITH COMPLICATIONS

I was a complicated person. Events and situations had become unmanageable. The demands required by my false self were holding me hostage. ***I despised my actual self with all its inconsistency.***

I seemed to be drawn to the very circumstances that had started all the trouble in the first place. And there seemed to be little choice in the matter. Over and over, I would act out the same types of problems. I felt stuck.

I have found a way out; the program. ***I am relieved to know that I am not the only one, attempting to deal with my powerlessness as it relates to dysfunctional settings.*** I am learning to 'just say no' to unavailable people. I am learning to avoid toxic settings altogether. Thus, my life is growing less and less fraught with trouble.

By attending meetings regularly, I am coming to believe that I will be set free of the entanglement that binds me. The practice of doing the same thing over and over again, expecting different results is diminishing. ***My Higher Power is giving me back the freedom of choice.***

Those in my group serve as a reminder: there is no difficulty too great to be lessened. I am facing life…

LIFE ON LIFE'S TERMS.

April 25
LEARNING TO APPRECIATE MYSELF

Time and time again, the events that I encountered over the years mimicked one another. My interpretation of those experiences seemed to always fall into the same familiar shades: life's not fair; my parents are crazy; people can't be trusted; I'm so stupid; people are mean; others can't do anything right; I have to do everything; people are 'nuts'; nothing ever works out right.
The list grew.

I held on to these old ideas and the result was usually the same: frustration, anger, shame and resentment.

I am making choices about my old judgments. Steps Four and Five are giving me a chance to review my past thinking; my old value system and my expectations attached to that system.

I am hearing my own voice with less exaggeration about who I should be all the time; consequently, I am able to view others with greater tolerance, as well.

My struggle to become my genuine self has not been easy. I appreciate that struggle. In my effort to navigate this new path of emotional awakening, I give myself permission to stumble from time to time.
The trail is not always well marked.

Two paths often diverge in the wood; sometimes I take the road less travelled, other times not. Either way, I emerge wiser for the journey.

April 26
BEING PART OF A GROUP

Whether I was in a relationship, out of a relationship; married with children, not married with children; employed, not employed; I rarely felt comfortable 'in my own skin'.

In other words, **_there seemed to be a disconnect between myself and others._**

I had a very difficult time being in the moment. Sometimes my anxiety level made it impossible to remain 'present' and so, I would distract myself: have another drink, make more food, go shopping, read my text messages, surf the web, binge watch. I would simply 'check out'.

Showing up is one of the most difficult things I do in recovery. ***I am always a little anxious about going to a meeting.*** I am often uncomfortable with the 'meeting before the meeting'. Making simple conversation is a struggle. The 'meeting after the meeting' is difficult, as well.

I see my home group as a place where I can practice being who I am in a social setting. Practicing being myself at a meeting is one of the most important components of my recovery.

My group is a ***bridge to activities outside recovery***; activities in which I want to participate.

The weekly meeting serves as safe place where I can try out being me. **_I can take risks,_** knowing that I will be welcomed back the following week; and the week after that; and the week after that.

I love the sound of ***KEEP COMING BACK!***

April 27
ABANDONING THE FALSE SELF

It seemed like a good idea at the time; taking on beliefs; devising strategies designed to get through the difficulties and distortions that was 'home'.
It seemed like an even better idea to absolutely insist that I behave accordingly, all the time; thus, assuring my 'safe' passage.
A plus B equals C; a no brainer.

The good news? I survived. The bad news? I abandoned my true self in the process. In order to stay focused on my performance, I had to squelch the presence of my genuine interests; those splendid curiosities of childhood that sometime lead to meaningful careers, life-long hobbies and sincere friendships.

I couldn't be distracted with feelings, perceptions and concerns. The barking sound of my inner voice shut down my real self: *'This is no time to get emotional! Snap out of it! Pull yourself together. Get over it.'*

I am looking at the old ideas connected with 'slugging it out' in order to endure life. At the core of all these notions lies one common culprit; the hyper-critical, 'all-knowing', unrelenting, authoritarian dictator know as my false self. Fear based and forever worried, this distorted nucleus is being de-constructed, one belief at a time.

Step Five invites my declaration of the exaggerated demands on myself and the uncompromising claims on others that drive me.
I own the false program I have co-created. I admit it…
to God, myself and another human being.

Step Six and Seven begs the question: *Am I ready to let go?* Am I ready for a new start? Am I willing to move freely through life as my real self; absent the inner regime of a brutal dictator?

Not only am I willing, I am thoroughly able and ready. *I escort my false self out of the building and off the property.* I embrace my real interests. I embrace my own empathy. Thank you, program.
Thank you, God!

April 28
ADJUSTING MY EXPECTATIONS

Disappointment seemed to be my constant companion. Setting up conditions rife with opportunity for hurt had become a habit. *I had become 'comfortable' in acting out the old equation of the past.* The formula? Move toward people who were unavailable, create expectations around the false hope, 'this time it will be different', take a risk, be disappointed.

Eventually, I grew cynical about ever really trusting. I practiced keeping my guard up. Trust was for the feeble hearted and weak willed.

I am connecting with my core self. I am aware of conditions that are eerily familiar. *I have no time for 'no shows'; people who consistently say one thing and do another.*

I trust people in the program who make themselves available; friends who usually do what they say they are going to do. In other words, I no longer go to the hardware store to buy groceries.

With the help of the program, I am becoming more available to myself. Instead of attempting to do ten things in three hours' time, I am lowering the demands to a more manageable time frame; perhaps three things in four hours. *My well-being is my number one priority.*

When I see a yellow flag, I proceed with caution.

When I see a red flag, *I stop.*

April 29
CONFIDING IN SAFE PEOPLE

I wasted a lot of time and emotional energy trusting the wrong people. *I hoped things would be different in 'new' relationships and situations.* For a time, events seemed safe enough and then, as though a fuse had blown, the lights went out. The discounting of observations, the dismissing of emotions, and the moralizing of how I 'should' be all the time, appeared in a variety of situations and circumstances.

For me to grow, I must be ***allowed*** to grow. I function best when support does not wish to control, does not wish to shape, does not wish to impose, does not wish to 'inform', does not wish that I submit.

On this journey, I share with people who can meet me right where I am without rescuing, caretaking or fixing me. *I expect support from people who simply listen;* people who allow my emotions; people who merely hold my hand as I struggle to navigate a new path; people who sit with me as I rethink my approach; people who encourage my own effort in solving my own problems.

<u>*I ask for help from reliable sources.*</u> I don't go to a voice teacher to learn how to dance. I don't go to a dance teacher to learn how to do math. I don't go to a math teacher to learn how to swim. Whether I am dancing, swimming or doing the math, I know this one simple truth:
When the student is ready, the teacher will appear.

I am awakening to a safe world and a safe world is awakening to me.

April 30
TOLERATING OTHERS

This disease came in many shapes and sizes. None of the sizes seemed comfortable in the beginning; and yet, as time went by, I grew intolerably 'comfortable' with the hand-me-down wardrobe. Dysfunctional and ill-fitting as it was, I had little choice in the matter. ***I took on the look of the family***. I found my role. I played my part.

I have stepped off the 'family' stage. I have turned in my costume. I have found clothing more suitable to who I am. I am adjusting the size and shape to accommodate my own comfort. Instead of acting out, I am living free. ***I choose my part.*** I choose complimentary roles more suited to who I truly am.

I meet others who are still stuck; still complaining of their role; whining about the unfairness of it all; bemoaning their fate, 'if things had only been different!' They are not to be pitied. However, I can validate their struggle. I can avail myself to be of some support. I can listen.
At the very least, I can employ common courtesy.

Today, I meet almost everyone right where they are on their journey, allowing them the dignity of their own struggle. ***I don't have to GO on their journey;*** don't have to change their perspective on their journey; don't have to stop them on their journey; don't have to 'suggest' they are going East when, in fact, they 'should be' going West.

I don't have to change anything about someone else in order to **BE** who I am. ***I can fully…LIVE AND LET LIVE.***

And what of the 'family' stage? I still go to the theater from time to time. I love a good show. ☐

MAY

May 1
SEARCHING FOR EMOTION

The past seemed to be a locked box. I had little or no interest in 'dredging up' old memories; and yet, by shutting down certain 'unwanted' feelings, I had inadvertently disconnected from my real self.

In trying to erase the painful events, I unknowingly blocked the more pleasant conditions, as well.

My false self was working overtime to keep my emotional life 'manageable'; the idea being: 'If I perform perfectly going forward, I'll never *have* to look back.'

The central component in my effort to find and recover my lost self is my ability to feel. I am encouraged to feel my feelings. Much like learning to ride a bike all over again, I practice. With the help of meetings, I can talk about events of the past without fear of being interrupted, discounted or dismissed.

I can own my emotions.

The work of awakening prepares me for the moment when I am ready to assume responsibility for my full recovery by taking Step Four. I am preparing to review my past experiences and subsequently, the emotions *attached* to those past experiences.

In doing so, I discover the old ideas that drive the old behavior. My emotions serve as guideposts on the road toward finding my real self.

Today, I talk. I trust. I feel.

May 2
ALLOWING MY EMOTIONS

I was a human doing rather than a human being. I held myself to a very high standard. The desired objective was nothing short of perfection. **<u>Mistakes were intolerable.</u>** When I failed, I hated myself. When others failed, I despised them.

Whether the demand fell to achieving success in all endeavors; or always loving others; or relying only on one's self; I rarely felt much of anything except excitement or shame, anger or humiliation. ***I bordered on being either depressed or anxious much of the time.***

I know that emotions have a very broad range of description; I can feel: pleasant, satisfied, passionate, upset, distressed, dejected, uptight, mad, outraged, timid, uneasy, frantic, uncomfortable, apologetic, worthless, glad, lost, disgusted, insecure, cheerful, elated; and all in a day's time!

Whether I am feeling mad, sad, glad, afraid or ashamed, I can feel it. I can own it. I can talk about what is going on. I can write about the emotion in my Fourth Step. I can continue to inventory my daily events in the Tenth Step.

I feel it to heal it.

May 3
KNOWING THE PLAY

Emotions ran my life; only I didn't know it. I was secretly terrified of abandonment not only by others, but by myself, as well. The old idea seemed to go something like, *'If I always perform well, I shall always meet with approval; if I don't, it's all over'.* With the advent of mistakes and failures, I berated myself. I feared other's rejection.

I would 'double down' on getting it right the next time. The false strategy I had created in order to avoid rejection by myself and others had taken over. *I felt trapped.*

Having taken all the Steps, I am aware of my true interests today. I tap into my core self. I know how I feel most of the time. Knowing my real self, I choose to act accordingly. I am thoroughly confident in my effort to become who I am. My decisions are generated by a pro-active stance.

With the help of God and others, I reason out my next move, praying only for the knowledge of His will and the power to carry it out. **Sometimes I fail, sometimes I don't.** Somethings I choose to perform are easier than others. I make a smashing cup of tea! Other things prove more difficult like going back to school, moving to a new house, changing careers, moving away from an unhealthy relationship.

Regardless of the task I choose to undertake, I am fully assured of one thing; the discovery of my real interests shall continue. I can *know* where I want to go; *know* the preferred destination. And the best part? Early arrival, late arrival or no arrival, I appreciate the adventure.
(most of the time)

And *then*, I make a cup of tea.

May 4
ACTING WITH CONFIDENCE

For the most part, I acted as I should always act and expected others to do the same. Regardless of my real interests, the 'shoulds' won out most of the time; and when they didn't win out, **<u>I felt ashamed of myself.</u>** In other words, when I did something that I wasn't 'supposed' to do, I caught hell from a false self.

As a result, I approached most everything I did in an uncertain manner; afraid of not doing it 'right'. *My false self was in the driver's seat with its excessive demands and harsh criticism.* I remained anxious and depressed most of the time without really knowing it.

In exchange for taking the Fourth and Fifth Steps, I receive a clean slate; a slate upon which I can create my own system of values; my own moral structure. Naturally, there are old ideas I want to keep. And yet, there are new ideas I want to establish as my very own through the Eleventh Step. My real self is emerging. I am recovering my true self.

I remain true to myself with all confidence. I *know* who I am. I *know* what I want. When the moment of truth presents itself, I act decisively. **<u>When the path is uncertain, I rely on prayer</u>** and the trusted counsel of others more experienced than I am.

When I do act, I need not fear the result. Win or lose, I am becoming who I am; I am fulfilling my determined interest; I am establishing my real self.

'To thine own self be true and as certain as night follows day, thou canst never be false to another.'

May 5
TAKING WHAT I LIKE, LEAVING THE REST

I felt compelled to chronically 'adjust' to my family situation in order to survive. I had to swallow everything regardless of its lack of appeal. <u>**I often forced myself to accept the unacceptable.**</u> Long after I left home, I remained a prisoner to similar settings. I was 'comfortable' with the dysfunctional familiarity. I hoped that the conflicts of the past would be magically resolved under 'new' conditions.

I arrived at the doorstep of my group uncertain of my staying power. ***I had little or no 'skills' in doing life.*** How could I possibly conform to this program? What about this God stuff? 'Surrendering' my will and my life? Reviewing my past? Saying no to old distractions; mood altering and otherwise? Being honest? Talking about my feelings? Taking the Steps?

I am as one who has been given, for the very first time, the original owner's manual to a car I have possessed all my life; a car moth-balled in my garage. <u>***I learn new things each day.***</u> Some techniques I use immediately, others I reserve for later. I still can't operate the radio. I didn't even know I had a radio! The dimmer switch is tricky. What's a sunroof? How do I open the hood? Where's the spare tire? What is 'tire pressure'? How do I start this thing?

In the meetings, I learn at my own pace. I don't have to accept ***anything*** until I am ready. I don't have to do ***anything*** that isn't comfortable. What works for one person in the room may not work for me; what works for me may not work for another.

I am remaining true to my emerging self. I can hear 'suggestions' for what they are; **suggestions.** <u>***I keep coming back.***</u> I can…

TAKE WHAT I LIKE AND LEAVE THE REST.

May 6
CARING FOR MY TRUE SELF

I indulged myself in all manner of activity in order to avoid my feelings. Emotion was not my friend. The pain, the hurt and the disappointment seemed to be stacked layer on top of layer.

I had immersed myself in many distractions. Whether I was tirelessly helping others or working endlessly on a new project or simply avoiding others altogether, I was in full flight from my actual self; the self that rarely lived up to my demands.

I am on a new track, embarking on a new journey known to billions over thousands of years; the search for my true self. I care for my genuine interests. I develop healthy relationships; relationships in which I am respected and supported in this timeless quest to recover my lost self.
My spiritual path is *now*.

Having taken Steps Six and Seven, I am gaining ground. I am partnering with a power greater than myself. I am entirely ready to have all the old ideas behind my shortcomings removed. In freeing myself, I find new ideas; new interests. I say yes to healthy situations.
I embrace safe people.

I allow the awakening process to begin, knowing that I meet the people I need to meet in order to learn what I need to learn; some call them angels, others call them passing acquaintances.

Still others call them trusted friends.

I am not alone.

May 7
SHARING AT MEETINGS

Over the years, I had become awkwardly reserved when talking to others about things that really mattered. I didn't know how. The ***'don't talk, don't trust, don't feel'*** rule had been in place for a long, long time. I had made it a practice to avoid a 'touchy' subject, to change the topic, to distract when necessary and dodge the 'sensitive' question. I needed to keep my emotions constantly in check, lest I 'lose it'. Certain conversations were off the table altogether, never to be broached.

I am faced with a setting in my home-group where folks are *expected* to talk about what is going on, honestly. My meeting is reasonably safe: no cross talk, no interrupting, no side-bar comments, no fixing, no rescuing, no caretaking.

I am free to either share or not share.
I feel no pressure to be anyone more than who I am.

I speak up when I *want* to speak up. Sometimes I know exactly what I want to say; other times I don't. ***I talk in order to hear my own voice.*** I need to put words to my thoughts in front of others no matter how faltering the sentences may seem.

I especially need to say how I feel. I do this for sheer practice. If someone relates to what I say, that's great. If someone can't relate to what I say, that's OK, too. I do this for ***MY OWN*** recovery.

I have discovered individuals with whom I can speak before and after the meeting; people that I trust. There are occasions when I say even more after a meeting than I say during the meeting.

Either way, ***I am suiting up and showing up***. I am trusting the process.

May 8
LOOKING AT MISTAKES

I spent many years trying to avoid mistakes. I lived in fear of causing an accident, doing something 'stupid'; getting caught. The stakes were very high as I had come to falsely believe that *by making a mistake, I was a mistake.* Without really knowing it, I felt ashamed most of the time.

I remotely entertained the notion that someday I would feel better. The only requirement? Total perfection, all the time. Failure was not an option!

I am under new management; the idea being:
I can, in fact, learn from my mistakes. I even embrace my mistakes, realizing they are all part of a greater process; the process of becoming who I am.

New settings bring new challenges. My recovery journey is all about new settings and new challenges. I take risks. I make mistakes.

I approach Steps One, Two and Three, realizing that my false ideas drive old behavior; that my unaided ability to sufficiently manage these old ideas is of *NO* consequence; that my demand for perfection in myself and others is entirely out of control; that my need for others' support (in order to heal from all this) is of ABSOLUTE necessity. I stand at a turning point.

I ask for God's 'protection and care with complete abandon' as I venture toward the dark lane leading to my past; my Fourth Step. I am prepared. I know this is the right path. I know others who have gone before me.

I know where to go for safety and support should the process get tough; my weekly meetings. *I am not alone. I am not ashamed. I am not afraid.*

May 9
FACING A PROBLEM

I devised a calculated strategy over the years to avoid problems. ***'Reality' was not my friend.*** The pressing issues of the day proved overwhelming. I found ways of going around the 'road-blocks'.

I had grown to distrust most of the major players in my life; and as a result, I came to believe that I alone, by myself, would be the one to solve all of life's troubles. My greatest tactic had a three-part approach:
Deny, **D**elay and **D**istract; the three ***D's***.

When a conflict arose, I would first deny that it even existed. When I could no longer avoid the issue, I would simply delay looking. When I could no longer delay, I found a convenient distraction or combination of distractions to 'take my mind off things'.

Today, reality ***IS*** my friend. My feelings alert my attention to things in the environment that are uncomfortable. ***I have options.***

I find a trusted friend. ***I can 'process' what is going on; talk about it.*** If allowed to have my thoughts and emotions without intervention, I usually come up with an approach to the problem that will work for me.
I move forward. I am no longer stuck.

Once I have arrived at a solution, the problem goes away. It's impossible to be in the solution **AND** in the problem at the same time. ***The trick is staying in the solution.*** Sometimes my solutions work; sometimes they don't.
I can always change my mind around what, in fact, is a solution.

What works today may not work tomorrow. I stay in the solution…

ONE DAY AT A TIME.

May 10
CHANGING MY THINKING

I had become convinced that my false self with its old demands, even superstitions, was my only 'true north'. My mission had become to satisfy every unrealistic expectation attached to my old ideas: who I should be all the time; who they should be all the time.

In fact, the pursuit of fulfilling these notions had become an obsession. I was compelled. I held myself and others in contempt when these requirements were not met. I was not a 'happy camper'.

I use a slogan: EASY DOES IT. I am lowering my demands on myself. I am lowering my expectations on others. ***The 'should always' is becoming, the 'perhaps sometimes'.*** As a result, I am reasonably happy most of the time.

When conflicts come up, I have one of two ways I can go. I can change the environment. ***Or I can change my thinking about the environment.***
The latter, I have found, is the easier softer way.

When troubles arise in relationship, even when I take the risk of stating what I am seeing, how I am feeling and what I need; the truth is:
sometimes people change, sometimes they don't.

I find a more favorable outcome when I lower my expectations not only of what others can do, but what I can do, as well. It becomes an 'inside job'. With God's help, I change my thinking.

LIVE AND LET LIVE…takes on a whole new meaning.

May 11
FINDING SOLUTIONS

I had become so overwhelmed over the years that I despaired of ever finding a way out of the trouble that seemed to never go away. I had been dealing with trouble since my childhood. I was exhausted. Without realizing it, I had created a story; a story of my victimhood: if only I had been treated better, if I only I could have gone to a good school; if only I had applied myself; if only, if only, if only.

The Twelve Steps are solutions. I am seeing the deeper meaning in the old saying, 'Life is something that happens to you while you are planning something else.'

<u>*I am taking the Steps. I am in the solution.*</u>
<u>*I am no longer a victim.*</u>

Life is still life: in-laws to be tolerated, rent to be paid, jobs to be found, situations to be avoided, cars to be repaired, dishes to be washed, floors to be swept.

I don't really have 'problems' today; just issues. I am applying the Steps daily in my endeavor to awaken; my endeavor to awaken spiritually, emotionally, intellectually, and physically. I stay in the day. I stay in the moment. *I make it a habit to pause often. I am still.*

The solution often lies in simply doing the next thing that is in front of me. I make a daily decision to turn my will and my life over to the care of the Steps. I allow me to be me; *feelings and all.*
<u>*I allow life to unfold.*</u>

I have what I need *at this moment* to be entirely who I am.
And that is enough.

May 12
FEELING MY FEELINGS

I had become a master at shutting down my feelings and emotions. I had developed countless strategies designed to shield my real self from the trauma of the past. I had created a false self for protection; a security guard of sorts: always alert, always in charge, always knowing exactly what I 'should' do. Feelings had no place; only hyper-vigilance.

As a result, my real self is still alive, but not well; not well at all. As though being locked in a remote room and told to remain quiet until help arrives, *my real self, after years and years of hiding, is virtually dead;* emaciated, almost deaf from the silence, almost blind from the darkness, uncertain of a 'real' world, afraid of leaving the 'safe' room.

The first sign of 'help on the way' is my ability to register and express feelings again; feelings of any kind: anger, sadness, fear, joy, hurt, rage, contempt, compassion, betrayal, frustration, satisfaction, guilt; any feelings of any kind will work.

I have the rooms of the program now. I am free to move beyond my one room isolation. I am free to explore my world. I am free to be myself.
I am free to talk about how I feel.

Make no mistake, my false self is still on duty, barking orders, over-reacting, demanding. I deal with those false feelings of fear, as well.
And yet, *I am returning to my real self:* staying safe; befriending available, non-toxic people; remaining awake; exploring new possibilities; accepting help in the Steps and yes… feeling my feelings.

I FEEL TO HEAL.

May 13
RECOVERING MY TRUE SELF

The restrictions that came with obeying the demands of a false self eventually proved unworkable. Regardless of the mounting notions which I had attached to specific survival strategies over the years, **the 'results' remained virtually the same; dysfunctional and confusing.**

The stress connected with maintaining the impossible 'shoulds', coupled with my self-destructive distractions made life impossible to manage. In sailing terms, I was sea-sick and way off course. In fact, I had hit bottom; my vessel trapped and under false command.

I find movement returning with the high tide; the fellowship, my program friends. The small voice of my true self is calling from somewhere. Recovery is taking a lot of effort. I am in earnest to set sail again. ***I am intent on discovering that mysteriously familiar voice; my genuine self.*** This is my solemn mission. I remain sober. I take the Steps to get underway.

In the beginning, my false self is battling for control, barking orders, demanding that I return to my 'assigned' post. There is mutiny in the air and my false self knows it. I am afraid. I need backup. I need meetings. I awaken to my feelings. I talk about events. I trust the process. ***I find my true self.***

I am allowing my real self to take its rightful place; the captain's chair. I have returned to my own voice! I have new interests, new ideas, and new direction. ***I am free; free to explore, free to risk, free to be who I am.***

And what of my false self; my mean old nervous Nelly? It's still on board; always fussing about something; always making a ruckus somewhere below deck. Poor thing. I understand the view is simply *terrible* from down there. Four bells and all's well!

May 14
BECOMING TEACHABLE

I relied on hardly anyone. I had grown leery of trusting other people. A lot of the people I had counted on let me down. Instead of embracing an ever-broadening circle of family and friends,

I found myself crawling into a narrow, isolated box. ***If I were to learn, I would learn it on my own.*** As a result, my options were limited. Fear kept me tethered. False pride kept me isolated.

An old song goes: *'Desperado, why don't you come to your senses? Come down from your fences and open the gate.'*

My admission of utter defeat is the 'coming down' from my fences. Taking Step One is my opening 'the gate'. And upon opening the gate, **the fellowship meets me right where I am**: no rules to obey, no promises to keep, no dues to pay, no 'minimum requirement' to meet; only a simple suggestion, ***'Take what you like and leave the rest.'***

According to the co-founder of Alcoholics Anonymous and author of the basic text, 'Alcoholics Anonymous', Bill Wilson wrote, ***'our Steps are meant to be suggestive only.'***

With the help of the program and many others who are trudging their own roads of happy destiny, I am returning to my genuine self. I am returning to love; the greatest teacher of all.

'It may be rainin', but there's a rainbow above you.
You better let somebody love you...
Before it's too late.'

May 15
TAKING STEP FIVE

I had no interest in seeing myself as a perpetrator; a person who had 'wronged' others. In fact, I balked at the notion of taking a moral inventory at all. *I had been the one born into circumstances beyond my control;* circumstances that would shape not only my view of the world, but more importantly, circumstances that would shape an ***ENTIRELY WRONG*** view of myself. Had I not truly been a victim of this disease? How was I to blame in all this? I had been the one wronged!

The man who wrote this Step in the late 1930's would later state in the same publication, 'We realize we know only a little; more will be revealed.' Webster's thesaurus gives me a broader array of words besides the single word, **'wrongs'**: sins, crimes, injuries, wounds, harms, errors, mistakes. The point is simply this. The author chose the word he chose at the time he chose it. Perhaps today, he would have chosen another word.

Regardless of the word, the truth is simply this:
I CAN COMMIT NO ACT, LEST I HAVE A THOUGHT *PRECEDING* THAT ACT.

<u>*The 'exact nature' of my error always lies in my thinking.*</u> All my dysfunctional behavior is but a symptom of my disease; **a disease of distorted OLD IDEAS** about myself and the world around me.

By taking Step Five, I own my unrealistic demands on myself; 'I should always under all conditions do this or that'. I own my exaggerated expectations toward others; 'they should always under all conditions do this or that'. *I cease playing God.* I genuinely realize the wrong, the error, the harm, the mistake *in my thinking*. I am preparing to have the *behavior caused by my thinking* entirely removed.

I admit to God, to myself and another human being when excessive 'shoulds', based on false pride, set me up for failure;
dysfunctional behavior. I am ready to get honest.

Step Five is the gateway to freedom; Steps Six and Seven, the bridge.

May 16
ACCEPTING THE DISEASE CONCEPT

I viewed the identified addict's behavior with disdain. I cringed at the antics of my alcoholic mother and father. I was ashamed. I was angry and bitter. How could they act in such an irresponsible way?

I said that I would *never* become like them. And yet, ***I became an alcoholic myself***; even married an alcoholic! How could I have been so stupid? I must have been out of my mind!

Blaming an addict for being addicted to something is like criticizing a crocodile for dining on gazelle. ***It's in the genes!*** The scientific and medical community **both** confirm the disease model for addiction. Knowing this in my head and accepting this in my heart are two very different propositions.

I would no more ridicule a victim of cancer than I would a victim of cerebral palsy or muscular dystrophy; and yet, when it comes to those afflicted with addiction, the story is often too familiar:
he could quit if he really wanted; he's irresponsible; she's had so many chances to stop; she should quit for the children; he's killing his mom and dad; what a loser!

As with all losses in my life, I go through a *process* of becoming OK with it all: first denial, then anger, then the bargaining, then sadness and finally, acceptance. The undertaking rarely proceeds in a straight line; the phases seldom predictable. Some days are better than others.
And so, the recovery process goes.

BUT FOR THE GRACE OF GOD, THERE I GO.

May 17
ALLOWING REALITY TO BE MY FRIEND

My life played out like a train wreck in slow motion. **<u>Reality was not my friend.</u>** An emotionally unavailable mother and a physically abusive father left me with one very real conclusion at the age of six. I'm screwed.

I didn't have to be a junior Einstein to know that life was going to be at best, a challenge; at worst, a nightmare. It proved to be a little of both.
Without knowing it, I devised strategies to assure my survival;
my not being abandoned. I created a whole belief system around how I should behave all the time. The good news? I survived.
The bad news? I lost my real self in the process.
Hyper-vigilance comes at a cost.

My false self, hell-bent to survive, had fully taken over by the time I turned eighteen. My real self in exile, I merely tried to stay in lock step with my false self's marching-orders. And when I failed, there was hell to pay…
in shame. It seemed I was a failure. **Distractions galore eased my anxiety:** drinking, smoking, eating, watching T.V., working, getting into relationships, getting out of relationships, acting out sexually, starting school, moving to a different town.

By taking Steps Four, Five, Six and Seven, I reclaim my real self. My false self sits in remission like a lion with its claws clipped; **my distractions, to a large extent, are in retreat.**

I surround myself with available people. I create safe conditions.
I naturally care for myself.

I am awake. I am aware. Reality is my friend.

May 18
LEARNING TO LIKE MYSELF

I can remember the moment when I consciously turned on myself. I had finally graduated from college. My actual self, even with all its mistakes and failures, had achieved something. There was only one problem: *I felt nothing;* nothing except depressed. I believed and had believed for years that regardless of how I dressed me up, irrespective of any achievements, at the very core of my being dwelt a failure.

In short, I hated myself. The diploma had not fixed me. *I set out to destroy myself with drinking; all under the guise of being 'care-free'.* Following four mental hospitals, a few jails and a world-renowned treatment center, I would almost die three years later; homeless, on the side of the road.

I know who I am today. I go to great lengths to review my old ideas and the perverted 'survival' demands associated with those old ideas. With the help of the fellowship, I let go of old dysfunctional demands.

The result? My real self is emerging with new ideas, new interests and new dreams. It's OK to be who I am! I take risks. *I ask for what I need.* I surround myself with supportive people. I **CAN** get there from here! Oh, wait; I **AM** there! 'There' *IS* here. Now is now.

My genuine self is out of exile; no more 'shoulds'! I am free; free to make mistakes; free to fail. When I act according to how I truly think and feel, I get a boost. Sometimes I win, sometimes I lose; it doesn't matter. I am alive. I am awake.

I exercise my God-given right; to be flawed and fully human.

May 19
TAKING WHAT I LIKE, LEAVING THE REST

Beginning at a very young age, ***choice played little significance in my overall behavior.*** I was free enough; never locked in the basement, chained to the water heater or tied to a fence post. And yet, I was held hostage by an unforgiving tyrant; ***my false self.***

My fear of abandonment dictated most of my strategy when it came to making peace with my dysfunctional environment. This skewed tactic formed my moral 'survival' code; a code I would attempt to enforce for years to come.

Most of my old ideas had little to do with reality; furthermore, I had applied no conscious effort in forming these so-called coping skills. They simply took hold and took over as a clinging vine might consume a perfectly healthy tree.

The program gives me my life back. I meet with others on a regular basis who are working out their own new strategies about living. The concept of ***keeping an open mind*** plays a big role in my forming new ideas and reforming old ideas. ***I am getting to know who I am.***
I am being true to myself.

I am under no pressure. ***I take what I like; and I leave the rest.*** And, I take it at my own pace. I am persuaded subtly, most of the time, that a new way of looking at old problems might work.

I realize that choices abound, regarding family and friends of the past.
I am, at long last, able to grow in a healthy way. I am free of the clinging vines. I am free of the clamoring demands.

I am free to choose; free to be me.

May 20
LEARNING TO ENJOY MY OWN COMPANY

I had become locked out of my own life. I placed so much importance on surviving a distorted and chaotic world, that I lost touch with my real self; my real interests; my real feelings. *My false survival-self eventually commandeered the bus, MY bus;* making incessant demands of my behavior: how I should sit, where I should sit, when I should sit, when I should stand, when I should look out the window, when I should sleep, when I should wake up.

It was as though I was being policed around the clock. I spent all my energy, trying to behave as I should. Exhausted by my failed efforts, I checked out emotionally and tried one distraction after another in order to relieve my growing self-hatred. At times, I had moments of hope that the trip would get better; *it didn't.*

As a hostage finally rescued; as one coaxed from an abandoned bus; *I cautiously step into a new freedom, a new light;* the rooms of recovery. At first, I am uncertain of it all; so strange, seeing people coming out of their own confinement; so unusual, watching others cry; so peculiar, hearing my own laughter; so awkward, having my freedom; so scary.

I am slowly returning to my real self. *I have moments when I can be alone with my own interests; my own feelings; my own hopes and dreams.* I have moments when I act spontaneously.

I hear my own voice; "I want to…". *I am becoming my own best friend.*
I am making new friends. I search for ways to enjoy my freedom.
I am learning how to drive the bus.

I'm an excellent driver; **definitely,** an excellent driver.
And with God's help, I'm really going places now!

May 21
LISTENING TO THE WORLD AROUND ME

I used to experience life, for the most part, as if looking in a rearview mirror. ***I was compelled to review my behavior:*** had I performed well enough, had I said the right thing, had I looked good enough?

The moment was lost on all the demands I put on myself or the unrealistic expectations I placed on others. ***I rarely enjoyed a situation in the present moment.*** Whether I was at a wedding, a party, a picnic; I was anxious most of the time, feeling disconnected and out of touch; separated.

I connect with myself today. I hear my own voice; feel my own feelings in the moment. I am available not only to myself, but to others, as well. ***I listen***. I connect.

The sounds of the day take on a new meaning. I am alive. I am awake. My senses are working for me. I am growing more and more intuitive. I am handling situations, once baffling.

I take the time to pause often, practicing Step Eleven, trusting that my Higher Power is guiding my every encounter throughout the day. **Where am I to go? Who am I to meet? What am I to learn?**

I listen with my heart. The answers appear sometimes quickly, sometimes slowly. And at the end of the day, I return. ***I rest.***

I listen to my own heart. ***I hear my own voice.*** I feel my own peace.

May 22
ACTING WITH CONFIDENCE

I rarely had the lasting strength to endure challenges throughout the day. Minor mistakes would become horrific 'situations'; nightmares to be endured. I had reached a place where no paths seemed to exit the very dark wood of all my troubles. Eventually, I would avoid decisions altogether.

I had, for all intents and purposes, checked out of my own life. I was acting out of habit, terrified of moving too far outside my 'comfort' zone. I was 'comfortable' alright; and **STUCK!**

I am awake today. And because I am awake, I have options; options that I can utilize in order to get unstuck. With the help of the program, *I move with a new certainty*, trusting others and God. I am no longer all alone. The dark path is becoming brighter and brighter.

I can know the play; I can take the shot. Sometimes I win; sometimes I lose. I can *always* learn.

'Repetition strengthens and affirms habit; faith then becomes natural.'
I consider all of life a practice.

I act with assurance, knowing that my is not dependent on how perfectly I perform every task I attempt; rather, *my worth is an absolute; a given.* I need not fear my mistakes. Indeed, I celebrate my mistakes.

I celebrate my humanity. I celebrate my freedom to attempt the 'play'; I celebrate my freedom to fall short. Win or lose…

I celebrate myself with confidence.

May 23
ABSORBING THE PROGRAM

I used to view most everything with a full dose of skepticism. I trusted nothing. I harbored the old idea that anything could go wrong at any minute. ***I placed confidence in very few; and, I left myself an "out" should things go wrong.*** I would often pick a fight in order to create an excuse to leave. It seemed the only person I could really trust was me and toward the end, even that belief was growing weak.

The program requires nothing from me. I may attend meetings once a week, once a month, once a year; or not at all. ***The choice is all mine.***
I move at my own pace. I have no leader to please,
no committees to join and no obligations to meet.

Step Two, at least for me, suggests that I can "absorb" the program. I can rely on a power greater than myself to speak through the individuals of the group or the group at large. I take what I like and leave the rest.

This process of allowing new ideas to freely pass through others so that I can learn, and grow is an amazing phenomenon. I usually 'hear' what I need to hear at meetings. Osmosis is a mysterious and wonderful thing.

I suit up.
I show up.
I stay awake.

And then? I go home and go to sleep.

May 24
CREATING A SAFE PLACE

Toward the end of my going it alone, before I found the recovery rooms, I literally had no safe place to go. Why? Because everywhere I went, there I was. I had become my harshest critic; and, I was rarely 'available' to myself as I had 'checked out' with all kinds of distractions.

In short, ***I hated my actual self;*** and would go to any length in order to avoid the anxiety associated with my not living up to the demands of a false self; a false self, hell-bent on perfection. ***FEAR*** (***F***alse ***E***vents ***A***ppearing ***R***eal) dominated most of my waking hours.

I could easily imagine the worst outcome before an event even had the *appearance* of unfolding. My thinking, for the most part, had become distorted.

Today, I create and maintain a safe place; first in my head and second, in my surroundings. The two usually go together. In other words, I cannot have one without the other. Prayer and meditation help.

I say no to exaggerated demands on myself. I say no to others who attempt to manipulate with anger and intimidation. I say yes to everything that is healthy.

I live in the moment, relying on my healthy self to guide me in all my activity.

I am free.

May 25
NURTURING ONE ANOTHER

The reality I had created for myself demanded unrealistic outcomes most of the time. **Mistakes seemed to reinforce my old idea that I was a mistake; a loser.** Most of my so-called relationships were about manipulating others in order to get what I thought I needed in order to 'survive'; in other words, in order to avoid being all alone.

There was a 'pay off' in most everything I did. Even when others manipulated me with anger or shame, I 'tolerated' their behavior in the name of 'going the extra mile'.

I am finding people with whom I can talk honestly; people with whom I can be direct; folks upon whom I can reasonably rely. They are available when they say they can be available.

They can listen without interrupting, without trying to change my mind, without debating.

I am in process. I am awake to that process. I pick people who respect my journey and give me the dignity to arrive at my own solutions in my own time, rather than giving advice. I am allowing others their struggle, as well.

There remains a 'pay off' in most everything I do. The difference today? Perspective. Rather than moving through life afraid,
<u>I am moving through life in confidence.</u>

I connect with my true self, allowing all the emotions that go with being who I am; and I am allowing others the freedom to do likewise.

May 26
LIVING THE DREAM

Most of my days, before the program, were spent slogging through life at half speed. Why? *I had ceased hoping that anything was going to truly help my disintegrated feeling of isolation.*

I was dying from the inside out. My actual self was exhausted of all the demands. My false self was working over-time; trying to 'keep it all together'; controlling everything.

I am returning to my real self. I am awakening to my own voice. I am intuitively sensing a psychological, emotional and spiritual shift in my perspective. I view the world with wonder as I reconnect with an inner self; a real self. I am eager to act on my own behalf. I am dedicated to my own well-being. 'Self-sacrifice' is not part of my vocabulary.

Each day presents a new opportunity to genuinely act according to my emerging core self; the self that has been there all along with its curiosities, interests, hopes and dreams. ***I can be who I am.***

I am thinking and feeling what I am genuinely thinking and feeling.
I am available to myself. ***I have all I need at this moment to be who I am.***

The destination *is* the journey…
and the journey is the destination.

May 27
FIGHTING FAIR

My actual self, the self that attempted to carry out all the exaggerated demands of my false self, often felt overwhelmed; often shifted the blame for 'failure' to an outside source, usually other people. ***I didn't know how to stand up for myself in a healthy way.***

Incapable of reviewing the old ideas behind MY distorted thinking, I often viewed adversity as something strange and mysterious; something happening ***TO*** me; some menacing element coming from outside myself.

Preoccupied with trying to be perfect as to avoid rejection, I lacked the presence of mind and skill to care for my true self. ***I fought with myself; hated myself.*** I fought with others; resented others. I felt like a victim.

My real self has only a few needs: safety, inclusion, support and expression. When I am not feeling safe, I can use my voice in order to ask for what I need. When I am not feeling included, I can 'check' my perception with others directly: 'Are you rejecting me for some reason?'

When I am ***NOT*** supported and when I ***CAN'T*** express myself freely, I ***RESERVE*** my real self. I lower my expectations. I move away from unavailable people. I move toward my available self. I enlist the help of others whom I ***CAN*** trust; God included.

There are times when I stand up for myself; times when I am willing to fight in order to protect what is sacred to me. *I state what I am seeing, I state how I feel when I see it; and I state what I need going forward.* Sometimes things change; sometimes they don't.

I access my voice in order to establish clear boundaries. I can negotiate. And yet, ***I am willing to walk away if necessary.*** I give myself total permission to take civil or legal action when needed.

My days of volunteering to be a victim are ***OVER***.
'No' means no. 'Stop' means stop.

May 28
STAYING IN PROCESS

My greatest dysfunctional skill was denial: denial of what was happening, denial of how I felt about what was happening; denial of personal problems; denial of needs attached to my personal problems. Everything was *FINE*.

Uncomfortable as it may be at times, I am awake to my feelings. I no longer live in the shadows of an idealized self with outrageous demands. I am aware of my process of thought and the subsequent emotion attached to my thought.

I resolve to return and rest with my real self. In quietness I find strength. I pause. I check my thinking. Sometimes I call a friend who listens without advising. Sometimes I go to a meeting.

I say no to old distractions. I embrace new ideas and interests. I act on those new ideas and interests.

Having taken a Fourth and Fifth Step, I am able to identify old ideas that keep re-triggering old emotions. With God's help, *I review the wrong ideas in the Tenth Step,* and release the unrealistic demands of the past.
If I behave inappropriately, I can always apologize.
If I do regress for a time, it's OK. Hopefully, sooner than later, I simply return to my process.

I seek through prayer and meditation to improve my conscious contact with God, praying only for the knowledge of His will for me and the *power* to carry that out.

May 29
EXERCISING THE POWER OF CHOICE

I had become so distracted with the noise of my clamoring false self that any effort at acting on a genuine interest was virtually impossible.
I was exhausted; easily distracted. Past decisions based on old
ideas were stacking up. Consequences were knocking at the door.

I was unable to think clearly because I had, in fact, lost myself to the process of my disordered world. 'Solutions' that had worked before no longer applied. I felt as though I was on auto pilot headed into a nose-dive and there was no pulling out of it. I chose to jettison the aircraft rather than go down in a blaze of 'glory'. In other words, I went to my first meeting.

I choose to still go to meetings. I am reclaiming my true self.
<u>I am reconnecting with my feelings.</u> As a result, genuine interests
are appearing on my 'screen'. Being able to know what I like and what I don't like gives me new perspective on how I *want* to spend my time. Doing what I 'should always' do is giving way to doing what I am *truly* interested in doing. More and more, it is becoming an obvious and simple choice.

Old habits formed in order to avoid emotions are falling away. I no longer distract myself at the first sign of 'trouble'. ***I am facing my fear.***
I am navigating new terrain. With the help of trusted friends,
I am talking about problems *and* solutions.

By taking the Steps, I am returning to myself. I have a chance to know who I am and what I want. With God's help, I know where to go and I know how to get there. With each passing moment, I can ask for the knowledge of His will and the power to carry it out.
The choice is all mine…

ONE DAY AT A TIME.

May 30
REQUESTING SUPPORT

I had placed myself in such an isolated position by the time I found the rooms of recovery that I had abandoned all hope of getting out of my troubles. My options had grown fewer and fewer with each passing day. I felt boxed in; damned if I did something; damned if I didn't.

Without really knowing it, I had ceased trusting anyone. The only voice I could hear was the overbearing demands of my false self. Obedience to the voice seemed to be my only comfort; distraction my only respite.

The Steps have freed me from the past. With God's help, I can define a problem and I can solve a problem. The program encourages my willingness to move away from a problem and toward a solution. Once I have discovered a solution, the problem goes away; at least for the moment. Applying a solution requires asking for help.
God often works through other people.

My security lies in trusting a *greater* process. I am using what I have in order to create what I need. I don't always get what I want, but I am growing more and more confident that I always get what I need at the exact moment I need it. I don't give up five minutes before the miracle.

I recognize good fortune when I find it: food, clothing, shelter; **trusted** friends and family.

I thank God for another day.

May 31
OVERCOMING THE EFFECTS OF THIS DISEASE

Whether I was smoking another cigarette to calm my nerves, taking another drink to give me confidence, watching another episode on TV to avoid life, having another slice to 'treat' myself, surfing the web for another purchase, taking on a third job to make more money, trolling the bars for another connection or combining all the above, the motive behind the distraction was the same; to avoid the hate I had for myself.

My false self with its unrealistic demands had sent my actual self into a state of chronic shame. When I wasn't despising myself, I was blaming others. Not only had I made mistakes; I believed that **_I was a mistake_**. Others were not to be trusted. The destruction of my actual self was, in fact, out of control.

By taking the Fourth and Fifth Steps, I examine my old moral system designed to keep me alive. I discover my false self with its distorted, antiquated demands.

I meet it face to face. I challenge head-on that part of me that has incessantly required more and more. *I confront the great accuser;* I turn a deaf ear to the belittling name-caller.

I don't do this alone. I am supported in this effort by another person. With the help of God, **_I challenge every exaggerated claim that has set me up_** for past disappointment and failure.

The *exact* nature of my wrongs? I should always…they should always. These never-ending demands are poison to my soul, and they're being replaced: sometimes I do, sometimes I don't; sometimes they do, sometimes they don't. The truth? **_Nobody is perfect_**. **_NOBODY._** This is…

LIFE ON LIFE'S TERMS.

JUNE

June 1
TAKING RESPONSIBILITY

Depending on the nature of certain circumstances, when things went wrong, I blamed others. And I shamed myself. I would be more careful, perform better next time; even perfectly. ***Only I couldn't perform perfectly all the time.*** Eventually, I would create a 'victim' story that covered *all* the bases.

Without really knowing it, I had re-created similar childhood situations of the past in order to 'act out' my current story of being victimized. I had come to rely on the story for strength. I shall overcome! I'll show those bastards. They can't do this to me and get away with it! I will kill them with kindness; love conquers all. I simply won't play. I'll run away, then they'll miss me. *<u>I was stuck in my own victim story.</u>*

By showing up at a meeting, I am moving toward a solution. I am stepping out of the problem for one hour and placing myself in the answer. I am doing what I *can* do in order to take care of myself at least for that one hour.

I am hearing others share of their old distorted ideas 'acted out' over the years; old ideas accompanied by expectations for different results. I am coming to believe that a power greater than myself can restore me to sanity.

I stand at a turning point. I inventory my old moral system; the old ideas at the core of my dysfunctional, self-abusive behavior. ***And with God's help, I let go of the victim story; what others could have or should have done better.*** I begin taking care of myself.

NO SHAME, NO BLAME

June 2
SEEKING GOD'S WILL

I had become an extreme cynic without really knowing it. **By the time I found the rooms, I had ceased trusting most people.** I had diminished my actual self with extreme criticism, fearing and loathing anyone that appeared to have authority over me.

Why? Because my own self-hate had grown by exponential proportions over the years. **The critical voice of my false self continued non-stop.** Any correctional voice from the outside seemed like someone screaming at me: you're a loser and you don't belong here!

When the program suggests that I turn my will and my life over to the care of God in the Third Step, my thought is: *no way!* Someone shares that the group is their higher power for now, until they've had a chance to review their moral system and their old ideas surrounding God.

I take a Fourth Step. I take a Fifth Step. I see where a lot of my old ideas were wrong, overly exaggerated. I hear someone share that these <u>misguided concepts can be removed</u> in Steps Six and Seven. **I move through the rest of the Steps.** I arrive at Step Eleven, a different person than I was at Step One.

God no longer appears as my demanding false self. I have confidence that I can pray for the knowledge of His will for my life and the power to carry it out. I have confidence in my *new* belief system.

June 3
BEING HONEST

I lived in denial most of the time. Denial said what you are seeing and what you are feeling is not true; forget about it; move along; there's nothing to see here. Having been pushed around by a false self that only cared about surviving another day, ***I hit the rooms completely unaware of my real self.***

I had become a slave to my own voice, obsessed with carrying out 'the orders' of who I should be all the time. And when I failed, **_I shamed myself and blamed others._**

I am no longer a slave to anyone. My false self is manageable most of the time. Why? Because I am beyond the old days and the old ways. ***The need for mere survival has been replaced with a genuine desire to live.*** I connect with my core self and act accordingly. Reality is my friend.
I own my accomplishments and I own my failures.

I talk about what I am seeing and how I am feeling. I ask for help when I get stuck. ***Solutions often present themselves naturally as I am supported by those closest to me;*** those who can listen; those who can withhold judgement; those who do not advise unless I ask for their advice.

I own my process. ***I have no fear in being who I am today, as I am merely one amongst billions of others***. I bring integrity to my own experience.

I connect. **_I am complete_**. I am real.

June 4
WELCOMING NEW IDEAS

I could not or would not let go of old ideas even though they had ceased working. I was entrenched in the notion that 'this time it would be different'. ***By the time I found the rooms, I was fatigued; call it battle fatigue.*** I had been a hapless captive in a war between my actual self and my false self; my false self with all its distorted ideas about how things should always be. Failure was ***NOT*** an option.

I am open minded today, having found a collection of people who share honestly and courageously each week about what, in fact, *is* working and what *is not* working. *I take what I like and leave the rest.*

Most of the time, I hear what I need to hear in order to move closer and closer to recovering my true self. I am hearing that the entire purpose of the program (and the Twelve Steps it represents) is to bring me into a correct relationship with my real self, my God and other human beings.

I replenish myself by relating to others on a similar journey.
I nourish my growth each time I show up at a meeting.
The more I know, the more I want to know.

With each passing week, I become more and more willing to try new approaches to old problems; ***sometimes they work, sometimes they don't.*** Failure ***IS*** an option. 'Failure' is where I learn.

At the very least, ***I keep an open mind.***

June 5
ENJOYING LIFE

I carried with me the notion that life should be absent of conflict. With each new problem, I cringed at the possibility of turbulence. *I feared certain projected outcomes, terrified of falling into the same anxiety I had experienced as a child.* I remained on guard and avoided trouble;
or sometimes I would throw caution to the wind and
move directly toward risky situations.

Without really knowing it, I was addicted to excitement. On some level, I 'needed' the distraction. *It seemed ironic as time after time, I created disruptive situations akin to those I had been trying to avoid.* The balancing act of always being in control took up a lot of energy.
I lost myself in the drama of it all.

Today I connect with my real self. I know my genuine interests. *I act in a way that is true to who I am.* I have more energy. Life seems to flow. Even problems take on a new dimension as I awaken to fresh solutions.

I am in process with all that I encounter: physically, mentally, emotionally, and spiritually. I am awake and aware. *<u>I do what I WANT to do.</u>*
I don't do what I don't want to do.
The choice is mine.

Having done the hard work of Steps One thru Nine, *I maintain my sense of wonder by practicing Steps Ten, Eleven and Twelve daily.* I share what I have found and discover that this is perhaps the greatest joy of all;
giving it away.

I GIVE IT AWAY, IN ORDER TO KEEP IT.

June 6
LETTING GO OF BEING THE VICTIM

I had come from a situation fraught with adversity. By the time I was five years old, *I was dealing with conditions that would have frustrated a full-grown adult.* I did not have the option of leaving; of heading for higher ground. I had to hunker down. I had to take it.

Day in and day out, one stupid situation followed another; some tragic in proportion. *I was exhausted at the age of sixteen,* having become addicted to sex, alcohol and work.

I have choices now. And by reviewing my old belief system through Steps Four and Five, *I am discarding those ideas of the past that kept me stuck.* With God's help, I am creating new values; genuine morals that really work to keep me happy, joyous and free; ideals that emanate from my real self.

I let go of the past. I live in the present. *I move toward people and situations that are healthy for me.* I actively engage with my own desires. I dream. I am proactive with *my* future.

I celebrate large and small victories in my recovery. *If it feels good and it is healthy, I do it.*

Today is the day. Now is the time. This is not a dress rehearsal. This is my life and I am living it to the fullest…

ONE DAY AT A TIME.

June 7
GOING WITH THE FLOW

I was stifled by my inability to measure up to the exacting standards established by my false self. *A part of me, my actual self, was frustrated at almost every turn.* I could not perform perfectly all the time, according to the ideals generated by my false self; the 'shoulds' devoured me.

In trying to maintain control, I had grown rigid. My real self was all but dead. Having fun was out of the question. Surviving was serious business. **Life had become a spectator sport.** I had, in effect, disconnected with myself and others. I had 'shut down'.

I am invited to 'let go and let God'. *My concept of God is changing dramatically.* The God of my understanding is 180 degrees north of the understanding of my God upon entering the program.

Circumstances seem to synchronize as I act in a way that is true to myself. *I no longer fear the worst as I know that I have the capacity to weather the storm.* I have a self. I have true friends. I have a program.

I am becoming my own best friend. *I allow situations to serve me rather than my sacrificial serving of situations.* Reality is becoming my friend. I wear life as a lose garment. I move toward serenity.
I let the river carry *me.*

'The water is wide. I can't cross over. And neither have I wings to fly.'

I am building a boat that can carry me.
I know I can make it, now.
And I shall row, 'neath the deep blue sky.

June 8
BEING HUMAN

Most of my life, I had been driven by unrelenting demands; specific demands related to precise strategies which I had created in order to survive. I had been left virtually alone to navigate a distorted and dysfunctional world. *I had a certain false pride attached to my perceived ability to live up to those exaggerated expectations.*

On the flip side, I had also developed a sense of shame each time I failed. I vacillated between shame and false pride. *I held others in contempt, as well.* Their 'failures' lay at the core of my resentment.
I hated them. I hated myself.

I am taking a closer look at my old survival strategies. Many of them simply do not work. *I am becoming a functional human being, living in a real world.* The program presents a new world and new ways to view the world.

I am adapting to new conditions; conditions upon which I can build a solid new belief system; *a value system that requires only a simple willingness.*

I let go of the mandate for perfection. I give myself permission to stumble and fall on this new journey. I allow others the struggle and joy of their own journey.

I am one of billions on the planet; billions of folks, merely trying to find their own way in a sometimes very confusing and frightening world.
I celebrate my being human.
I celebrate my new-found gift to…

LIVE AND LET LIVE.

June 9
FACING CHALLENGES IN RECOVERY

Problems in the past seemed to be insurmountable and yet, I continued to apply the same approach. *I had some very limited ideas to work with:* always be on time, never leave a job half finished, always be polite, never shirk responsibility, always be honest, never tease someone, always be loving, never let anybody push you around, always report trouble to the authorities, never be a snitch, always be courageous, never doubt yourself.

The list of 'always' and 'nevers' was unceasing, unrelenting and unwavering.

I am letting go of my old ideas in exchange for new solutions. Breaking the habit of practicing old strategies in order to solve new problems is my greatest challenge in recovery. *<u>My thinking is changing slowly.</u>*

The conflict of not performing perfectly all the time is being replaced with the more realistic proposition; *sometimes I perform perfectly and sometimes I don't.* 'Mistakes' are part of my process for learning.

The 'sometimes' of life allows my entry into the human condition. *<u>I am not God.</u>* I am a mere mortal, capable of striking out at any time; proficient at getting a hit, as well. Sometimes I even hit a homerun!

I am beyond merely staying alive; avoiding abandonment; surviving. I am living. *Challenges are there. Choices are made. Actions are taken. Outcomes are unpredictable.*

Most of the time, I know the play; I take the shot. *<u>Sometimes I win, sometimes I lose.</u>*

That's life. (That's what all the people say)

June 10
READING THE SIGNS

I was so 'checked out' before I found the rooms that I rarely relied on my five senses to guide me, even in the most obvious of ways. I seemed to be immune to pain, emotional and otherwise. **When matters indicated 'proceed with caution', I raced on 'full speed ahead', never looking back for fear 'they' might be gaining on me.** I functioned as though sailing in a dark sea with nothing but a flashlight to guide me.

I am awakening to a world that invites my return to reality. I am trusting my own perception more and more. **No longer hamstrung by seeing life the way I always should, I am experiencing life the way it is.** I adjust accordingly. I rely on my sense of sight, smell, taste, hearing and touch to guide my responses. I no longer live in denial.

<u>I intuitively know how to handle 'situations that used to baffle' me.</u> Remaining loyal to my real self is my beaming light; my true north.

I view others as they are. Sometimes people move toward me; sometimes they move away from me. **I allow relationships to ebb and flow, as I am no longer terrified of abandonment.** Even when folks move against me, I can respond in ways that assure my well-being.

I can allow others to be on their own path, fighting their own battles. I take 'things' less personal. **<u>I can detach.</u>** I remember at the end of the day…

TO THINE OWN SELF BE TRUE.

June 11
WEATHERING A CRISIS

I rarely learned from life's experiences due to my obsession with avoiding conflict. One way or another, *I hoped I could side-step the struggles with which others seemed so easily entangled.*

And yet, life being what it is, I would find myself embattled with my own incongruencies or at war with outside issues; enmeshed, entrenched and immersed. *And when the crisis had passed, I was the last to know; most often, having learned very little.*

Life is my school room now. Having taken Steps Four and Five, I am launching into a world where adversity leads to greater freedom. *God is removing my old 'crisis control' system.* How? By placing people and situations in my life so I can consciously walk through old childhood emotions attached to new events.

New situations shed new light on old 'survival' ideas. I identify current errors in my thinking by taking Step Ten. *I can feel the feelings, identify the old erroneous demands and with God's help, promptly let them go.*

Often, old events will present in new ways more than once; indeed, some lessons are harder learned than others. *I find myself stuck at times and yet, with each passing day, I awaken to how I genuinely feel.*

I know a crisis when I see one. I am aware of danger. *I realize God is doing for me what I cannot or will not do for myself.* I trust the process. And when I get to the other side, out of harm's way; I know it. I feel it.

And to date, there is no greater feeling, for me, than knowing that a power greater than myself has seen me through, yet another storm.

June 12
JUSTIFYING MYSELF TO NO ONE

It seemed at every turn I had to create a reason for my being in the world lest I be abandoned. I felt compelled to defend my very existence. ***I sought through several strategies over the years to gain the respect of those from whom I needed approval.*** In the beginning, I moved toward everybody.
I was a nice boy, well-mannered.

Later I would adopt a plan of mastering all that I set out to accomplish.
I would gain the admiration of all. ***I secretly prided myself falsely in being above the rest of the human fray.*** Exhausted from trying to please everyone, I eventually moved away from others entirely
with various distractions.

My worth as a human being is no longer up for debate. ***My reason for being in the world is not dependent on how well I can serve the needs and wants of others.*** I am enough just the way I am.

Having settled the score on that issue, ***I am free to be who I am.*** I am happy to be complimented by others and yet, I need validation from no one.
I am present for and appreciative of myself.

<u>I act according to my genuine interests.</u> At the end of the day, as it turns out, it *is* all about me. If I meet someone and that person likes me, great!
If I meet someone and the person does not like me, that's OK, too.
I no longer need anyone else's approval in order to live freely.

Thank you very much.

June 13
TAKING STEP TWO

Having created the best plan I could devise in order to deal with my desperately deplorable conditions; conditions distorted beyond the realm of reason, I remained convinced that my strategy would eventually work. ***That is, I hoped that my world would eventually be free of conflict.***
I clung to the notion that all would eventually be well. I lived in denial of reality and remained frustrated most of the time.

Admitting the obvious is sometimes difficult; acquiescing to the notion of defeat, virtually impossible. Meeting with others who take Step One on a regular basis is like being reminded that tornadoes do, in fact, still exist. ***I cannot over-power a tornado.*** Dysfunctional worlds are beyond my control.

Rather than my taking Step Two, I allow the Step to take me. I attend meetings regularly. I see others moving away from their personal tornadoes, disengaging, detaching; otherwise, letting go.
The group is a power greater than myself.

By attending meetings, I am breaking the cycle of denial. ***I am beginning to believe that there is a solution;*** that I can eventually get free of my trouble.

A sense of well-being is returning; sometimes for a few moments, sometimes for a few hours. I move away from the tornadoes;
I move toward the available shelter.

Hope is returning.

June 14
TRUSTING OTHERS

I wanted to trust the so-called responsible people in my life. In fact, I needed to trust the adults in order to flourish; in order to fully become my real self. Due to repetitious displays of unavailability, toxicity and abuse by my 'grown-ups', *I forced myself to stay on high alert, willing to do whatever I had to do in order to survive another day.*

Eventually, I had to abandon my true self with its genuine interests and curiosities. The things that really mattered had become a liability. *I trusted practically no one.* War zones do that to people.

I have standards now; standards by which I gauge whether a person or a situation is who or what they seem to be. *I am becoming more and more available to myself.* I am allowing my real self to emerge, free to explore. I am treating myself with respect; turning down the volume of screaming demands of my false self; the 'shoulds'.
War zones are becoming less and less attractive.

<u>I want to connect with safe people;</u> people who usually do what they say; people who can support me right where I am; people who allow my struggle without fixing me; people who speak of their own struggles; people who share their own emotions; people who are reasonably predictable.

Some say this is a tall order! Indeed. No one person is everything to me all the time. No situation is always the same. *Human beings are human beings and yet, I can choose how much time I spend with another;* I can choose how much I share with individuals I encounter. I can choose the pace at which I want to move toward others.

I can move away from others when I require privacy.
AND, I can choose when to *end* a relationship altogether.

June 15
OWNING MY BEHAVIOR

In my emerging world of little or no accountability, I discovered quite by accident the art of denial. **When I could no longer deny, I played the 'blame others' card.** I could always justify my thinking. I could always litigate my resentment. I could always rationalize my behavior.
After all, I had witnessed the masters; those of my own family.
(See, I just did it again.) Old habits die hard.

I no longer live with the fear of abandonment. The rules have changed.
I care for myself, first. I am beyond mere survival. *I do what I do in order to care for me.* This is not up for debate. Caring for myself is not a fleeting fancy. It is an absolute must.

Ask any fireman what goes through their mind before racing into a burning building; any lifeguard what they consider before jumping in the water to save someone else; *self-preservation, first.*

Reality is my friend. I *want* to participate in my own recovery.
<u>*I want to admit when I have made an error in thought, word or deed.*</u>
I have the Tenth Step that affirms that I am not only going to make mistakes, but that it's OK to make mistakes, as well. I can learn from all my experiences.

With the help of God, I stand on my own two feet, unapologetic of who I am, unafraid of admitting my mistakes; thoroughly convinced of my human nature, adequately confident in all my endeavor and *perfectly willing to be myself…for I can be no other.*

June 16
MAKING DECISIONS

I had been confined to the demands of a false self which I had constructed in order to minimize, or eliminate entirely, what I considered to be conflicts in my world. For example, in order to prevent my mother's anger, ***I would comply on every level***; I would master every task required of my teachers; I would always be seen and not heard.

The 'shoulds' I had created required very little thinking; only obedience. My actual self, rarely validated, remained in a constant state of anxiety and depression.

I review the old ideas attached to my survival strategies of the past. ***I regain entry to the region of my real self.*** I give myself permission to consider new alternatives to old problems. I am making decisions that are designed to enhance my self-realization. I want to become who I am.

In Steps Six and Seven, I am inviting a God of my understanding to remove beliefs generated by my false self. I decide what needs to go.
I am creating a new moral structure; one that is 'me friendly';
one that I can employ with all assurance; with all my heart.

In my morning meditation, I pray for the knowledge of His will for my life and the power to carry that out. ***I am acting according to how I genuinely think and feel most of the time.*** When I remain true to myself,
I feel productive at the end of the day.

I remain awake to *all* the interests in my life.

June 17
TREATING OTHERS WITH RESPECT

I was consumed with hating myself and resenting others. ***Not only had I failed to live up to my own exaggerated demands, I had come to see others as hopelessly flawed, as well.*** I moved from shame to blame and back. I was exhausted. I rarely seemed to be able to simply relax. My worth depended on how well I was doing and when I was doing well, I feared the time would come when all would collapse.

By the time I found my first meeting, most everything had collapsed. ***I could no longer manage.*** I considered myself a failure. I trusted hardly anyone.

The opening reading in my group states, 'We respect where each person is in relation to their own recovery…' I give myself and others the latitude of a new understanding.

Knowing some of the personal details of others in the group through their sharing, ***I am aware of their struggle and because I realize their struggle, past and present,*** I naturally respect their journey.

I see the playing out of a universal human struggle: to separate from the old, to embrace the new; to fall, to get up, to move on.

I am one among billions on the planet, all of whom are challenged in one way or another. ***<u>I have come to see the beauty in most people</u>***: their wrestling with the human condition; their playing of the cards dealt; their traversing the course of this life, defying setbacks, overcoming hardships.

Each day, I am viewing ***myself*** with more compassion as I… *'trudge the road of happy destiny'.*

June 18
REMAINING TEACHABLE

In my attempt to overcome the distrust generated in my family of origin,
I grossly over compensated. I was convinced that asking for help was
not a good idea, as it merely validated my self-perception;
that I was an inconvenience to those around me. I had ceased asking for
anything. *I didn't want to appear weak, nor did I want to be a burden.*

I had incorporated the three dysfunctional **D**'s: **D**on't talk; **D**on't trust;
Don't feel. *I mostly heard the voice of my false self,* barking orders;
criticizing, discounting and shaming.

I keep an open mind today. In my effort to recover my real self,
I am discovering 'direct routes' to certain 'points of entry',
the Twelve Steps; points of entry that lead to the recovery of my lost self.
I take what I like, I give it a try;
perhaps it works, perhaps it doesn't.

Nevertheless, *I am willing* to use road maps in order to navigate my desired
journey toward self-realization. The destination is worth it!

I am practicing the ***HOW*** of the program; ***H***onesty, ***O***pen-mindedness and
Willingness. I am talking in meetings. I understand that my sharing may
help someone else. ***I am not an inconvenience.***

I am an asset. I admit through Step One that I have been unable to manage
my life alone. I listen to others speak of their experience, strength and hope.
I come to trust that there is a clear way out of all this mess.

And with God's help, I move with confidence through the Steps; in my
own time, in my own way. I reserve the right to change course at any time.
The choice is all mine.

June 19
MAKING A LIST

In my effort to conform to all the exaggerated demands dictated from my false self, **<u>I had mercilessly beat down my 'actual' self;</u>** that part of me that attempted over and over to live up to the idealized values I had adopted and created over the years; strategies devised in order to survive a world wrought with conflict.

I regularly abused myself with distorted thinking and quite naturally, I resented others. ***The distractions I employed to alleviate my pain had, in fact, become a problem in and of themselves;*** addictions of one sort or another.

I embrace Step Eight as one reading a bill presented by a contractor, having completed most of the work on remodeling my damaged home. There is debt. There is responsibility. ***There is a reckoning of sorts for the damage done over the years.***

Step Eight requires that I simply become willing to make a list. I have three categories: 1.) amends to myself 2.) amends to others toward whom I have acted harmfully, and 3.) ***NEVER AMENDS***; those remedial actions toward others whom I ***NEVER*** want to see or speak with ever again.

I move through the process with a solid confidence that ***God*** is doing for me what I cannot or will not do for myself. I place myself on the 'installment plan' when it comes to footing the bill for damages done. I place myself at the top of the list. ***I take this Step for me. If others are eventually helped, I am glad of the outcome.***

This Step is about being ***WILLING*** to clear away the wreckage of the past so that I can live as my true self; so that I can live freely; ***so that I can live with who I am.***

June 20
TAKING STEP NINE

I tried to avoid conflict. I had gone to great lengths to eliminate situations and circumstances that might lead to trouble. And yet, trouble seemed to always follow. Naturally, I was always 'on the scene'; a reluctant participant. *I had formed distractions in order to avoid the pain* that goes with difficulty and much to my sad surprise, these distractions had become compulsive in nature.

In other words, I had started doing things that I knew were abusive to myself and others. *I did them anyway.*

I saw others in three basic ways: those I would avoid, those I would move toward and those I would move against; I would shun some, manipulate others or directly hurt the ones who remained. *On most every occasion, my 'actions' were not of my choosing.* They were reactions based on my distorted, diseased thinking; reactions formed on a subconscious level based in fear.

I have a list of those that I have harmed, including myself. *I seek to own my detrimental behavior toward myself and others by making direct amends.* I do this in order to live with myself.

I am at the top of the list. I take every opportunity to be gentle with me; no more beating myself up for not doing 'it' perfectly. *Where others are concerned, I have one goal: to address old mistakes directly.*
Some are supportive; some are not. That's OK.

I am taking this Step to further my *OWN* recovery; no one else's. I am responsible for delivering the message, not for how the message is received.

I go forward, knowing that I am meeting the moment of compensation directly; neither regretting the past, nor wishing to shut the door on it.

I am beginning to know a *new* freedom and *new* happiness.

June 21
TAKING STEP TEN

I seldom admitted when I was wrong due in large part to having *NO* esteem for my actual self. I had convinced myself that I had to be right all the time, lest I appear to be weak; sub-standard. *I guarded with great vigilance the high expectations toward myself and others*, always insisting on perfection.

I denied those times when I would fall short. *I had become unfeeling; rigid in my thinking without really knowing it.* Self-examination was out of the question; beyond my purview. The 'blame and shame game' was full on.

My ability to feel is returning. I know when I am disturbed or upset. I try not to distract myself; rather, I go to the thought behind the feeling. *I know the process very well, as I have completed Steps Four and Five where I review my series of life events laced with emotions;* emotions based on false ideas and exaggerated demands.

Fleeting though it may be, a thought always precedes any action. *When I am 'wrong' in thought, word or deed, I can review the old demands setting up the thought, word or deed.* I can process the event with another trusted friend in the program. *I correct the problem BEFORE it gets out of hand.*

My occasional over-reaction, emotional and otherwise, is part of the journey. Being awake is part of the journey. *Being able to correct my over-reaction is part of the journey.* It is the gift of a true conscience.
I maintain a current inventory of my emotional well-being.

With the help of God, I am connecting with my real self;
no shame, no blame; just honesty.

June 22
TAKING STEP ELEVEN

By the time I found the rooms, I had not only alienated myself from my real self, I had alienated myself from God and others, as well. *I had surrendered to a false self; demanding, criticizing, and abusing.* I was exhausted from trying to squelch the voice; tired of trying to be perfect.

I resented others without really knowing it. I had been unmerciful with my actual self. Some of my distractions had grown to compulsive proportion.

Reconnecting with my genuine self, I am at ease with the big questions. Who am I? What shall I do? Where shall I go? With whom shall I associate? *Steps One through Nine have given me my life back.*

I am reasonably confident about who I am. I lower the unrealistic expectations on my actual self. I downsize the exaggerated claims on others. I am at peace most of the time. People and places that are no longer 'emotionally' safe are off my social calendar.
I don't go looking for trouble.

In taking better care of myself and my interests, I naturally enlist the help of God on a regular basis, usually in the morning. *I ask for His protection and care with complete abandon much like one would trust the captain of a huge cruise ship.* I am then free to roam about the ship and enjoy the excursion.

I pray for the knowledge of His will for me and the power to carry that out. *Some days I connect as one soaring with the eagles; other days, not so much.* Either way, I need look no further than the first day I entered the program in order to realize how far I have come.

BUT FOR THE GRACE OF GOD, THERE I GO

June 23
SHARING MY EXPERIENCE

Even in the old days, before the program, I had accumulated some marvelous adventures; marvelously scary! ***My experiences rivaled some otherwise 'normal' lives.***

I had seen and survived a lifetime of peculiar conditions, the likes of which few others had seen; the fights, the screaming, the leaving; the return 'all-is-forgiven' moments, the sanctity of a few fleeting moments of peace, the thrill of distraction. ***Life had been a series harrowing roller coaster rides.***

After all, hadn't I been the one ***attracted*** to excitement? Like the proverbial moth to the flame? Yes. ***And I had paid the price.*** Battered and bruised, sick and tired; I had earned my seat in the rooms of recovery.

I share a common dilemma with those raised in dysfunctional, if not addicted homes; the dilemma of finding a ***REAL*** self; abandoned, neglected and exchanged for a ***FALSE*** self. ***I am surviving the catastrophe of this shipwreck-of-a-disease.***

In search of myself, I naturally want to help others. I want to disclose related events; circumstances upon which I can find common ground. ***I am aware of a power greater than myself when I hear someone else share;*** when I hear of their emotions; when I hear of their similar grief and frustration.

I listen more intently to the person who is new in the room. Why? I want to be reminded. Indeed, I need to be reminded of the chaos, the pain and confusion that is the distorted world of addiction. I do not want to return to a life of disconnect. ***I want to remain with my true self,*** exploring new interests, new ideas and new paths of curiosity. Every time I share, I move closer to recovering my real self.

June 24
VENTING MY ANGER

I had experienced enough frustration and disappointment by the time I was fourteen to satisfy a lifetime of circumstance and condition. *I had 'stuffed' much of the anger that accompanied the promises broken, the thoughtless words spewed, and the harmful acts perpetrated.* In other words, I never talked about all the trouble and how I really felt.

These events stacked up. *My rage was like molten lava trapped just beneath the surface of an inactive volcano, waiting to explode.* Pressure, pressure and more pressure; building, building, building.

I need to rage. I need to express my fury. *<u>I use my voice and scream;</u>* sometimes into a pillow, sometimes in the middle of the woods, sometimes in workshops designed to support me in my grief.

I need to get angry. I need to express my anger. *I use my voice and tell a trusted friend what is going on.* I choose a person who does not want to fix me; someone who can allow my rants and my raves.

At the end of the day, I have choices around how I am going to deal with hurts; how I am going to deal with disappointments; how I am going to deal with frustrations. My therapist is invaluable. *I can own my emotion and process the events of my life.*

I break the rule of: 'Don't talk; Don't trust; Don't feel'. I am free of shame. The clinging vines of self-hate and resentment are removed…

ONE DAY AT A TIME.

June 25
KNOWING HOW TO HELP

I had built an entire life around being able to read other people's situations;
thus, inserting myself in a way that would appear worthy of notice.
I hoped for inclusion. Practicing this tactic in my alcoholic home
was rather like showing up to play football with a violin
or going to the paint store for tomatoes.

It did not work. And yet, ***I tried over and over, hoping for connection***,
persevering with my strategy in 'pleasing others' in order to be included;
in order to feel appreciated.

Today, I go to the paint store to buy paint; not tomatoes. I have my own
experiences. I have my own strengths. And I have my own interests.
All three serve me well, as I am connecting with my real self.
I know that I can, in fact, stand on my own two feet.

Desperation is receding; fear of abandonment is in retreat. ***I am stepping
into an 'actual' self that is not harangued*** and criticized with the
occurrence of every mistake I make common to man.
I am a ***human being***; not a ***human doing***.

I talk about things. ***I have a 'buddy system'.*** I trust others who are safe.
I step ***INTO*** my feelings and emotions. I am becoming my own best friend.
I hear my own voice as compassionate, considering all the events that I have
encountered and survived.

I see others as independent of the need to be fixed or otherwise, rescued.
I support people right where they are in their journey. ***I do this by simply
listening.*** I listen by:
1.) turning off my phone 2.) maintaining eye contact
3.) letting the other person know that I have heard them
{a simple nod of the head, a few words; Oh, I see; Wow; Hmmm…}
4.) validating the other person's thinking and feeling, ***unconditionally***.

By attempting to live fully unto myself, capable of solving my own
problems, absent of harsh judgment; and by allowing others the dignity to
do the same, ***I am free of the need to have all the answers.***

I am free to…***LIVE AND LET LIVE.***

June 26
CREATING NEW VALUES

Most of the old ideas I had formed over the years had arrived in my 'bank of morality' quite on their own, without any conscious effort or responsible consultation on my part. ***They had merely appeared.***

For the most part, I had been attempting to compose my own symphony with someone else's scraps of sheet music; with an unrelenting conductor barking directions, listening for every little mistake. <u>***I felt under pressure much of the time.***</u>

A lot of the ideas I had formed over the years were common to most: no stealing, no lying, no killing, no cheating, no giving up; ad infinitum the list. ***Other ideas had been inspired by distorted conditions and custom designed by my false self:*** always win, never lose; always love others, never get angry; always be independent, never ask for help; always help others, never be a burden; always know the score, never make a mistake; always be 'cool', never let them 'see you sweat'.

I have new music and a new conductor… ***ME***. I am conscious of the process as I form and reform my own moral values. ***I am free to explore new concepts related to all people, all places and all things around me.***
I consider each day to be an opportunity toward a higher education.
I am awakening to the possibility of a new life.

I am aware of the responsibility I play in maintaining my own belief system. No longer a victim, <u>***I choose with confidence my own path,***</u> my own interests and my own alliances.

I live with earnest intent, as though my very life depended on it…

JUST FOR TODAY.

June 27
WANTING WHAT I HAVE

I never seemed to be enough. I never seemed to have enough. And what I *did* have seemed to be at risk most of the time. ***I maintained a constant vigilance toward being more, having more or keeping what I already had.***

Perceived loss was sometimes unbearable. My grief from childhood seemed to be a breath away from being re-triggered, day in and day out. ***My false solution? Get more stuff!***

I am using what I have in order to create what I need. ***Today, I have everything I need in order to discover, recover and be my real self.*** I have food, clothing, shelter, trusted friends and family.

The first Nine Steps of the program allow my letting go of a false self; a dictator. Steps Ten and Eleven welcome my stepping into a new world; a world in which I enlist the help of God, myself and others to do one thing: ***become the real person that I am and always have been.***

The program requires, for the most part, my undivided attention. ***I put the program FIRST in my life FOR my life.*** I go to meetings. I talk about my progress. I talk about my setbacks. I naturally return to my genuine nature: the desire to love and be loved; the wish to be fully active in my own self-expression.

I use my voice to ask for what I need from sources capable of helping me. ***I allow what I ALREADY possess to sustain my recovery.*** My glass is, in fact, half full. I need but add a lemon and some sugar. Bingo, lemonade! And ice is nice, as well.

Now. I wonder if Joe from next door has some ice cubes?

June 28
RELATING TO HEALTHY PEOPLE

One of the reasons for establishing and maintaining dysfunctional, even abusive relationships was the distorted need to 'act out' my past conflicts in order to resolve underlying issues. Much of this effort was forged from an entirely unconscious state of mind. *In other words, my old 'solutions' had become habitual.*

My false beliefs regarding myself and others had driven most of my behavior. Without really knowing it, I had established a blueprint for staying stuck. *I remained a victim.*

I am considering new alternatives; new options. I re-assess old loyalties. *I measure the value of 'good friends' in new ways.* Are they emotionally available? Are they self-supporting? Are they reasonably capable of following through on a commitment? Are they capable of letting me arrive at solutions on my own? Are they willing to allow my struggles and the emotional process that goes with those struggles? Are they reasonably content on their own journey? Are they free of any addictive distractions?

I relate to those who are awakening, conscious of the feelings that go with the ups and downs of their everyday life; people who are talking about what is going on in real time; people who are trying to be transparent. I am being direct with others about what I need, what I want and what I expect. *I welcome honesty.*

A tall order? Perhaps. *And yet, my recovery is worth it.* I am worth it. My choosing a co-dependent relationship is like a recovering alcoholic taking the first drink. Therefore, I make healthy choices.
I create a safe space for my emerging true self.

I put the program first *IN MY LIFE, FOR MY LIFE.*

June 29
REMAINING CONSCIOUS

Before I found the rooms, I functioned on 'auto-pilot' most of the time.
I had emotionally 'checked out'. Life had become a constant, unconscious reaction to crises of various kinds; one crisis bleeding over into the next. *Most of my reactions were backed by a line of reasoning; my own custom designed strategy.* The endgame? To survive, of course; to not be abandoned emotionally; to not be 'turned out, into the cold of night'.

The disease of addiction didn't care how clever my plan. *The world of addiction proved to be an impenetrable frozen tundra; a kind of death to 'all who enter here'.* Only, I had no choice in the 'enter here' part.
I was already there!

My tactic remained simple: do what I must in order to 'make it'; whatever that meant. From this effort, emerged a whole system of beliefs and ideas; an entire moral structure designed to do one thing: keep me alive. *The principle of not talking, not trusting and not feeling quickly became a primary approach.* There would be many other 'principles' to come.
In fact, discovering ways to 'shut down' and emotionally distract myself became a way of life. I became quite proficient.

Things are different now. *I give myself permission to feel what I am feeling at the time I am feeling it.* I talk about what is going on. I am transparent with those I trust. I own my perception of the world around me. I challenge my thinking. I remain awake. *I review a play… BEFORE I take the shot*; in other words, I respond rather than over-react to life's events.

There is an emotional intensity, the likes of which can be overwhelming at times. <u>*I am not alone.*</u> I go to a meeting. I pray. I talk. I feel. And if that doesn't work. I feel. I talk. I pray.
And then I go to a meeting…

ONE DAY AT A TIME.

June 30
PRACTICING MEDITATION

In the past, I rarely paused long enough to sit down and eat breakfast; always on the go. Maintaining a frantic pace seemed to be working. My reasoning? ***Smart people multi-task; I am a smart person; therefore, I should multi-task…ALL THE TIME!***

My demands for perfection often pushed me to the point of despair. ***I had, strangely enough, grown 'accustomed' to my depression and anxiety.*** I distracted myself in order to avoid these emotions.

I am centering my attention on the here and now. I allow my feelings to register. I honor my body. In returning to a safe place, I give myself permission to rest. ***I find my strength.*** I find my vision.

I am conscious even while performing a difficult task or a multiple of difficult tasks. ***I focus on my intention connected to what I am, in fact, doing.*** My mind and my action are one.

I take the time to enjoy my completed purpose.

When agitated, I pause. I can pray for the knowledge of His will and the power to carry that out. ***I find that the answers appear, often of their own accord.*** I find a half-speed and move with conscious grace through the events of the day.

I am aware.   I am awake.   I am alive.

JULY

July 1
STAYING FOCUSSED ON MY PROCESS

I would sometimes fall short of some presupposed result I was hoping to achieve. At the thought of having failed, I employed the 'skill' of denial. Living in denial became a way of life. All of reality lay just beneath the surface. *I counted on being able to blame others in order to avoid my own sense of shame.* What shortcomings I may have exhibited were unconsciously transferred to others. I made my inside world about what was going on in the outside world.

I am discovering my universe within; my 'moral' structure. *Emotions of anxiety, depression, rage and shame are my guideposts.* When exaggerated demands on myself and others appear,
I STOP.
I LOOK.
I LISTEN.

I have the process of self-examination today; a process that allows the hearing of my false self's voice and the relentless declaration of distorted ideas about who I should be all the time and who others should be all the time; the 'shoulds'.

The Fourth and Fifth Step invite my awakening to an otherwise unconscious process; my old thinking. *When I find myself resenting others, justifying my own abusive behavior or rationalizing some unhealthy action, I go back to the drawing board.* I review old strategies attached to old conditions; methods meant for a different time, a different place.

Steps Six and Seven give me a way out. *I let go of the old ideas that are no longer working.* I rest in the process. I rest in the new concept: that God is doing for me what I cannot or will not do for myself. I attempt to…

LET GO AND LET GOD

July 2
CULTIVATING SPIRITUAL GROWTH

My approach to anything spiritual had been rigid and 'well defined'.
I followed certain rules. Or I didn't. Period. There were universal spiritual axioms I employed when convenient: 'what goes around comes around, give and it shall be given to you, do unto others as you would have them do unto you, judge not lest you be judged'.

<u>The spiritual growth idea was not one of my top priorities in life.</u>

When considering the notion that someone or something, undetected by the five human senses, could be participating throughout the course of human events, I remained doubtful; sometimes confused and angry. *Where had this omnipotent force been for the unfolding of MY glorious and dysfunctional nightmare?*

I am considering new ways of looking at things. *I have found others who have found a way out.* I hope for a brighter day. Others who have gone before, assure me that there is something wonderful and mysterious called, *A LIFE.*

I begin where I am. I decide to trust this process; the process others call recovery. I am finding the courage to go to meetings. *I am changing the things that I can change; primarily ME.* With the help of others, I am growing more confident in my ability TO change.
I have a plan; the Twelve Steps.

Like the immortalized dancer, Fred Astaire, who once said to his partner Ginger Rogers, *'One step at a time, dear! One step at a time!'*
I am learning to dance again.

<u>Repetition strengthens and affirms habit; faith, then, becomes natural.</u>

July 3
CREATING NEW IDEAS

If my situation looked like anything it looked like 'stuck'. My strategies, my schemes, my skills and my actions had led me to one place; the emotional 'dead zone'; physically alive, yes; but emotionally deceased.

Adhering to the dictates of a false self, I had alienated my real self; buried my genuine interests, sacrificed my curiosities; all in the effort to survive an unsafe, sometimes hostile environment.

I am reasonably sane; always have been. What worked back then, however, does not work now. I am sometimes frustrated. I am sometimes confused. I am responsible for discovering what still works and what does not.
Going forward, the creation of new strategies to live is my top priority.

Fortunately, I have a process by which *I can prepare a new space for new ideas* that truly work. With the help of others, I am clearing out the old and making room for the new.

I inventory old ideas that continue to set me up for failure, disappointment and fear. I let go of the unrelenting demands behind those old ideas:
'I should always do this…they should always do that'.

With the help of God, I am wiping the slate clean; putting the trash to the curb; weeding the garden; draining the swamp. *I imagine the possibility of something they call A LIFE.* I am making room for new ideas! I act with confidence, using what I have in order to create what I need…

ONE DAY AT A TIME

July 4
FREEING MYSELF OF DYSFUNCTIONAL BEHAVIOR

I had established a system, a foundation of sorts, upon which my entire world functioned. I was convinced that my behavior could, in fact, influence the behavior of others; especially the people in charge. *I searched for ways to prove, beyond a doubt, that I was top-of-the-list material*.
This idea came with a price; the loss of my real self.

Pleasing others proved to be a full-time affair; morning, noon and night. I developed an entire belief system around what I thought would work, only there seemed to be one subtle problem; it didn't.

I changed strategies, made new rules and yet, the major players in my life continued to be exactly as they were; mostly unavailable, sometimes toxic.

My higher power is removing the old ideas that keep setting me up. *I am willing to allow the deconstructing of a false self in exchange for the promise of a new awakening;* an awakening to the constructing of a real self.

Steps Six and Seven merely suggest that I call on a God to help me with all the remodeling. By design, I visit circumstances like those of the past.

I re-feel what I could not or would not allow myself to feel in the first place. ***I am aware of misguided demands,*** unwarranted claims on myself and others. I allow the demolition of old ideas no longer suited for my needs.

I welcome the removal of the old.
I anticipate the arrival of the new.

I fully embrace *'a new freedom and a new happiness'*.

July 5
FORGIVING

I was gifted with a very good memory, especially when it came to things like touching a hot stove, bumping my head, tripping downstairs and the like. ***With each passing day, my mind registered all the elements in my environment that could potentially hurt me or keep me alive.*** I remembered especially those from whom the most pain had been delivered; usually the ones I loved the most. I grew to fear them.

I formed my young thoughts accordingly and eventually, I 'evolved'.
<u>I designed an entire method around one thing: surviving;</u> staying in favor of those who fed and clothed me; staying alive. The good news? I survived. The bad news? I lost myself in the process.

By taking the first Nine Steps, ***I have changed my old strategy when it comes to surviving at the hands of others.*** Today, I am aware of the human propensity for neglect. I am mindful of a universal narcissistic tendency. I know of the human will to do battle; to lash out in fear;
to abuse in anger; to kill in rage.

Thus, I concede with a certain premonition the mistakes of man; myself included. I am not perfect, nor is anyone else. ***On my best day, I don't even come close.*** What's more; I don't even want to be perfect. I do what I do; I did what I did. They do what they do;
they did what they did.

I am not impervious to the heat of hot stoves and yes, I still bump my head from time to time. I even trip down the stairs.
<u>I am a human being having a spiritual experience.</u>
Fools rush in where angels fear to tread. I tread lightly as I…

LIVE AND LET LIVE.

July 6
CARRYING THE MESSAGE

I had grown so accustomed to defending a position in order to survive that I rarely considered the needs of others. Life had become a power struggle; sometimes subtle, sometimes overt.

I had no genuine sentiment, only an agenda fashioned by my false self. I was compelled to remain true to the demands.

Whether I was helping others out of 'kindness', battling with others over 'principles' or detaching from others with pride, *I seldom acted from a place of genuine respect.* I was, in fact, driven most of the time; my only concern being that of staying alive.

I am in a unique position, having fully recovered from a state of hapless confusion, misguided reaction and compulsive behavior. *I am, in short, awake. I am aware.* I have my experience of walking out of a very dark night. I have my strength of knowing, with the help of God, how to navigate the path. I have the hope of a an even brighter day ahead, up the road; over the river.

I face the past. I own my old ideas. I change my strategy. I correct my course. I make myself available.

Whether I have one day or thirty years in these rooms, my message follows me wherever I go: there is a way out. *I carry the courage of living free. I carry the vision of standing true.* Spoken or unspoken, I carry the message of recovery.

I move forward…

ONE DAY AT A TIME.

July 7
RE-SETTING MY IDENTITY

I had come to see myself in context my past experiences; experiences primarily related to being raised and educated by some very dysfunctional people. *Much of how I viewed myself and the world around me came from a strict approach I had created when faced with conflict.*

I prided myself in staying true to the old ideas formed by my false self. In fact, I had idealized a rigid approach to life. *Every time life failed to unfold accordingly, I felt hate toward myself and resentment toward others.* I felt like a victim most of the time.

I am not my old belief system. No longer stuck in the past, I move forward, creating new ideas. My false self takes up a lot less room. Liberated from the unrealistic demands and critical dialogue, *I connect with my real self, safely.* I emerge with genuine interests. I participate in my own agenda. I *HAVE* a life.

When I know what I want and act accordingly, I establish my authentic self. *Win or lose, I am confident in my new ability to remain true to myself.* I am reasonably content with allowing life to unfold. I let go.

The element of spontaneity returns as my false rigid demands are removed; old notions of how I 'should always' be are challenged. *I break free of the old chains of perfection.* If it feels good and it is healthy, I do it.

Whether my responses are connected to my spiritual nature, my mental ability, my emotional condition, my physical capacity or a combination of all four, I rest assured of one thing: the growth of my real self.

I connect and I awaken. I am who I am.

July 8
ASSESSING OLD STRATEGIES

How I thought about myself and other people determined all my behavior. Most of my actions were motivated by unconscious forces, operating in tandem fashion to assure my survival. *I had practiced these reactions enough times that they had become routine.* Some would even say that my having a 'choice' in much of my behavior was mere fantasy.

And yet, I took great pride in this idealized moral system of right and wrong; good and bad. *However, this false pride, well established by adulthood, came with a high price when I failed its demands;* the price being, the hatred of myself.

And when others failed, I unleashed criticism and resentment. *Even in the face of great anxiety and depression, I marched on, hoping to finally appease this monster I had created.*

The Fourth Step suggests that I thoroughly review, as best I can, the moral system upon which I have based my actions of the past. I am allowed all the time I need. *I am encouraged to continue my journey regardless of the difficulty.* I grow confident in my search for old dysfunctional ideas, lurking at the core of my false self; old ideas that continue to set me up for disappointment.

The Fifth Step invites the review of my old moral system as it relates to one deciding question: how well is the system working? Am I better off, having demanded more from myself and others than could ever be delivered? Or is it time to lower my expectations? *Is it time to let up on my actual self to always perform according to the dictates of a distorted false self?*

This is my life. I have a choice.

July 9
PRAYING

I was a religious person; attended church, read the bible and said my prayers. ***Always more interested in the outcome rather than the process, I requested, even demanded, certain conditions;*** make me more saintly, send money for the rent, give me better grades, guide me in my career, let me marry the right person, show me which car to purchase.

For the most part, praying was reserved for when I attended church and when I had exhausted all I could do in order to solve a problem. ***When I did not get 'quick' results, I blamed God.***
I saw myself as a victim.

I am no longer a victim of life. I am a co-creator in my life.
I pray. I meditate. I act.

I pray for the knowledge of His will for my life and the power to carry that out. ***I meditate*** on the vision of what that would look like.
I act on the idea.

I creatively visualize what I truly want in conjunction with my real self. ***Sometimes I get it; sometimes I don't.*** God is always doing for me what I cannot or will not do for myself.

My prayer?

SHOW ME THE WAY.

July 10
FEELING GOOD ABOUT MYSELF

I had drifted into a state unconscious emotional disturbance, wafting between depression and anxiety; ashamed of what had happened, worried about what might happen. *I engaged in a regular practice of hating myself or blaming others.*

I distracted myself with all kinds of behavior, not wanting to feel anything. I rarely owned my contributing thoughts and actions. I merely stewed in shame, unaware of any process; unawake to any other way of life.

I am moving toward myself; my real self. I am turning down the volume on the demands of my fearful false self. *I give myself permission to feel what I am feeling.* I regularly talk with someone about what is going on; someone I trust; someone who can simply listen. I step into freedom. All options are on the table. I embrace the journey.

I grasp this process, fully aware of the challenges. I am reclaiming my life through the Steps. I have moments when I respond in a healthy way to current events. *I give myself credit.* I applaud my own effort. I allow the compliments of others. Feeling good feels good.

I reward myself often. I treat myself with dignity. I give myself latitude for mistakes made on this one-step-forward-two-steps-back mission of recovery. *I treat myself with respect.* I realize my moments in courage. I appreciate who I am. I marvel at how far I have come…

ONE DAY AT A TIME.

July 11
MANAGING MY LIFE

I had made a catastrophe of my life, attempting to not only control my own behavior, but trying to manage other's actions, as well. I was exhausted. ***I stacked one event on top of the other in order to entirely distract myself from life's conflicts.*** When a pleasant occasion did present itself, I rarely availed myself of any genuine emotion. I acted as I 'should'. The lights were on, but nobody was home.

I am encouraged to feel my feelings. I am encouraged to check-in with others. I am encouraged to talk about what is going on. I am encouraged to stay in the present. I am encouraged to be gentle with myself. ***I do all these things <u>as an act of my own will.</u>*** I implement a plan of recovery; a plan to reclaim my abandoned self.

It has been said by those who have gone before that humility is the 'sincere desire to know and do God's will'; that any use of the human will along these lines is, in fact, the correct use of my human power. ***I believe the program has been given to me in order that I may have life and have it more abundantly.*** I act with all confidence toward that end.

I go to meetings whether I feel like it or not. I take the Steps. ***I connect with my real self and I act in a genuine fashion, according to who I am.*** The process itself presents healthy options from which I may choose.

In the tough decisions, I pray simply for the knowledge of His will for my life and the power to carry it out. ***<u>I consciously ask for His protection;</u>*** His care.

And so, I trust my actions implicitly.

July 12
HONORING THE JOURNEY

Having created such a rigid belief system in order to survive my distorted world of addiction, I had great difficulty appreciating others' perspective in a genuine way. ***The view of myself and the world around me was narrow and presumptuous.*** Unable to respect my own struggle, I deflected my fear and anxiety. In other words, I blamed and criticized those around me; found fault at every turn.

This prejudicial limitation, subtle as it was, thrust upon me the absolute necessity to always be 'right'. ***I had established an entire moral structure that dictated how situations should always be.*** Genuine empathy was a rare bird. As time went on, my world grew black and white with very little grey. I avoided certain 'types' altogether. Some I even secretly hated.

With the help of the program, I am lowering the old demands of my false self. ***I am addressing a misguided moral structure through Steps Four and Five.*** By attending meetings and hearing others share, I realize the plight of others; a plight not unlike my own. In knowing others, I grow to respect others. In respecting others, I grow to sincerely care. And in sincerely caring, I respond quite naturally in a loving way most of the time.

I know of many episodes in my own travail. I reverence my process. I see myself as one among many. I care. ***<u>My heart is returning to love.</u>*** And when I scorn others as I still do, the thought comes to me: there go I…

BUT FOR THE GRACE OF GOD.

July 13
REMEMBERING THE PRIMARY PURPOSE

My emotional pain was off the charts. Opportunities for distraction had multiplied. I could barely sit with myself for more than a couple of minutes before I felt compelled to do **'something'**. And in the process of doing **'something'**, I often doubted my entire purpose for even taking **'something'** up in the first place. I would give up halfway through or finish the effort under half steam. Eventually, *__I came to doubt any purpose at all.__*

These days, I am on a quest of sorts. No longer running from my difficulties in fear, I am searching for myself; my genuine self. *I grow passionate as I discover real interests.* I have moments of joy as I complete small tasks **related** to those interests. I celebrate when I achieve a desired result; when I persevere.

I learn from my mistakes. *I grow a little smarter each day; some days I grow a lot smarter; other days, not so much.* I am coming to see the wisdom in the old saying: 'It matters not whether I win or lose, but how I play the game.'

The primary purpose of my recovery rests in one solitary effort toward one single outcome; to get my life back. *In short, I want to connect in as loving a way as possible with God, myself and others.* I do this by putting the program first in my life for my life. I have a game plan in the Steps. I stick to the plan and the plan sticks to me. Distractions come and go. Sometimes I win; sometimes I lose.

__The Steps shall always remain.__

July 14
OWNING MY FREEDOM

I had restricted my behavior in order to protect my true self; my vital self; that core component essential to all lively pursuit. ***Not wishing to disturb or more to the point, not wishing to be disturbed, I fashioned into my life specific strategies designed to eliminate the conflict.*** For example, I moved toward those in 'power', hoping to please; later, I would rebel; and still further on, I would withdraw altogether.

These positions came with relentless demands, some often conflicting with others. I would comply on one level and hate myself for not standing up. I would stand up and hate myself for not being more gracious. I would ask for help and criticize myself for not being more independent. And so, it continued for a long time. ***I had imprisoned my real self in the effort to secure the peace; the terms being dictated by my false self.***

I step from a world of self-imposed exile, uncertain and afraid. ***What will become of me if I let go of the old plan?*** Who am I if not the person obsessed with survival? How shall I function if I am no longer defined by my pain and misery?

The Second Step suggests that I can, once again, embrace the peace that comes with operating from my genuine self; that I can enjoy the freedom of my actual self in its search for meaning; that I can, at long last, fully embrace my own worth, wonder and dignity. ***I am safe in the program.***

I explore the freedom of a new world; the world of recovery.

July 15
BEING PRODUCTIVE

I came to believe that anything and everything I had attempted to do was flawed. *I may have achieved ninety percent of what I had hoped for, but the remaining ten percent kept me up at night;* the ten percent of imperfection: a mis-spoken word, a 'thoughtless' action, a mistake, a detour in the plan, a setback, a deed misapplied in haste.

The self-appropriated tightrope upon which I insisted to perform had ceased serving me. *<u>My obsession often left me paralyzed emotionally;</u>* discouraged, anxious and afraid.

I am connecting today with an old friend, myself. Having cleared away the wreckage of the past, I am free to pursue sincere interests long abandoned; genuine curiosities newly formed.
I am alive again.

When I act in a way that is true to my core value, I always feel productive regardless of the outcome, perfect or otherwise. I am accepting of most mistakes made along the way, as they have come to be my teacher. *I take great delight in accomplishing the smallest of tasks:* a cup of tea well made, a dinner served for friends, a chore tackled, a book revisited.

I am discovering the art of simply being. I choose to define myself according to who I am, rather than what I do. *<u>When who I am meets up with what I do; absolute bliss!</u>* And when the outcome is what I have hoped for; ecstasy! And what of the imperfect ten percent?

I don't sweat the small stuff anymore. *Oh, and by the way, it's all small stuff.*

July 16
DEALING WITH INNER CONFLICT

I had operated for a long time with specific beliefs regarding how I should act all the time. Most of these ideas revolved around three basic approaches when dealing with others: complying, resisting or withdrawing. ***In the beginning, I sampled all three. Eventually, I would pick one.***

I 'evolved' to the extent that I created over time a rather permanent false self, hell bent that I perform perfectly all the time. For example: ***I should always be thoughtful of others, kind to strangers, charitable toward others, etc.; a compliant, 'loving' position.***

At the same time, the other two approaches were operating in the background. When the time came to stand up for myself and resist injustice, I often felt unable to respond and when I did respond,
I felt ashamed; 'Loving people never fight.' The same was true of withdrawing from others, which I saw as neglect; 'Kind people never withdraw support.' The point is simply this:

I was damned if I did perform according to the false self's dictate and I was damned if I didn't. I was in conflict most of the time.

Thanks to reviewing my old ideas by taking the Fourth and Fifth Steps, ***I am realizing a new idea: all three approaches can operate at the same time; indeed, it is natural.*** There are times when I comply in order to get along with others; no shame. There are times when I resist in order to stand up for what I believe; no shame. There are times when I withdraw in order to create a private moment; no shame.

I lower the demands of my false self. ***Distorted old ideas are being removed.*** I celebrate the freedom of my true self. Whether I am moving toward others, against others or away from others,
I am always moving toward becoming who I am.

July 17
EMBRACING THE PRESENT MOMENT

I spent a lot of time pining over the past or worrying about the future.
I rarely enjoyed a moment's rest. *My mind criticized past actions involving myself and others; not guilty one day, guilty the next.* Back and forth it would go, the volume out of control; loss upon loss; error upon error.

I told myself the future would be different. I would better control unfolding events. I would perform better. *I would not make the same mistakes.* I would maintain a vigilance unmatched in the past and
this vigilance would assure the outcome I wanted.

Even when the 'good times' appeared; *even when I got what I wanted, there appeared the "what if's":* What if my grades aren't good enough? What if she says no? What if the car breaks down? What if the plane crashes? What if we can't find a hotel? What if we run out of money?

Today is the day. Now is the time. I have what I need in order to be who I am, right now; food, clothing, shelter, trusted friends, and reliable family members (perhaps). *Regardless of where I am in the Steps, I have hope;* hope that 'things', while they may not get better **overnight**,
will most assuredly get different **over time.** They say, time takes time.

I practice staying in the moment. <u>*I practice feeling my feelings.*</u>
I practice remaining awake.

I find with each moment's passing that I am, in fact, buying time; time needed in order to recover my lost self. Some moments are 'better' than others. *Each moment is strangely different.*
And for me, 'different' is a good thing.

July 18
ANCHORING MYSELF

There were times when I attached myself to various scenarios, hoping to feel connected. Whether I was the one calling the shots or the one reacting to the shots being called, the outcome seemed better than the alternative; being all alone; being unemployed; being left out.
Denial of my condition kept me stuck.

Fear of the unknown kept me going back for more. ***Circumstances dictated my state of mind.*** Oddly enough, these situations felt familiar; almost comfortable. Pain was a strange bedfellow.

I am returning to home base; my real self. ***In my returning, I find a sense of clarity;*** a sense of solid well-being; a sense of something indicative of a 'true north'.

With the help of the program, I am finding a place in the world that is reasonably safe; reasonably predictable. ***In the meetings, I find people who are searching for healthier solutions, willing to establish new boundaries, and hoping for a more solid foundation going forward.***
Little by little, I find my truth.

Home is defined as, a place established to encourage the nurture and growth of those who enter therein. ***Each week when I attend my regular 'home group', I feel as though I am walking through a door upon which hangs the sign, ENTER HERE ALL WHO SEEK SAFETY AND PEACE.***

Thanks to the design of the meetings: the rotating chairperson, the no crosstalk expectation, the non-affiliation with any outside organization, and our primary purpose; ***<u>I am free to explore my truth.</u>***

I am free take what I like. I am free to leave the rest. I am free to come. I am free to go. In short, I am free to be who I am.

July 19
SORTING OUT THE TRUTH

I had grown up in a world where blaming and labeling others were common practice. How I saw myself, at best, was often distorted. *I came away with the notion that I was not enough.*

And I acted accordingly, often dangerously exceeding realistic limitations in order to 'prove' myself or pathetically limiting my activity as to not feel embarrassed upon possibly failing.

The voice of my false self, with its relentless demands, blaring at full volume, hounded my every move. *I fully participated in beating down my actual self;* that part of me that was on the hook to always perform well, if not perfectly.

The accusations were endless: you're so stupid, you should always think first; you're so careless, you should slow down; you're so thoughtless, you should consider others; you're such a liar, you should always be honest; you're such a braggart, you should be humble; you're so mean, you should never get angry.

I no longer address myself with inner dialogue using the word, 'you'. The word 'you' presumes there is an audience. *I constitute only one member in my 'audience'; my real self.* I have, in effect, eliminated the middleman; the critical dictator of all 'truth'.

I am free of the 'shoulds'. *'Should' is not in my vocabulary.*
I am who I am, period.

Thanks to the self-searching invitation of the Twelve Steps, *I am realizing my own truth:* the truth about myself, the truth about my world and the truth about how *I AM TO BE* in that world.
This is my privilege. This is my responsibility.
This is my truth. This is my program.

July 20
RESPONDING TO EMOTION

In order to appear 'fine', I denied my feelings and emotions. When one is struggling to stay alive, pausing to 'get in touch' with how one is feeling is not an option. I reacted and I moved on. The time in between critical events seemed to grow shorter and shorter. *I moved from loss to loss with little or no awareness.*

Opportunity for resolution rarely presented itself. I grew more emotionally 'numb' by the year; more anxious of the future; more depressed about the past.

I am encouraged to feel what I am feeling. I take the time to talk about events that prove difficult; events that sometime trigger past trauma. *I am fully re-assured that this is part of the recovery process;* the process of breaking up the denial associated with my experience.

When I feel angry, I can check my 'pulse'. Sometimes my anger is associated with something in the environment that requires my immediate attention. *I ask for what I need in order to feel safe.*
I act in order to care for myself. *I move on.*

When my anger turns to rage and continues longer than an hour, I know to look beyond what just happened. *I have been triggered.*
I am reacting to old events. *I am stuck.*

I process my emotions with someone who is safe; someone who is present; someone who allows my autonomy; someone who can listen without 'intervening'; someone who allows me the dignity to discovery solutions that work for me.

I plan my action. I act according to my plan. I stay connected. I remain involved in my own process. These are my 'educational moments'.
I need this awareness in order to recover.
Remaining emotionally awake is a **good** thing.

Responding to life, rather than reacting is even better!

July 21
CARING ABOUT OTHERS

I cared more about other's approval than I cared about others. And yet, there were times when I 'sacrificed' in order to help. My primary concern was to avoid conflict. ***I sought out relationships where I was either the one needing support or the indispensable one, giving support.*** All the while, I was unaware of my process; unaware of the 'bargain struck' with the other individual or institution.

In order to carry out the survival demands of my false self, I had to have an audience of some kind. I could be gracious at times, seeing myself as the benevolent savior; at other times, powerful and demanding, an all-knowing authority concerned with the best outcome for everyone. ***Either way, I always lost myself in the process; my real self.***
I was, in effect, on 'auto-pilot'.

I see others as privileged; privileged to be on their own journey. I no longer need an audience in order to 'act out' an unresolved issue. I talk it out. ***<u>No longer am I compelled to control anybody.</u>*** I am satisfied to extend the same dignity granted to me in the program; the dignity of discovering my own values, defining my own problems and arriving at my own solutions ***in my own time***.

I am unable to manufacture care and concern for others simply because I 'should' always be caring and concerned for others. ***What I CAN DO is take the time to know someone by listening politely to their story.*** In knowing them, I come to respect who they are. In respecting their journey, I grow to ***genuinely*** care about their process; thus, I respond in a naturally caring way.

No longer compelled to rescue, caretake or fix other people, ***I am free to allow others the dignity of sorting out the details of their own adventure.*** I 'lend a hand' upon request, provided I have a free hand to lend as I…

LIVE AND LET LIVE.

July 22
CHOOSING MY OWN VALUES

Having been raised in an alcoholic home, I created a 'value' system primarily designed to keep me alive. *I rarely had a conscious choice in the matter of morality.* I merely made up strategies as I went along.

I adapted. The television provided a package of ideas suggesting what was right and what was wrong. Each network had to comply with a 'code of ethics'; the good guys always winning, the bad guys always losing.

I single-handedly devised a rather complicated matrix of ideas; some based in reality; others not. For example: *I believed that if I copied the behavior of one of the 'good boys' on TV, that my mother would stay home at night;* that she would act like one of the 'good mothers'. Try as I might, I rarely got the desired results and yet, I tried again and again.

I am reviewing these old ideas. *The Fourth Step creates a space so that I can decide which values are to be maintained and which ones are to be abandoned.* I awaken to a new freedom.

I am participating in my own process; a process that will determine my new thoughts and behavior going forward.

I am creating an open area in my mind much like one would do if beginning to decorate an old tired room. *I am encouraged to look at as many experiences of the past as I can in order to determine the beliefs that emerged from those episodes.*

I lay the groundwork for the building of a new moral structure; my moral structure; a moral structure that I *choose, consciously;* a moral structure that really works.

July 23
PUTTING VALUES INTO ACTION

I functioned from a place that defied reason. At an early age, I employed ideas and notions that eventually evolved into deep-seeded values; values which, for the most part, were an entire mystery in their origin. *I performed as I performed because I 'should', rarely giving my actions and reactions a second thought; rarely feeling anything.* If I stayed within the 'guidelines', all seemed to go well; only, all did not go well.
And yet, onward through the fog I would trudge.

I review my current values on a regular basis. *I am fully aware of their origin; MY OWN MIND.* The Tenth Step invites my participation in re-creating a moral system that really works. I am awakened to circumstances both past and present that contribute to how I see myself; how I see the world around me; and more to the point, how I respond to myself and the world. I allow my feelings. I am in touch with my emotional landscape.

Origins of new ideas are no longer a mystery. *I have a lot of sources for new ideas:* music, books, movies, documentaries, colleges, trusted friends and professionals, art. The list goes on.

I reason things out with another, embracing the new; letting go of the old. Step Eleven suggests that I can employ the help of a higher power in order to know what I believe.

Having established, IN A CONSCIOUS WAY, the values upon which I rely, I can act with all assurance as I move through my current circumstances.

I am entirely confident as my real self directs the action I take. I go forward. And what of the results? I leave the results up to God.

I LET GO AND LET GOD

July 24
LENDING AN EAR

I had rehearsed and 'acted out' a lot of scenarios before I found the program. I knew my part line by line. I had grown rather 'proud' of myself in a false way. I considered my 'ideals' to be profoundly brilliant. ***However, when I failed to live up to these ideals, the voice of my critical self could be figuratively deafening; nevertheless, I still considered myself to be above the fray.*** My strategy? I would simply do better next time. And in the meantime, I would cover up my mistakes; embellish the truth; deny my failures; and manufacture a story.

I am invited in meetings to 'share'. There is a strict 'no cross-talk' rule which assures that no one will interrupt my sharing, criticize my sharing, interpret my sharing or otherwise cut me off from my story. ***I have the freedom to talk about as much or as little as I want.*** There are no topics that are off the list as I relate my story to recovery. I can tell the same story over and over. The group listens respectfully.

I hear other people tell their stories; sometimes in the meetings, sometimes before the meetings, sometimes after the meetings, sometimes one-on-one over coffee or dinner. ***The guideline established by the no crosstalk rule gives me direction when dealing with another person's telling me of their situation.***

I simply listen without interrupting, without criticizing, without interpreting. I sometimes ask for clarification if I am not certain of points being made and yet, ***I extend a common courtesy;*** the courtesy availing one the opportunity to finish their thought.

By giving someone the time to hear their own voice, I extend the gift of dignity and respect which the program gives me.
I allow another's autonomy.

I am given one of the greatest gifts that earth has to offer; the gift of ***trust*** by another human being.

July 25
LEARNING TO RELAX

I functioned with a very high level of anxiety. Somedays I was more anxious than others. *I had my distractions available to keep my life 'manageable':* work, school, food, relationships, social media, television, mood-altering chemicals; to name a few.

Even when I 'relaxed', I rarely let down entirely; always running from my emotions. Depression dogged my every step. *I lived in a state of shame without really knowing it.* The dictates of my false self rarely let up: I should be more, do more, have more…*ALWAYS.*

I am aware of the old ideas today; the old ideas that no longer work. I am turning down the volume on the demands that hold on from the old days, the days before I found the program.

<u>*Some days I am more, do more and have more; some days, not so much.*</u>
 I am OK with ordinary. I am wearing life as a loose garment; allowing the ebb and flow, the ups and downs.

I am taking it slow. I am setting aside moments during the day when 'things' stop. *I usually have a cup of my favorite tea, review the events of the day, and sit with how I feel.* If need be, I call a trusted friend. I connect. *I VALIDATE MY ACTUAL SELF.*

Lighting a candle, taking a bubble bath, building a nice fire, practicing a favorite hobby or simply going for a long run; I take care of my absolute need to treat myself with kindness.

<u>*I hear my own voice with compassion.*</u> I create a safe place where I can simply be me, uninterrupted. I remember…

EASY DOES IT.

July 26
BUILDING A LIFE

I had created a sick plan, without really knowing it, to keep me alive during the days spent in my dysfunctional family setting. ***Whether I played the hero child, the scapegoat, the lost child or the mascot, certain ideas had become ingrained.*** I acted on those ideas, reviewed those ideas, honed those ideas, to the point that I came to believe that I was, in fact, those ideas. I idealized this false self.

My so-called moral structure, for the most part, had been formed in reaction to a distorted world. ***I would spend a great deal of time attempting to fashion my actual self to accommodate these 'moral' demands.*** I allowed my false self to reign supreme.

I am taking back my life. Having reviewed my old beliefs and their origin, I am prepared to examine the 'exact nature' of their wrongs; their errors in perception; their unrelenting demands.

Taking Steps Four and Five prepares the way for a sense of new beginning. I embark on a new adventure; the adventure of connecting with my real self, acting accordingly and becoming who I am.

I clear a path for new ideas and interests. ***With the help of God, I am freeing up the space once occupied by neurotic obsessions.*** I am entirely ready to have God remove all these ideas and behaviors; behaviors which no longer serve my genuine growth.

The connection with my real self and its genuine impressions, true feelings, sincere interests and natural curiosities guide the action I take today. I am true to my own journey.

I am true to myself.

July 27
TRUSTING THE RECOVERY JOURNEY

Even though my family of origin was anything but predictable, safe and nurturing, I had come to 'trust' the practices, routines and roles of those I lived with. ***I adjusted and re-adjusted my approach to coping.*** At one point, I believed whole-heartedly in my solution; a solution constructed in order to deal with the unavailability and abuse which I encountered over the first eighteen years of my life.

The end game of my plan was to become such a great and wonderful person that everyone, family included, would avail themselves to me unequivocally and utterly respect what I had become.
I would emerge triumphant. (Yeah, right.)

I am reviewing the situation. The rooms provide a safe and predictable place where I can explore the old system. ***I keep what I need to keep.*** I am invited to explore a new system: talk about things, trust those who are trustworthy, feel my feelings, connect with my genuine interests.

The old and the new sometime clash. The process seems out of control.
I get frustrated. I am afraid and sometimes confused. I press on.

I reason that **I AM WHERE I AM** on this journey is due, in large part, to the choices I have made. The road is long. ***I allow the process of recovery to unfold at its own pace.*** Each day I stand at a turning point. Sometimes the choice comes down to a simple action.

I attend my regular meeting whether I feel like it or not.
I stay the course. I keep the faith.
I recover.

July 28
SETTING BOUNDARIES

I had a difficult time knowing where I stood in terms of identity. ***The role of each person often changed in my family, depending on the circumstances of the day.*** The unifying idea behind the entire operation was the notion that we all needed to stick together regardless of the upheaval,
the conflict or the dysfunction.

Anger would turn to resentment; resentment to rage. Sometimes, I seethed in silent fury; other times, my temper spilled over. ***In order to maintain control, I began constructing walls; brick by brick, stone by stone.***
I ceased talking. I stopped trusting. I closed off my emotions.
The lights were on, but nobody was home.

I am entertaining some new ideas thanks to the program: I can be me, you can be you; I can use my voice to ask for what I need; ***I can be politely direct in stating what I can do and what I cannot do in a relationship;***
I can walk away from any form of abuse.

Having taken the Steps, I stand on my own two feet. I have a self that is independent of the 'role' I may play in any relationship. ***I am free to establish that self.*** Indeed, the primary purpose of my program is to be who I truly am in the world around me; to connect with God,
myself and others in a healthy way.

I use my anger as an early warning system; a warning system that lets me know that something is not quite right in the environment. ***I can ask for what I need directly.*** Sometimes I get what I want, sometimes I don't; the point is simply this: I am making the effort to establish my real self; to take care of myself; to guard my recovery.

I know where I end, and others begin.

July 29
EMBRACING CHANGE

The most constant source of discomfort in my family proved to be the advancing force of change and the fear of uncertainty that often came along for the ride. Stability was not the order of the day. *And so, I established my own order, according to an emerging false self that dictated the 'absolutes' of staying alive; of not being abandoned.*
By the age of six, I was prepared for anything. **NOT.**

As time went on, I grew more and more afraid. Reality was not my friend. The 'changes' were too much to handle; loss upon loss; hurt upon hurt. *It seemed that nothing was too sacred for the vigor of change; all could be re-defined in the blinking of an eye.* Eventually, change would become the agent by which I dysfunctionally 'thrived'.

Having constructed a false self to see me through, I grew addicted to excitement without really knowing it. *Old ideas would be acted out over and over in varying scenarios.* There was a certain 'comfort' and familiarity in all the drama; a peculiar sense of security.

Having fully embraced Steps Six and Seven, I am ready to have all my distorted ideas and the behavior attached to those old ideas thoroughly removed. <u>*I am willing to go to any lengths to recover my true self.*</u>
I know my process. I have reviewed a good portion of the events of my life. I have felt the emotions attached to those events. I know from whence my old ideas have developed; my false self.

I move toward the future and the certainty of change, knowing full well that events like past episodes will occur. <u>***Changes will come.***</u> I will be 'triggered' emotionally. I have my 'hot buttons'. I use these new events to process old notions that are incorrect and no longer work. The Tenth Step assures 'safe passage' regardless of stormy weather. Change is constant.

REALITY IS MY FRIEND

July 30
ALLOWING LIFE TO UNFOLD

By the time I found the rooms of recovery, I had gone far past a state of mind whereby I had to be in control. *I had, in fact, adopted a 'carefree' attitude with the help of my major distractions: alcohol, travelling the road and relationships.* And although my anxiety rarely surfaced consciously, I lived with the constant fear that the beast would be awakened.

Whether I walked on eggshells or ran like the devil, there was always hell to pay; the creditor being, my false self; the constant critic; the judge and jury. *I was exhausted.* The longer I lived, the deeper the debt grew.
I acquiesced to my silent fear and depression.

The Steps give me a way out. I find a portion of my real self (Step Four) in discovering the old ideas of the past. Having viewed what appears to be, upon first sighting, an otherwise healthy oak tree, *I am entirely ready to have God remove all the clinging vines that hold me down;* the clinging vines that distort the beauty and wonder of a growing entity, my true self.

I am aware of the conflicts of my current events. I know much of my life experience is repeating itself so that I may learn from these events.

__Adversity is my opportunity to choose differently;__ my opportunity to let go of the old; my opportunity to embrace the new. I welcome the future.

I awaken to my real self; healthy, energetic, alive and well. I act in tandem with my genuine interests. I keep me safe. *I connect with a new world of abundance and support.*

I permit the support of my Higher Power. I thrive.

July 31
READYING MYSELF TO LEARN

I was in full flight from reality; and for good reason. ***Life had become insufferable.*** I had developed not only a process of distraction strong enough to divert my attention from the core of my life, but I had created a belief system designed specifically to make all the conflict go away, both internally and externally. I surrendered to a false self in the hope of one outcome; to be loved, to be respected.

Admitting that my best effort no longer works is difficult. ***Conceding that I am powerless to do anything about my best effort not working? Next to impossible.***

Step Two affords the time necessary to trust a process greater than myself. I come to meetings. I come to an awakening. ***I come to believe that a power greater than myself can guide my search for and eventual recovery of, my real self.***

I commit to this new process in Step Three; a turning point. ***That is, I act on Step Four.*** I do the work it takes much like one digging a tunnel to freedom. I pray for God's strength and go to a meeting. I keep digging. And if that doesn't work, I go to a meeting and pray for God's strength. Either way, ***<u>I don't give up five minutes before the miracle.</u>***

I am feeling emotions that I have not felt in years, if ever. I am talking to others whom I trust. I am sharing in meetings about specifics.
<u>I am uncovering my real self, huddled and hidden.</u>
I review the exact nature of my old demands.
I am now ready to learn.

I humbly ask God to remove the clinging vines of distorted ideas and demands from the past.

When the student is ready, the teacher will appear.

AUGUST

August 1
RELEASING THE VICTIM STORY

I had experienced episodes in my family as a child that quintessentially defined words like neglect, abuse, abandonment and disrespect. *__I was victimized.__* I had been born into my circumstances without the convenience of being consulted first. I did not volunteer for membership, nor did I cherish the experience. Naturally, in order to tell the tale, I had to be somewhat honest about the facts. I created a story
that would become 'my' story.

Whether I smoothed things over or embellished details for effect, I came to rely on my story as my 'truth'. *I practiced the story; edited the story; updated the story.* My story came to define who I thought I was.
I acted accordingly.

By reviewing my troubled past in a Fourth Step, I identify the points of trauma, the episodes of embarrassment and humiliation, and the scenes of disappointment. *I feel the grief: anger, rage, shame, sadness and hurt.*
I give myself plenty of time to 'be with the pain'.

Without really knowing it, I am letting go of my role as a victim. I am taking full responsibility for my recovery. *__The story no longer serves me.__* I may not have been the one to start all the trouble, but I am the one left to resolve it. Nobody else can do it for me.

And yet, I am not alone. I talk things out with a trusted friend. *My therapist knows what I am trying to do and supports my effort to unravel the past.* I identify the 'exact nature' of the old ideas associated with my past; the unrelenting demands on myself and others; the non-stop critical nature of my false self.

The process of Steps Six and Seven is the crossing over. I am letting go of the old story. *__No longer a victim, I welcome new ideas.__* I embrace my true self, I assure my safety, and quite comfortably, I am becoming who I am.

August 2
UNDERSTANDING GOD

I had a firm grip on my established beliefs concerning God. I lived under an illusion that I had come to terms and made peace with my defining moral code, having conjured what did and did not work theologically in my distorted world of dysfunction. ***I did not regard my perception as limited.*** Quite the contrary, I took pride in my position, 'knowing' that I was right.

I am confronted with the 'God thing' almost from the beginning in the rooms of recovery. I am uncomfortable, even angry. My reasoning? How is God going to do anything about this? After all, isn't this 'all powerful' God the one behind my pain? ***Where was God when I needed him?*** Why was I distributed to a family that victimized me? Why had I been allowed to suffer?

I am disturbed at the thought of turning my will and my life over to the care of this thing which I don't understand. I entertain the thought of not going back to meetings. ***I grow impatient with my so-called progress.***

I am at a crossroads. I can remain a victim or I can take responsibility for my recovery. God or no God, I choose to take responsibility. I consciously move *off* my victim story. ***I begin my Fourth Step in search of the antiquated ideas of the past that have driven me, shape me and kept me dysfunctional.*** I take the Fifth Step and talk of the mythical demand for perfection on myself and others; the exact nature of my wrong thinking and behavior.

I emerge realizing I know only a little of the 'big picture'. The mystery has become even more mysterious and yet, ***I am willing to own my old ideas formed by my false self.*** I let go. I am willing to move on. I am becoming teachable.

I don't fully understand the mystery that is 'God'. To understand that I don't understand God, *IS* to understand.

In other words, E=MC squared. Aren't I the little Einstein?

August 3
SAYING 'NO'

Objects of my affection had dwindled to a precious few; usually people toward whom I gravitated in the hope of getting what I needed and desired. ***Theory of reciprocity being what it is, my thinking grew along the lines of 'you scratch my back, I'll scratch yours' or 'one hand washes the other'.***

Often, I would say, yes; 'loving people should never turn away a request'. ***Often, I would regret it.*** Often, I would do my duty; 'masterful people should never shirk their responsibility'.

Having recovered my real self, I embrace my own interest first. As one locked away for years, I am happy to get on with **MY** life. ***I am released; released from a self-imposed prison of 'shoulds' and 'oughts'.*** No longer constrained by the notion that my very survival depends on how well I please others, I explore the core nature of who I am and what I want.

I help others because I want to, not because I must. I am loyal to the discipline of my chosen activity because I am, in fact, *interested* in my chosen activity. ***I move away from some because I want time to be with myself, privately; not because I must habitually escape their oppression.***

<u>I am free to choose how and with whom I spend my 'down time'.</u>

I celebrate boundaries by being able to say what I mean and mean what I say: I am not interested in attending an event; or, I cannot engage a request due to other priorities; or, I would prefer not to participate at this time; or, I have changed my mind. ***These responses say 'yes' to me.***

<u>I can pause before responding to a request,</u> politely state my intention and confidently stand firm in my decision.

August 4
IDENTIFYING ILLUSION

I labored under many illusions, not the least of which was the idea that I could become the idealized image which I had created in order to survive. Given enough time, I would realize all the lofty notions which I rehearsed, day in and day out; the pay off? ***The respect and love of all; family included.*** I hoped to become untouchable in my commanding admiration of all.

I came very close. I even convinced myself at times that I had, in fact, arrived. It is indeed very lonely at the top. ***I would eventually fall from my lofty perch, my chief critic, my false self, reminding me of my imperfection every step of the way.*** And yet, 'I will try harder next time,' was my usual reaction after the shame subsided. 'How could you have been so **STUPID***!*' was usually the nucleus of my inner voice.

My real self does not have to 'perform' in order to live. It simply lives. **<u>My actual self has no levels to exceed</u>**, **no mountains to climb, and no people to impress.**

If new levels are achieved as a result of my acting on genuine interests, fine and dandy. If I climb a mountain out of an interest in hiking and I reach the top, super! If I impress someone with my effort, all the better.

However, satisfying endless demands in order to 'prove' my worth is no longer a priority. ***That circus has left town.***

I feel my feelings. I am centered. I meditate. I creatively visualize activity; activity for which I have a true interest. ***I act with purpose, hoping for certain outcomes.*** Sometimes I get the outcome I want; sometimes I don't. My worth is no longer dependent on how well I perform.

I am enough.

August 5
SUPPORTING OTHERS

I had grown weary and bored with helping others; burned out. I rarely got the results hoped for. My advice went unheeded most of the time. And worse, I had been blamed at times for meddling in others' affairs.
Admittedly, I took some secret delight when observing their struggle.

My critical assessment having proved true, I could say with pride, 'I told you so; I saw that one coming; I tried to warn them'. Often, the very issue with which I was struggling, was the issue I could plainly see in others; *'spot it, you got it!'*

My fatigue stemmed from an old fear of not being seen; a fear of having no actual value. The logic went something like: ***'Make yourself useful, prove your worth and you won't be cast away'.*** By the time I found the rooms, I had essentially imploded. I had collapsed in my effort to establish my reason for living.

Having dismissed the false self in Steps Six and Seven, I am returning to a real self. No longer terrified of abandonment, I am free to express myself which, among many other things, includes helping others.
I am aware of my first loyalty; ME.

I put the program FIRST in my life FOR my life.

Step Twelve suggests that I carry this message to others and practice my program. I increase my chances of a full recovery when I share freely of what I have been given; namely, a genuine self: available, supportive and awake. ***I allow others the dignity of exercising their own solutions in their own time, in their own way.***

I politely listen as problems are defined and stories are told. Most importantly, I validate feelings when they are expressed. ***I don't have the answer to anyone else's problem.*** I realize that resolution for most comes from within. I respect the journey of others.

I LIVE AND LET LIVE.

August 6
CONTINUING THE RECOVERY PROCESS

I had always been able to start most endeavors with great enthusiasm. I was a visionary. I had hopes for the future: the right girl, the right career, the right place to live, the right friends. At times, it seemed that I was getting these things and more. *I grew anxious with the unfolding of each year;* what would happen if I could no longer 'pull it off'?

Eventually, slippery slopes would appear; dreams would die; phantoms would haunt. I conceded defeat on some level. Hope had left the stage. I was, in fact, terrified. *Strategies I had tried in the past in order to make my life work had stopped working.* What was I to do? How was I to continue? On some level, I knew that doing the same thing again and again, expecting different results, was insane.

I enter the program not knowing what to expect. I am anxious. I am cautious. I am doubtful. *My first meeting sheds light on 'the problem'.* I am encouraged to keep coming back; that all I need to do is, 'bring the body and the mind will eventually follow'.

I return. I read the literature. The first Nine Steps take me to a different place. I move into a 'maintenance' phase of my recovery, Steps Ten, Eleven and Twelve. *I continue to go to meetings.*
I practice my program.

New events trigger old emotions. I stay with the process. I own my feelings, identifying the lingering distorted beliefs driving my dysfunctional behavior. I talk it out. I pray. *I go to a meeting.*

And should that not work? *I go to a meeting.* I pray. I talk it out.
There it is.

August 7
FEELING THE FREEDOM

Much like the elephant tethered to the stake unaware of its own strength to break free, I functioned at half power before I found the rooms.
My real self was rarely consulted about anything.

I reacted out of habit most of the time, demanding specific outcomes, holding myself accountable. And when I failed, out would come the hammer of shame and blame; shame toward myself, blame toward others.

Any genuine interest was overshadowed by the compulsive need to always perform according to the distorted 'values' associated with staying alive. ***Remaining 'right side up' in a frightfully upside-down setting was a full-time job;*** the task master, unrelenting. 'Row, row, row!'

Thanks to Steps Six and Seven, my false self is now delegated to rather menial chores and confined to a small, somewhat comfortable room in the basement where he lives and takes all his meals; poor old chap:
always afraid, always anxious, always muttering obscenities.

I have no room in the house for a dictator. I tolerate this grumpy grouch-of-a-man much like one would love an old uncle who helped during desperate times. I have made peace.

I make plenty of room for my true self, me; IN ***MY*** NEW HOME. I am finally free to act according to who I am; ***NO SHAME***!

New interests appear. Old interests resurface. In response to these interests, ***sometimes I get what I want; sometimes I don't. It really doesn't matter.***

My value is no longer dependent on how well I perform; how 'timely' the destination; how 'sensible' the approach. ***It's about the journey.***
It's about the adventure of it all. It's about the freedom.
The joy of life returns.

August 8
HONORING MYSELF

I was often loyal to situations that had ceased being in my best interest. *My fear of abandonment kept me tethered to the very people who were NOT helping.* Old ideas around what relatives should do for one another; what friends should always be to each other; what employees should always perform in the line of duty; all these expectations regarding relationships weighed me down.

And what's worse, I was often disloyal to myself. *I dismissed my own needs and interests.*

The program gives me permission to place my needs at the top of the list. I respect that I am but one of many, most of whom are thoroughly capable of taking care of themselves. When I take the focus off others, I have more room to take care of myself.

I can be present for my own needs. *I can respond to my own voice.* I can take direction from my heart-felt interests. I can remain true to myself.

By facing the old demands of my past through Steps Four and Five, I can position myself in such a way in Steps Six and Seven as to partnership with God. I am willing, able and ready to change.

I can sincerely ask for His protection and care with complete abandon, knowing that He is doing for me what I cannot or will not do for myself.

With each new day, *I trust the process.* I trust myself.

August 9
TAKING THE DAY IN STAGES

I lived life from the vantage of gazing into the future. I hoped that someday 'things' would be different. I believed that I would never make the same mistakes as my parents. ***Reality was not my friend.*** There seemed to be disturbances all the time; disturbances so intense that they consumed what little space I had for myself.

I devoted most of my time to the fine art of coping, still clinging to the notion that life would get easier. Living in the moment had become impossible. The moment was the last place I wanted to be. ***I was unconscious emotionally for most of the events in my life.*** Distracted, in large part, by any means available, I survived the thoroughly unpredictable episodes of trauma and chaos.

Having a program that returns me to the center of my genuine core being, I am functioning at a higher level. ***I am remaining true to my emerging healthy self; my real self.*** I am alive with interest and authentic hope.

I choose my activity for the day with consideration. I appreciate the effort required to move through the day. ***I am allowing my real self a voice in what I attempt to do.*** I am connected.

Whether I am making a simple cup of tea or attempting to land a man on the moon, ***<u>I know the play; then, I take the shot.</u>*** Sometimes I score, sometimes I don't. I am more accepting of setbacks as I lower my demands on life. Reality is my friend. I potentially learn from ***all the events of the day*** regardless of whether I 'win' or 'lose'.

I create a safe space for myself today. In returning and rest, I find strength. I limit my ventures into the future. ***I remain in the day, recalling the high points and the low points.***

I take my 'progress' in stride.

August 10
RE-ESTABLISHING MY TRUE SELF

I had spent so many years marching to the orders of a false self that I had great difficulty imagining another way of life. The old ideas, and the behaviors attached to those ideas, had become habitual in nature. And the habit of thought had become 'comfortable'. *I prided myself in acting out this idealized image which I had created.* And yet, when I failed to satisfy the impossible standard, the myth of perfection, I berated myself and blamed others.

The hate I felt for my actual self and the resentment I held toward others proved too great. Underneath it all, I operated from deep state of perpetual grief. I would distract my attention away from the problems of depression and anxiety, choosing rather to move toward *anything or anyone* that could stop my emotions from bleeding into reality.

These obsessions/addictions, abusive by their very nature, fueled my false, critical self. I grew more and more impaired to fulfill my 'obligations'. My real self was all but dead.

Having de-constructed my false self and the accompanying program of 'shoulds' by taking the Fourth and Fifth Step (not an easy task), *I move into a new beginning of sorts;* a willingness to embrace the future as I let go of past demands; a willingness to create new ideas more in line with my real self, my genuine interests.

The old self is not easily moved. Loyal Captains never give up the ship. *With the help of God and others in the program, I usher this bossy, boisterous old chum to more appropriate accommodations…below deck.*

I reclaim my rightful place at the helm…*OF MY OWN SHIP.*
God as my true north, I am now free to choose my own course.

I know what I want and apply my effort to that end. Regardless of the outcome, I usually feel productive. *<u>As I practice staying true to myself, I come alive.</u>*

Come what may, I awaken to a new world of options.

August 11
CHOOSING MY PATH

Although I had made choices, I rarely felt connected to those choices. ***Life had become something that was pushing me;*** a habit; something to be endured rather than enjoyed. In fact, my false self with all its unrealistic demands was driving the bus. And it was my bus!

I 'came to', seated in the back of the bus, the night I attended my first meeting. I had little or no idea of who I was, where I was, or where I was going. ***A false self had taken full control***. I was just going along for the ride. Eventually, others informed me of the truth: this is *your* bus, *you* can drive your bus, and *you* can go where *you* want to go.

With the help of God, the fellowship and the Steps, I am happy to report that I am driving the bus! ***My false self sits in the back now***.

He will always be along for the ride and yes, I tolerate him much like I would a crochety old uncle who used to help me with my math a long time ago.

At the end of the day, I consciously choose where I have gone.

I am responsible for my own journey.

August 12
FACING THE PAST

As one in full flight from reality, I found it impossible to 'be in the present'. Depressed about the catastrophe called, 'my past', ***I lurched into the future, clutching anxiety in one hand and old beliefs in the other.*** The sense of loss and the grief associated with that loss drove my false self to declare, 'never again!' My hyper-vigilance would 'see me through'. Denial would protect me.

The 'never agains' would stack up. I would become an alcoholic. I would marry an alcoholic. I would forfeit opportunity. ***I lived in a state of shock, grief and bewilderment most of the time; and yet, I would tell others that all was 'fine'.*** Running from one distraction to the next, I often placed the focus outside myself; 'I'm not the one with the problem, they are! In fact, they *ARE* the problem.' Run, run, run.

I am in recovery. I am slowing down now. ***The rooms of recovery give me a safe place to sit and rest.*** I find others recovering from their own intimidating exhaustion, their own silent pain. Having been exposed to the raw elements of this condition, I realize that my hyper-vigilance is not enough to 'see me through'. And yet, for the moment, I am out of harm's way.

I feel powerless over this disease. This rampaging nightmare is out of control. ***My life is unmanageable.*** Denial no longer serves me. The past is close behind. I am desperate. What am I to do?

Keep coming back, they say. And so, I do. ***I begin to hope for the return of sanity*** and in some small way, a semblance of clarity does return. Feelings emerge.

I stop. ***I am at a turning point;*** go on as before or lunge into the program; walk away or take the Fourth Step. *F*orget *E*verything *A*nd *R*un (FEAR) or *F*ace *E*verything *A*nd *R*ecover? This is the question before me.

Keep coming back, they say. ***And so, I do.***

August 13
RECOGNIZING MY REAL SELF

I had been a person more concerned with results than reality. I denied how I felt and pressed on.'Mine is not to question why, but to do or die!'

<u>**It mattered not that I had little or no interest in what I was doing.**</u>
Pleasing the 'significant others' around me was the order of the day; sticking to the script.

Like a pirate stealing a ship, my false self, with its demands and fears, stationed itself at my internal helm, barking orders and making judgment calls; my real self, overwhelmed and restrained, being ushered to a small cabin below and silenced. Only one thing mattered to my actual self on deck;*obey the orders, follow the rules, honor the code and ignore the voice coming from below.*

Feelings are the conscious voice of my real self. <u>***I listen to my real self.***</u> I allow my real self to guide me. I am one with my real self. I am who I am, and I act accordingly; no shame, no blame.

Reality is my friend. I recognize events in the environment that are healthy, thus, inviting my genuine curiosity and special interest. I respond in kind. I also detect elements that are remnants of the past, dark passages; I allow the education, but have no interest in returning, as *I have moved on to higher places.* I am reasonably happy most of the time.

My real self is back at the helm. *I chart my course. I set sail.* I move toward fulfilling my dreams. I recognize safe people and safe people recognize me. I move toward healthy relationships.

I embrace all that is me.
I celebrate my recovery.
I celebrate myself.

August 14
VISUALIZING MY BEST INTEREST

Resentment and shame contaminated most of my waking hours. *Whether I blamed others or myself, the result was usually the same; constant distraction from what really mattered;* what had always *really* mattered, my best interest.

Survival was a strange teacher. The lesson seemed to go something like this; come what may, only three things matter: *stay loyal to those in charge, do what you are told, make yourself useful.*

Having cleared away the wreckage of the past by taking the Steps, I am at last free; free to serve my **own** best interest. I consider what is best for me. <u>*I put my program first in my life for my life.*</u>

Naturally, I am limited. I balk at creating new ideas. *I hesitate to try new approaches.* I stop short of taking risks. I restrict the use of my own voice.

In times of indecision, I creatively visualize a perceived interest and how that interest would, in fact, play out in real time. *I use my imagination.* I play with possible outcomes. I generate what I really want.
I improve my conscious contact with God.

I am creating a safe place where I can insure my best interest; a healthy space with healthy people. <u>*I move toward my best interest as I visualize conditions that assure my well-being:*</u> spiritually and emotionally; physically and intellectually.

I befriend myself. *My best interest is my number one priority.*

August 15
LOWERING MY UNREALISTIC DEMANDS

I had become a monster to myself and others. *Regardless of how I presented myself on the outside: nice, friendly, calm, collected; I felt horribly anxious most of the time.* I had become a tyrant.

My false self required nothing short of perfection, regarding my idealized notions of how everyone ought to behave all the time; myself included.

My false self is no longer running the show unchecked. I have a kind of built-in radar that alerts me when I am over-reacting to an event. I can pause; 'take five'. *__I can retreat, regroup and return.__*

In doing so, I give myself time to 'push-back' with my own belief system; how realistic is it to expect 'this' from myself or another person?

Sometimes my 'over-reaction' IS realistic; sometimes not. The point is that I am willing to grow along spiritual lines. I can factor into the human experience the 'human' aspect of it all.

Sometimes I behave in an ideal way, sometimes I don't.
Sometimes others behave in an ideal way, sometimes they don't.

I can better experience…

LIFE ON LIFE'S TERMS.

August 16
GROWING THROUGH DIFFICULT TIMES

Inundated with catastrophes, great and small, I shut down emotionally and grew skeptical of ever finding any peace in this life. In order to feel anything, I created my own drama.

<u>I had become rather addicted to excitement.</u> Whether the thrill came from a wild, intoxicating night on the town or a 'knock-down, drag out' fight with a loved one, the end game was always the same: to feel ***SOMETHING***.

I am aware of my feelings today. Feeling what I am feeling, at the time that I am feeling it, about what I am feeling it about IS my true north. I **want** to feel my emotions. ***<u>My emotions are the guideposts on my journey;</u>***
the journey toward becoming who I am.
I am aware; therefore, I am awake.

Someone once joked that the entire meaning of life can be summed up as follows: Inevitably there will be in life, mountains to climb, dangers to overcome and pit-falls to avoid; the object is to climb the mountains, overcome the dangers, *avoid the pit-falls and be home by five o'clock.*

I am guided by adversity. Life is something that happens while I am planning something else. ***<u>I can appreciate my own struggle today</u>; my struggle to fully realize who I am.*** I can know how it feels to face my fear. I can know how it feels to exhibit courage. I can know how it feels to move through a difficult event, get to the other side and rest assured that I am still complete; my real self, intact; even stronger.

By God's grace, I move ahead…one mountain, one mole hill at a time.

August 17
MOVING TOWARD CHANGE

Change, that universal element unrestricted by individual complaint, moved through my life like a freight train. *Whether in my family of origin or in the world at large, change was on the march.* I had great difficulty in finding 'safe' episodes in which to let down; times when I could genuinely explore what it meant to be me: what I liked to do, who I liked to be with, where I liked to go.

My real interests took a back seat to the primary purpose of my life, survival. Time that might have been spent playing out my curiosities was spent developing methods to cope with distorted conditions. *The program of managing an unsafe world was always running in the background.*

I acquiesced to this programming, this false self; and came to rely on its demands made on my actual self and others. This, or so it seemed, kept my world stable. *Preoccupied with maintaining a steady grip, I abandoned my true self.* Security trumped spontaneity. My sanctuary became a prison.

I am in recovery. I am confronted with the prospect of change; change in my thinking. I am told in jest that the only thing I need to really change is everything. *My old ideas are like glue.*

Eighty percent of what I do comes from a moral structure obscured by unrealistic demands on myself and exaggerated expectations on the world around me. Much like viewing a film of my own biography, I am invited to revisit the past for as long as it takes in order to gain a new perspective on who I am. Why? Because I am getting ready to make changes.

With God's help, I review my old belief system with all its components: what experience contributed to ideas formed, how did it feel at the time, who was involved?

I move through my events at my own pace. *I get a clear picture.* I brace myself for change…*always* moving toward the recovery of my true self.

August 18
ACCEPTING OTHERS

I used much of my time, before I found the rooms, comparing my 'insides' to others' 'outsides'. I was either better or worse. I held myself to a pretty high standard of behavior and when I would 'fail' on occasion, rather than feel the shame, I would naturally blame others. *Eventually, those things which I despised most in myself were often the first things I would notice in others.*

I projected my self-hate onto others. Imagine my dilemma.
Everywhere I went, there I was in despicable form.

Whether I took pride in my kind and giving nature, or my free and independent spirit or my commanding, 'take charge' attitude, *I seldom fulfilled all the performance demands required by my emerging false self.* I couldn't be loving all the time. I couldn't be completely independent.
I couldn't always be masterfully competitive.

During my early compliant phase, I was intolerant of others who were delinquent in the face of authority; I feared the angry and rebellious. *While in my independent days, I found people repugnant who were 'needy'.* And when I grew rebellious myself, I despised the conformists; wimps!

Having found the rooms, I am now under new management. *I challenge the old ideas that drive me.* I participate with a power greater than myself in removing incessant demands perpetrated on others. When I witness an offensive act in others, I am often seeing something internal;
that thing that I *cannot or will not* accept in myself.

When I have prolonged feelings of embarrassment, humiliation or anger, I take Step Ten. I process my emotions. I lower the expectations on myself and others. *I am tolerant of my own shortcomings; therefore, I am growing more patient with others' imperfections, as well.*

Usually, *WHEN I SPOT IT, I GOT IT. Ouch*!

August 19
CREATING RELATIONSHIP

I had a special talent for picking people who were usually unavailable. In fact, I was drawn to those who were emotionally and sometimes, physically unable to 'show up'. ***I was addicted to the excitement of uncertainty.*** And on some level, it was 'comfortably' familiar.

I was unavailable, as well. ***Acquaintances substituted for friends;*** casual friends for intimate friends. I viewed most relationships as necessary inconveniences. I had a 'high turnover' of friends with whom I shared on a deep level, both physical and emotionally.

I had grown alienated from others; distrustful of the process. Seldom did I feel any real 'connection' at all. I exhibited loyalty even in the face of betrayal for fear of sliding further and further into the 'abyss of alone'.

I am available to myself today. ***Because I can hear my own voice, I can hear the voice of others.*** I realize that **process is everything** when it comes to creating a solid friendship. Time takes time.

I allow the acquaintance phase to evolve naturally so that when the time comes to invite someone to coffee; say, having met them in a class or at a meeting or at a party or at church, ***I can be reasonably assured that they will, in fact, show up*** without some flimsy excuse for their late arrivals, no calls or no shows. If a person cannot be reasonably available on a physical level, how can they possibly be counted on, when the time comes, to be available on an emotional level?

I employ the skill of listening to my friends. I expect the same in return. My friends are reciprocal in nature; that is, ***I give my time and energy and I reasonably expect the same in return.*** Loyalty where loyalty is due.
I no longer 'sacrifice' for anyone, knowing that even the most 'charitable' act is attached to some form of personal 'pay off'.
I am satisfied with honestly being me.

I allow others to be others.

August 20
CREATING DEEPER RELATIONSHIP

Most of my relationships were at best superficial; even the ones that involved physical 'intimacy'. I was unable to talk about feelings. As a matter of fact, *talking to family about what was really going on and trusting that they could and would be supportive was not a part of my survival strategy.* Don't talk, don't trust and don't feel was the 'play'.

Now I have the freedom to select with whom, how long, and on what grounds I relate to certain individuals. I have acquaintances that I only see when I attend common activities. *I have casual friends with whom I share common interests: sports, theater, dance, cooking, recovery, religion, politics etc.*

I have friends that I absolutely count on for emotional support and unconditional love; *intimate friends*. I even have one friend with whom I am intimately committed, both emotionally and physically; my wife. *What a joy!* (most of the time)

I have the gift of availability. I am present emotionally, spiritually and physically not only for my actual self, but for others, as well. I can listen to my own voice; my real self. *I can listen to the voice of others without internal distraction; the residue left over from the old days of rescuing, caretaking and fixing.* I celebrate others' autonomy. I extend to them the dignity and privilege of owning their individual process; of expressing their feelings; of defining their issues; of solving their own problems.

I expect **intimate friends** to do the same for me. When we meet, they listen without judgment. They are present. *They allow our occasion to sometimes be all about me when I need to vent strong emotions and sort things out.* I can let down; be myself. These moments are the very fabric of my life; the tapestry of my existence.

I have the gift of setting boundaries; this is what I can do right now, this is what I can't do right now. *I can be honest about what I need without the fear of being rejected for having a need.* I fully embrace the opportunity for intimacy; the spice of life; the context for connection; the meaning of existence. I am alive.

August 21
GRIEVING THE LOSS

In order to survive, I had to essentially lock up my real self. I had to 'shut down' the feelings that go with being young and alive; curious and spontaneous. Life got serious very quickly. I was on high alert most of the time. ***Much like one living in a war zone, I had to stand guard.*** I had to know when to act and when not to act; who to trust, who not to trust; what to tell, what not to tell; when to 'duck and cover', when to run.

Over time, I developed a strategy. Like the monotony of war, my world became a daily routine of endurance and distraction. *I focused on what I 'should' be and used all my energy to maintain the status quo.* I lost my true self in the process. Over the years, I became a virtual automaton; the lights were on, but nobody was home.

I attend my first meeting. I hear of a new process. I connect. I go home. I tell myself that life is messed up, but 'they did the best they could with what they had'. I go to more meetings.

Breaking free of denial, I am entertaining the idea that my life IS unmanageable; that something HAS gone terribly wrong in my development. I hear others tell of their abandonment and abuse. I relate.

I speak of my own neglect. I feel anxious and afraid, but somewhat hopeful. I tell more of my story. *I feel angry; sometimes enraged.* I feel stuck as a victim. I come to believe there is a way out. I don't have to remain a victim.

I take the Steps, reasoning that I can recover by clearing away the old ideas and wreckage of the past. *On some days I feel sad, angry, confused and overwhelmed; other days, I feel overwhelmed, confused, angry and sad.* I have moments of spontaneity; even laughter.

As I approach Step Ten, I have seasons of true acceptance; acceptance of the whole picture: who I am, who 'they' are, what I can reasonably expect from myself, what I can reasonably expect from 'them'. *I connect with my true self; **Step Eleven***. I connect with others; Step Twelve.
I am accepting who I am.

August 22
RELYING ON THE PROGRAM

I had grown skeptical of any association with institutions and rarely counted on a process that involved rules, methods and absolutes. Trusting authority was out of the question.

I would fearfully or grudgingly comply, sure enough; but seldom relied on anything or anyone for help.

Even though I did, on occasion, get some needed support, I feared the time would come when 'something' would go wrong. *I 'slept with one eye open', anticipating the moment when, once again, I would have to react to some 'crisis'.* I regretted the past, feared the future and *HATED* the present. I was trapped in a world of isolation and fear.

Today, I need a safe place; a place where my genuine confidence in humanity itself can be restored; a place to recover from a lifetime of hurt and disappointment; a place that I can trust. *My recovery home group is that place.* Here I meet others who claim only one endeavor: finding a way out of all the dysfunction.

<u>I am invited to take what I like and leave the rest.</u> I have the added option of remaining entirely unknown outside the rooms. *This is an anonymous program.* I am also free to create relationship beyond the doors with those whom I trust and relate.

The program is not allied with any sect, denomination, politics, organization or institution. I am not obliged to commit to anything. The Twelve Steps are mere suggestions.

I understand that everyone takes the Steps in their own way; in their own time, at their own pace.

I am free to come and go as I please. When I need a safe place to retreat and regroup so I can return to life's challenges, I always have an available seat in the rooms of recovery.

August 23
TRUSTING OTHERS WHO HAVE GONE BEFORE

I had grown doubtful of those who professed to have all the answers: politicians, preachers, teachers, parents and friends. ***I embarked on a solo journey; team of one.*** I devised an approach upon which I prided myself; even scoffed at others who dared take paths unlike mine. Whether I exalted the notion that I should always be loving and kind; or free and independent; or masterful and 'in control'; I seldom allowed an alternate route.
My mind was set.

The longer the journey, the more embedded the old ideas. My demands on others grew more intense, as well. Life itself was subject to my uncompromising beliefs. **<u>Nobody could be fully trusted.</u>** I avoided intimacy; shunned any activity that could leave me vulnerable.

I discover myself in a risky position when I get to the rooms of recovery. Even if I do have some of the dysfunctional characteristics, ***how can I be certain that these people can really help?*** What's the plan? Who's calling the shots? When do I graduate? What will I become?

A pioneer in recovery, upon writing the final chapter to the first book ever written, outlining a new approach called the Twelve Steps, had this to say: 'We realize we know only a little. More will be revealed.' This same man had earlier determined that if he were to recover, ***he needed another's help;*** someone with whom he could genuinely relate; someone whose story he could hear and thereby, be strengthened regarding his own recovery.
And so, Alcoholics Anonymous was born.

Whether someone has years of recovery or one day's reprieve, ***I need and respect the experience, strength and hope that EVERY person brings to the table.***

I don't need a guru. I need a friend.

August 24
WEIGHING MY OPTIONS

I had created a belief system that left little room for variance. In fact, I was locked in. The 'shoulds' ruled the day. ***Depending on the emotional need at the time, some demands were more hysterical than others.***

For example: I felt lonely; thus, people should always give me the attention I deserve; I felt disappointed; thus, people should always do what they say; I felt betrayed; thus, people should always be loyal.

I was relentless with the demands on myself, as well. I felt lonely; thus, I should always be independent and strong; I felt disappointed; thus, I should never trust this person again; I felt betrayed; thus, I should always retaliate in order to get even.

I am discovering my true self, covered in 'shoulds'. Like predatory vines clinging to the healthy branches of a sprawling oak, my old ideas and their exaggerated expectations choke the life out of my real self. ***I clear the vines from an otherwise healthy tree.*** I am taking Steps Four and Five.
I am looking at my old moral structure; what is working, what is not working? What is healthy, what is not healthy?

I can grow in the worst of weather; even in the face of adversity. I pray for the knowledge of His will for me and the power to carry that out in my effort to be who I am; in my progressive struggle toward self-realization.

I take opportunity to act according to my real self; to my genuine interests.

I connect with my revised core values and act with conscious intent.
I realize every problem has many solutions.

I have choices. I respond thoughtfully to events in the environment. ***I allow the ebb and flow of the day.*** Once I discover a solution, the problem goes away. I embrace the freedom to simply be me.
No shame. No blame. No muss. No fuss.

August 25
KNOWING THE DIFFERENCE

I reacted to inconvenience and catastrophe in the same way; alarm. Whether I was running late for an appointment or swerving to avoid a serious crash, my emotional barometer registered the same; panic. *I lived under extreme internal pressure and approached most everything as though my very life depended on a favorable outcome.* I had to be on constant alert. Mistakes were unpardonable. Failure was not an option.

The volume control on my 'perfection' panel was stuck on high. Due to my hyper-vigilant approach to maintaining my idealized self, I lived life as one walking a fine line between life and death every day. *The false belief? 'If I am an inconvenience, I will surely be abandoned. If I am abandoned, I will surely die.'* Every letdown, every slip-up, every blunder ignited a fire storm of self-hate.

Today, I know the difference between inconvenience and catastrophe. My very life is *NOT* dependent on how well I perform all the time. Confidence in my real self is returning. *No longer plagued with unrealistic demands for perfection, I am at ease most of the time.* I can let down. I can relax. I don't have to be in total control in order to survive. I respond rather than react.

I assess the risk in activities I choose to involve myself; the key word being, 'choose'. *No longer a victim without escape, I am free to participate in what I want to do.* And I am free to say 'no' to any activity with which I am uncomfortable.

Having had a few flat tires on the highway since recovery, *I am no longer compelled to call the local crisis hot line.* I merely phone a reliable wrecker service.

AMAZING **progress!**

August 26
TAKING CARE OF THE BASICS

I was a person who often abandoned my own needs in order to perform as I thought I should. Often skipping meals, working too many overtime shifts, missing necessary sleep, or multi-tasking to no end, *I would push myself in order to get what I thought I absolutely needed; approval from myself and others.* The pay-off rarely fixed me.

On the contrary, in my exhausted condition, I made mistakes. I encountered setbacks. And like a sitting duck, *I would suddenly come under attack by my false self with all its accusations and claims:* 'You're so careless; you're a failure; you can't do anything right; you're crazy; they're going to leave you; they can't put up with your reckless behavior; you are such a waste, an utter inconvenience!' I would do better next time. Shame, shame, shame; distract, distract, distract; run, run, run.

I establish my real self, having inventoried the erroneous demands of my false self and revealed the demands for what they are; distorted and unrealistic. *I nurture my real self.* I eat when I am hungry. I talk about my frustrations of the day with trusted friends. I connect with others whom I consider safe. I rest when I am tired. **Easy Does It.**

The incessant dictates of a false self with its unrelenting, idealistic requirements *ARE* in retreat. Sometimes I act in accord with my true self; sometimes I don't. I am no longer held to a mythical standard of perfection. I know the play, I take the shot; sometimes I score, sometimes I don't. I am still on the team.

With God's help, I am seeing my real self with genuine appreciation and compassion. I release my fear of abandonment. I embrace every opportunity to support and nurture me. I am alive.

Just a few of my favorite activities: going for ice cream, taking a nap, talking with a friend, going to a ball game, **working a regular shift, coming home, taking a shower,** going for a bike ride, reading a good book, working out, eating dinner; and finally, nature's way of letting me 'check out', going to bed. **Aaaaaah.** Cotton sheets are so nice. Nighty night.

August 27
ACKNOWLEDGING MY OWN GROWTH

I rarely seemed to be 'enough' in my struggle to maintain the exaggerated requirements made on myself in order to be me. *For example, upon completing a task (or not), I would quickly move on to something else, hoping for a 'self-esteem fix'.* I was sometimes uncomfortable with compliments, often pointing out what I could have done better or how I should have performed. I was quick to criticize my actual self, courtesy of the false self I had created in order to survive.
Old ideas and old ways held on for dear life.

Having prepared myself in the Fourth and Fifth Step for a thorough house cleaning, I venture forth with a singularly NEW idea: *God can AND will remove the distorted thoughts that continue to set me up for disappointment.* I need only ask. Steps Six and Seven are merely an extension of what I already know: I can't, He can, I think I'll let Him. But how? I am aware of my feelings throughout the day. Having taken a moral inventory, I am well versed in listing an event and registering the emotion that is attached. Moreover, I can identify the **BELIEF** behind the strong emotion. *In my new awareness, I admit promptly when I have fallen back into old patterns of thought.* I release these old ideas to which I cling. <u>I let go absolutely</u>.

As current events trigger old emotions, <u>reality becomes my friend</u>; thus, pointing me in the 'right' direction, to the proper 'rock' under which to look. I wish to leave as few 'stones unturned' as possible.

Step Ten introduces me to a whole new world; the world of honesty and growth. *Thus far, I have braved many a battle and slain my fair share of dragons in this process of recovering my real self.* I compliment my true self every time I own how I feel. I participate in my own recovery every time I talk about an activating event. I clear a new space in my clutter every time I admit my possible error in thought, word or deed.

<u>I take note of my progress often.</u> I compliment others. And when others express their appreciation toward me…I simply say, thank you.

August 28
STAYING THE COURSE

Distractions were my way of 'checking out'. When things got a little 'too real', I could resort to age-old methods guaranteed to put me in a 'better mood'. I could throw myself into my work.
I could dedicate my life to others.

I could alter my state of consciousness with a variety of legal and illegal chemical substances; my favorite legal substances being food, alcohol and nicotine. I could 'lose' myself in 'binge watching'. I could immerse myself in a relationship. I could travel to distant lands.

I am awakening to a rather new phenomenon; the presence of an emerging self that wants to feel and talk; wants to trust its curiosities. ***I actualize this true self by remaining conscious and staying present.***
With the help of God, I am available to myself.

No longer content with being half awake for the show, I consciously connect with my five senses: tasting, touching, smelling, hearing and seeing. ***I move through the day with a sense of heightened awareness toward the world around me:*** the taste of a fresh cup of tea with just the right amount of honey; the sound of my cat purring; the falling of summer rain;
the sight of freshly fallen snow; the soothing warmth of the hot tub;
my wife's sigh of relief, having found something once considered lost;
the uninhibited laughter of a child.

I can never go back; back to a semi-conscious state, as before the program. I am on a new path. My journey is turning out for the better. ***I measure my progress in inches now,*** stopping along the way to 'smell the flowers'; appreciating a significant moment in 'real' time; getting to know my evolving 'real' self; in short, truly living.
I move forward undaunted…

ONE DAY AT A TIME.

August 29
TRUSTING THE TRUSTWORTHY

Growing up in a family where bad judgement, lying and cover-up were the dynamics of the day, I lived in a constant state of unfolding contradiction. For example: On the one hand, my parent acted as though she loved me and yet, she seemed to say 'you're an inconvenience'; startling events would occur and yet, we would never talk about the events; harsh things would be said and yet, there would be no resolution, no apology. **<u>We would merely 'move on' to the next crisis of the month.</u>**

To make matters worse, the factor of 'unavailability' played into almost everything. The reasonable expectation attached to planned outings often dissolved at a moment's notice. ***Disappointment became a repetitive emotional condition; despair a constant state of mind.*** I grew to trust only a few. After my first eighteen years, I despised my parents. The essential building block of any 'loving' relationship, *trust*, was absolutely missing. Eventually, I would trust no one. I heard no voice but the demands of my false self.

I have a very difficult time trusting others to this day. The rooms are a safe and constant base camp. From this place, I can venture forth, exploring my world from a new perspective; the vantage point of recovery. ***No longer shackled by misplaced loyalties, <u>I see others realistically</u> and I adjust my expectations accordingly.***

I don't saddle a camel and expect to win the blue ribbon for barrel racing at a rodeo. Horses are horses. Camels are camels.

Trust takes time; time well spent in the ***ART*** of choosing and building genuine relationship. ***I determine 'deal-breakers' from the outset; what I will not tolerate, endure or otherwise suffer through, ever again.*** I want people in my life who are available; people who say what they are going to do and usually do it; people who show up. When I talk about how I feel, a trusted intimate friend listens without presuming I want them to fix me.

I trust people who are, indeed, trustworthy.
Trust is a *choice* for me.

August 30
SUPPORTING MY SELF

I was born into a world which mandated my total dependence on others. I did not choose my family. I instinctively trusted that the 'adults' in my life had enough resources and proper character to support my unmitigated need for survival. **When faced with evidence to the contrary, I created a false self in order to make it through another day.** Eventually, the progressive demands of this false self would deafen the voice of my real self.
I shut down and pressed on.

Remaining loyal to my false self's expectations became my number one objective. I took great pride when I acted accordingly. Upon failing, I felt ashamed. **_I grew, in time, to hate my actual self._** I saw myself as a 'loser'; a deplorable. 'What was wrong with me?' Depressed and anxious, I distracted myself with all manner and forms of activity,
legal and otherwise.

I am in a different place now. Circumstances are such that I have a safe place to go in order to recover my true self; a true and healthy self which I had to abandon years ago in order to survive. I purposely **LOWER THE DEMANDS** on my actual self; that part of me that acts on my behalf; that part of me that supports who I am. **_Sometimes I get an outcome I want; sometimes I don't._** I make mistakes just like everybody else. However, I am not a 'mistake'. I lose from time to time. However, I am not a 'loser'.

I accept life on life's terms. Trudging this mysterious course called life, when approaching the 'fountain of knowledge', I realize that 'some folks come to drink; and some folks come to gargle.' **_Sometimes I drink of the fountain, sometimes I gargle. No big deal._**

I support my real self's struggle to simply be, regardless of the expected outcome of the expression. It's OK. **_I go easy on my emerging self._**
Things seem to go better when I practice the slogan…

EASY DOES IT.

August 31
SEARCHING FOR THE REAL ME

There were times in the past when I would briefly tap into my genuine interests; weeks, sometimes months at a time. ***Eventually, something in the environment would trigger old ideas, old emotions;*** and off to the moon I would go. My functioning self would figuratively leave the planet.

Usually my 'checking out', would be an ***attempt to avoid something***, something I had been 'seeing', but not seeing for years; something of conflict within my own belief system; something often projected onto another.

The anxiety being too much, I would Deny, Dodge and Distract.
I **D**enied that a problem existed. I **D**odged the emotions accompanying the problem. I would **D**istract myself in order to not look. (the three D's)
Over time, this repetitive process snuffed out the real me.

Upon entering the program, I understand that THE BIG PROBLEM is my utter lack in acknowledging that I have NO functioning self; ***that I am powerless;*** that my life has become unmanageable; that I am stuck in my distraction.

The anger and anxiety that comes with taking Step One, I find, is a good thing: ***denial is no longer an option.*** Returning to earth has its very real advantages. Step Two assures me that there exists a real hope in reclaiming some semblance of sanity; that a 'reset to normal' is possible. I am relieved.

Making a solid decision to follow the rest of the program (Steps Four through Twelve), requires a good deal of soul searching. Do I remain as I am or change? Do I settle for 'stuck' or take a chance on moving forward?

<u>I abandon myself to God as I understand God</u> and prepare for the journey ahead…into the past. I go back in time, (Steps Four and Five), in order to move forward. The search for my real self is on!

SEPTEMBER

September 1
COMING TO BELIEVE

Prior to finding the rooms, a major false belief was formed: ***ALONE, I would serve as my primary source of strength; a source unto myself upon which I could absolutely rely in order to survive.*** All the rest had been imposters, phonies; utterly incapable of delivering what I needed. I feared God, but I did not 'believe' in God. I feared authority figures, but I did not trust them. In fact, I trusted only a few people at all.

Surviving the relentless demands, day in and day out, required an incredible amount energy. ***Life had become a series of navigational problems.*** Ironically, as many troublesome passages as I cleared, dozens more were created. I despaired of ever coming to rest. I was exhausted.

I find rest now in the recovery process itself: going to meetings, talking about how I feel, staying in the day, living in the moment, taking life one day at a time. ***I sometimes pray:***

'God, I don't _really_ believe you exist. Please show me in a way that I can comprehend that you do exist; and that you do, in fact, care for me. Amen.' (Step Two Prayer)

I experience 'incidents of coincidence'. I begin meeting people at the exact time I need to meet them in order to learn precisely what I need to learn in order to move forward in the search for my real self. My genuine self is beginning to trust again. ***My true self is emerging.***

On occasion, heartfelt desires come to pass. ***I have a 'connected' moment.*** Some say, God often works through other people. More and more, I am finding this to be true.

'When the student is ready, the teacher will appear.'
I am coming to believe that a power greater than myself can, in fact, restore me to sanity; the sanity I once knew; the sanity of my true self.

September 2
MOVING BEYOND THE 'MISTAKES'

At the center of my strategy to survive a confusing and distorted world, lay the core skill of perfection. I told myself that I had to eliminate 'mistakes', lest I draw the wrath of the person in charge and risk abandonment. ***The thought of being 'left behind' because I couldn't perform terrified me.*** Soon, I would spend more time trying to control my world rather than simply exploring my world. My real self was being replaced. My false self was taking over.

One mistake represented a lack of ability. Any lack of ability represented the possibility of becoming a liability. Any sign of failure reflected my overall worth. My reasoning went something like this: too many mistakes equals not enough worth; ***I must perfect my idealized self.*** I had to prove myself to myself. I had to prove myself to others. Gaining approval of others came at a price; the loss of my true self.

I make mistakes; however, I am not a 'mistake'. I fail from time to time, but I am not a 'failure'. ***Upon reviewing the exaggerated demands with which I pummeled my actual self, I realize the unproductive nature of trying to force myself to become some pre-conceived idealized image.*** I let go of the old ideas and embrace the new: it's OK to explore; it's OK to take risks; it's OK to make mistakes; it's OK to be human.

No longer distracted by the fear of abandonment, I am totally available for my real self. I pursue my genuine interest and in practicing this effort to become my natural self, I realize that sometimes things work out and sometimes they don't. ***I feel the joy of successful expression or I absorb the disappointment of having failed.*** Whichever the case may be, I keep moving toward my real self. I keep acting on my genuine interests.

Step Eleven always invites me to consider a change in course if I am continually frustrated. Reality is my friend. When agitated, I can pause and ask God for the next healthy thought or solution, and act accordingly. **<u>The process toward becoming my genuine self is, in fact, a struggle.</u>**

I am content with trudging the happy road. I am content with progress rather than perfection.

September 3
EXPRESSING RAGE

There were times in my dysfunctional family when I absolutely wanted to scream; wanted to hit someone; wanted to break something. Sometimes I did. Most of the time I didn't. ***Most of the time I shut down my emotions, distracting myself from the triggering event.***

After practicing this 'coping' skill for a long time, I became immune to episodes of calamity and disappointment. ***And yet, the silent stress and anxiety grew exponentially.*** I had become the proverbial silent 'ticking time bomb'. I had virtually 'shut down' my feelings; flat-lined my emotions.

In recovery, I am defusing the bomb. ***The range of all my emotions are on the table.*** I am particularly aware of strong reactions to any current event, especially my tendency to feel outraged at times. I have a person whom I can trust; a person who is aware of my effort in taking the Steps.

When taking the Fourth Step, I fully anticipate that old feelings will not only surface, but new feelings will 'come up' around old events. ***Sometimes, while processing an old event, a new event will trigger strong emotions from the past.*** I am prepared for a bumpy ride during this time.

Rage is not pretty. And yet, expressing my outrage is part of the mission I have chosen; the mission to recover my true self. ***I can use my voice to scream; a 'controlled burn'.*** I can beat my bed with a tennis racket and scream. I can climb a mountain and upon arriving at the top, I can scream. I can take a run in the woods and scream.

I can find a private room where no one can hear me and scream. I can take a hammer, beat pennies and scream; take an axe, cut wood and scream; go to a batting cage, hit baseballs and scream.

Is there any proven data that this 'method' works to restore 'long term stability'? None that I know of. ***But I sure do feel better after I do it.***

September 4
APPRECIATING A FULL RANGE OF EMOTION

While living in a dysfunctional world, I considered 'staying calm' an asset.
Limiting my feelings had its advantages: I could manage conflict better,
I could avoid trouble more often, I could maintain the 'peace'. *The ability to
'read the environment' could not be compromised by emotion.*
I had to remain aware of the demands of the moment. I had to survive.

As a result, my range of feelings diminished over time, leaving me with the
big three: shame, excitement and fear. *The big three morphed into chronic
depression and anxiety.* Ashamed of what I hadn't done correctly
in the past and terrified of what might happen in the future,
I was unable to live in the present.

I am awakening to feelings for the first time in a long time. I am aware of
my anger, my sadness and my joy. *I am encouraged by others to
'stay with' my emotions; feel the feelings.*

They say, don't *F*orget *E*verything *A*nd *R*un (FEAR),
FEEL EVERYTHING AND RECOVER.

I am uncomfortable. I distract myself, but I keep going to meetings.
I keep talking about how I feel. I keep owning my stuff.

Being able to allow my feelings gives me a new option; the option of
grieving losses, both past and present. *Often, events in the present will
emotionally mimic events of the past; events that gave birth to the old
ideas which set me up for deep shame and resentment.* I can take direction
from my emotions today in order to deconstruct the harmful demands of the
past; the harmful demands **behind** my emotions.

By opening the door to my 'negative' emotions, I also open the door to the
happy feelings, too. *I find that in order to feel joy, I must feel my sorrow,
as well.* One goes with the other. My real self comes as a total package.

September 5
BREAKING DENIAL

I employed the 'skill' of blocking emotions much like the soldier in battle who hears and sees the turmoil all around but stays focused under fire. There was little room for reality. **Roles must be acted out and strategies had to be obeyed.** My false self was calling all the shots.
Mine was but to do or die. Reality was NOT my friend.

Don't talk. Don't trust. Don't feel. *I relied on my old ideas surrounding loss to see me through;* 'stop complaining, pick yourself up, just leave, drop out, chin up, no whining, keep on trucking, don't look back, love until it hurts, never say no, always stick it out, be loyal'.

Reality IS my friend today. *At the first appearance of loss, I can admit the loss and feel the feelings; usually anger, sometimes rage.* When I do this, the phase of denial is broken. I am free to struggle with the totality of the assessed 'harm'. The 'I-can't-believe-it' phase is moving into the 'believe-it-and-deal-with-it' phase. I am moving through the grief process. This is a GOOD thing, as genuine acceptance of the loss lies just ahead; and ultimately, 'acceptance is the key to all my problems.'

I am in a better place to 'bargain' my way through the loss. For example: I lose my favorite pair of glasses. I can't believe it. I look all over.
No glasses. I still can't believe it. Damn! I look for my glasses the next day. Still no glasses. Son-of-a-$%#@#! I have REALLY lost my glasses.

I am now dealing with my actual loss. I reason what I must do in order to arrive at a solution. I am no longer completely stuck. *Some losses are greater than others.* Some have simple solutions while others require a great deal of effort.

My recovery process requires admitting my reality in order to reclaim my real self. I have a way out and it starts with moving out of denial and into the truth. *<u>Thank you, God, for the 'grief process'.</u>*

September 6
ALLOWING GOD TO BE GOD

The essential ingredient of any healthy relationship, trust, was missing in my family of origin. ***There had been enough disappointments, incidents of abuse and moments of neglect to 'poison the well'.*** In other words, the trust factor had disintegrated altogether, even though the outward appearance of loyalty remained. My family unit had fractured.

When it came time to look up at the sky on a star-spangled night and consider the creator of it all, I wanted to believe that something, someone was holding 'it' all together. ***I needed to trust that some power greater than myself 'had my back'; and yet, reality proved otherwise.*** The situation on the ground was not conducive to faith building;
in fact, fear ruled the day.

By taking the Fourth and Fifth Step, I am redefining my concept of God; I must, if I am to move toward recovering my real self. ***The process requires trust.*** I am willing to abandon the old ideas and misconceptions which I carry concerning God. For example: God is not my parents, God is not teachers of the past; God is not authority figures from earlier days.

However, I am the one who says what stays and what goes. **THIS IS MY MORAL INVENTORY**. Nobody else can inventory these beliefs about God *for me*. ***If I am to truly experience God, I must trust God.***
My simple request of God? Show me who you are
in a way that I can understand.

I experience moments where 'things' go as planned (what a concept!); items needed for expressing my real self are located; and people show up whom I need to meet in order to learn what I need to learn, so that I can move forward on my recovery journey. ***I entertain the idea that God is doing for me what I cannot or will not do for myself.*** I have moments when I trust that the universe is naturally unfolding; that my role in that universe is respected and supported; that my needs matter.

I can relax and let God be God. I can…***GO WITH THE FLOW***.

September 7
CRYING

In the old days, any sign of being 'weak' did not serve my primary purpose; to survive an unsupportive, sometimes hostile environment. The 'code of the road' seemed to be, 'don't trust; figure it out for yourself; don't let them see you sweat; *and whatever you do, don't let them see you cry'*.

My emerging false self was a harsh task master. Staying alive was a serious matter. Remaining true to the strategic demands was all that mattered. Whether the plan centered around being the most giving, the most independent or the most accomplished person in the room, *the common thread weaving its way throughout was the absolute need for perfection;* no excuses, no whining; failure was not an option. I prided myself on rarely deviating from my chosen course.

When I did miss the mark, I hated myself. My idealized self was firmly established; nonconformity could not be tolerated.

I find at the core of crying rests one thing; release. I release when I get mad. I release when I laugh. And, I release when I cry. So, whether I cry about it, laugh about it or get mad about it; I am simply releasing. **No shame.**

<u>I am moving toward my real self which experiences life from moment to moment;</u> event to event; feeling to feeling, spontaneously staying in the day. When I laugh, I laugh. When I get mad, I get mad. When I cry, I cry. **No shame.**

I surround myself with others who are safe; others who are available; others who are living in the now, rather than being stuck in the past, rehearsing and acting out some victim role. *<u>I am connecting with my real self.</u>*
I am on a new path.

I laugh, I cry, I get mad.

No shame.

September 8
RELINQUISHING THE BURDEN OF BLAME AND SHAME

Part of the 'plan' in trying to stay alive in a distorted, up-side down world
was to assign appropriate shame and blame to whom it belonged;
the result being, respectively, self-hate and resentment. ***This unconscious
plan yielded the exact opposite of what I had initially wanted;
relief from all the anxiety.*** When I could not perform as I demanded,
I felt ashamed, believing that I would do better next time. When others
disappointed, I grew resentful. By blaming, I removed myself from the
equation. I was 'off the hook'.

Whether I played the role of victim or perpetrator, the plan to shame myself
and blame others into submission had ceased working. I was depressed
about the past and when I wasn't depressed about the past, I was anxious
about the future. The back and forth nature of my dilemma proved
unmanageable. **_'I lived life mostlyss from the viewpoint of a victim.'_**

Losing my real self in the process, I chose to acquiesce to the false self
with all its demands and unrealistic expectations.

I am re-connecting with my true self. 'Performance' is not an issue. ***I let go
of the old idea that I must abandon my genuine nature in order to survive
a chaotic world.*** I step away from the confusion. I don't go to a football
game expecting to ride a pony. ***I go to watch the game.***

When I feel guilty for having not met a certain expectation for myself,
I can simply try again. No shame. In trying again,
sometimes I win; sometimes I lose.

When I feel angry toward a situation that falls short, I can simply access
another resource. I can use my voice to ask for what I need. No blame. In
asking for what I need, sometimes I get what I want; sometimes I don't.
The survival of my real self is no longer dependent on perfect outcomes.

I am who I am. And that is enough.

September 9
BEING REAL

I spent an inordinate amount of time trying to be the kind of person I thought I had to be in order to get what I needed: approval from myself and others. Eventually, I chose a specific role. I rehearsed the part. I acted out the scenes. ***My director, the false self, was unrelenting with its demands on my performance.*** I would enlist the effort of my actual self to study the play, learn the lines and deliver 'the goods'.

The one thing that got lost in all the activity was the one thing that mattered most, my real self. I had no time to explore curiosities, try new things or broaden my perspective. ***I was obsessed with pleasing the beast; the false self.*** At the end of the day, very little mattered except my ability to stick to the script; the 'should always' part of the play: I should always be self-reliant, independent; I should always love everybody, be kind; I should always be in control of my world, strong and courageous.

I dismiss the 'should always' concept today. The worth of my real self is no longer dependent on how well my actual self can perform some pre-scripted role ***all the time.***

In fact, I am no longer tied to just one play. ***Having taken the Steps, I am free to express myself without fear; the fear of being 'abandoned'.***
I connect with myself in a healthy way: I feel my feelings, I talk about what is going on and I realistically consider my options. I am real with myself and I am real with others who are safe.

No longer locked into a binding contract with the old director (my false self) now sitting back-stage grumbling and mumbling to himself like a tired old uncle, I explore ***MY*** true interests; ***MY*** genuine needs.
<u>*I am learning about my REAL self.*</u>

I ***CONSCIOUSLY*** decide what role **I will rehearse**; what script **I want to play.** I reaffirm the age-old truth taken from an age-old play: 'To thine own self be true and thou canst be false to no man or woman'. (I added the 'woman' part to the script…clever lad!)

September 10
WANTING WHAT I HAVE

I lived in a world where the future meant everything. Someday I would get a bike. Someday I would start middle school. Someday I would get a car. Someday I would go to work. Someday Dad would come back. Someday Mom would stop acting weird. Someday I could leave. ***The presumptive outcome was always the same: someday I will have what I want.*** **LIFE WILL BE BETTER**.

The irony of this belief proved out, time and again; when I got what I wanted, inevitably something was never quite right. ***The 'life-will-be-better' part of the bargain rarely paid off in full.*** Like the guy who shows up at the ice cream stand for a double dipped vanilla cone with chocolate sprinkles only to find that they're out of chocolate sprinkles, I 'felt short-changed'.

I am on new footing. I have a real self that simply wants to feel safe enough to express itself. ***I find that I have what I need in order to be who I am most of the time.*** I am living in the moment.

Today is the day. Now is the time. I have plans for the morning, for the afternoon, and the evening. ***Life is not a dress rehearsal.*** I have plans for the week, the month, the year and yes, I still dream about the future. ***The joy of expressing myself is no longer dependent on the outcome of my plans.*** Sometimes things work out; sometimes they don't. Regardless, I am connecting with my real self. I am recovering lost interests and I am discovering new ones. I act on my true interests.

I am aware of what I have at my disposal; my props. And I appreciate them all: my pots, my pans, my dishes, my cell phone, my shirts, my pants, my shoes, my bed, my table, my sofa. ***Acting on my behalf, I use all these 'things' in order to maintain the expression of my real self.***
As a result, I am reasonably happy most of the time.

Now, where the heck are my car keys!

September 11
ATTENDING GROUP CONSCIENCE MEETINGS

My family proved to be anything but democratic. There seemed to be a looming sense of dictatorship even when 'things' seemed to be going smooth. *I rarely knew when my actions would ignite the wrath of the despot, my parent.* The three approaches I had to choose from went something like: I can submit to Mom's demands, I can avoid her altogether, or I can rebel against her. Initially, I complied; then, I avoided; then, I rebelled. I had no voice in most matters.

Living under the harsh 'rule' of another, I abandoned my natural curiosity and playful instinct in exchange for staying 'off the radar'. *I created a false self.* I followed its demands. I took great pride in my ability to measure up. Whether it was couched in terms of always being a good boy, always being independent or always being a rebel, I gloried in the false self I had become.

I am seeing myself as one of many. *My home group reflects a safe image; a place where I can go in order to let down, be myself and talk about what is really going on.* My home group is one of the safest places I know. I have a voice. I have a vote. My opinion matters.

I restructure my extended family dynamic every time I go to a group conscience meeting. I practice participating in real matters in real time. *Some group conscience meetings are safer than others.* Personalities are free to mingle. I can move away from ideas I don't agree with, I can move toward ideas I do agree with. I can even move against ideas that I don't like; without feeling guilty. I can stand up for what I believe. My presence in the group matters. I can be who I am without fear of being thrown out, dismissed or shut down.

'Our leaders are but trusted servants.' *No one person is the boss, no one person has all the answers and certainly, no one person can do this recovery work alone.* 'Our common welfare comes first;s personal recovery depends on our level of unity as applied to our primary purpose'.

September 12
GRIEVING

Grief was very much a part of my life growing up, only I didn't know to call it grief. Experiencing loss, over and over, set up a numbing effect on my system. ***I became desensitized to pain.*** I streamlined my thinking in order to get through the events of the day. In other words, I became rigid in how I viewed myself and the world around me. My approach to life seemed to be working. At the very least, I was staying alive. Avoiding the extreme emotions of life was necessary if I were to navigate an unsupportive, sometimes hostile environment. ***I rarely considered real losses in real time.*** I simply moved on to the next distraction. I simply 'shut down'.

I recover my lost self by remembering the past and feeling the grief; a very tall order. **The Fourth Step suggests that I list the ideas driving my actions; an inventory of my morality.** In order to get there, I look at the events of the past that set up my belief system. And, as night follows day, emotions come up as I recall the events; usually feelings surrounding grief.

I go through the grief, perhaps for the first time. ***I face my pain. I get angry. I cry.*** The grief process is a ***gift*** and a ***mystery***. At first, I deny my pain. Then, I admit my loss; my anger. I bargain out the loss. I get sad. And finally, I accept my loss. It becomes part of the bigger picture called my life's 'history'. I absolutely rely on this established process.
That is the gift, but what of the mystery?

No two events are grieved in the same way or at the same pace. I can remain in denial about a certain loss and then suddenly, the event bursts onto the scene. I can get angry about an event, admit it, but remain stuck in the 'bargaining' phase. I can finally accept a loss and then, fall back into a sadness about it all.

I have accepted the grief process as a necessary inconvenience;
an absolute necessity to recovering my abandoned self.
I have come to trust the process.
I LET GO AND LET GOD.

September 13
ACTING IN THE MOMENT

One of the glorious benefits of being a child, which I missed to a large extent, was the wonderous spontaneity of it all: the thrill of being in the moment; alive and aware and awake; to have an idea and act on it; to see where the idea and the activity leads; to arrive at that new place of discovery; to enjoy the reward of a genuine interest pursued.

My freedom was often restricted due to my own hyper-vigilant, high-alert lookout for 'threats' in the environment; threats primarily from those who were supposed to be keeping me physically and emotionally safe.
I traded my spontaneous real self for the 'security guard';
my false self, rigid and demanding.

I am an adult. I am fully capable of taking care of my need for safety and essential provision. I am self-supporting through my own contributions. I dismiss my false self, with the help of God, through Steps Six and Seven. ***I no longer need an overbearing, demanding chaperone to manage my every thought, word and deed.*** I reconnect with my real self.

I laugh more. I cry more. I am OK with getting angry from time to time.
No longer 'shut down', ***my actual self is free to serve my genuine interests.***
I can act according to who I am rather than who I 'should always' be.
I embrace my curiosities.

I do things on the spur of the moment just because I can. I speak my mind in 'real' time. I move with ease most of the time; in tandem with who I am.
I act in accordance with my own best interest.
I pursue my own happiness.

I am free.　　I am alive.　　I am aware.　　I am awake.

September 14
QUIETING THE MENTAL CHITTER CHATTER

One of the problems confronting me before I found the rooms of recovery was the constant 'background noise' in my head. ***It was as though I had two programs open on my computer with forty programs running in the background.*** Old distorted ideas conflicted with even *older* distorted ideas. Some demands seemed to be in exact opposition to other demands.
The battle raged. Self-accusations jammed the airways.
The 'itty-bitty-shitty-committee' was in constant session.

The recovery process gives me a chance to 'de-program'; to recess the committee. ***I am letting go of countless distorted demands designed by my survival self; then, perpetrated onto myself and others.***

In fact, I am **entirely** ready to have God remove these slanted thoughts which have shaped my character.

Sometimes quickly, sometimes slowly; these incessant, exaggerated expectations foisted onto life are being removed by a power greater than myself. I ask for God's help with complete abandon.

A new space is opening. I get a fresh start. ***The 'sound' of the old chatter is faint.*** I feel safer somehow. I begin to re-integrate my *real* self into life. I can hear my own voice. I am more at ease with who I am. I seek through meditation to improve my conscious contact with God as I understand him.

In returning and rest, I find strength and confidence. ***In quietness, I find peace.*** I pray for the knowledge of His will for my life and the power to carry that out; and then… I take a nice hot bubble bath by candlelight; perhaps a nice hot cocoa, too.

Mmmmm…positively scrumptious!

September 15
CELEBRATIING MY REAL SELF

I spent much of my time, before finding recovery, putting myself down; denigrating any accomplishment; finding fault and imperfection. *I hated myself for not being able to live up to an idealized sense of who I should be.* Naturally, there was nothing to celebrate.

And what of the times when I did, in fact, measure up to the 'standard'? Did that satisfy the demand for perfection? Did that give me the 'glory' I desperately sought in order to be more? *And by being more, did I gain the genuine approval from myself and others?* No, no and no.

There seemed to be a bottomless pit into which most of my efforts were tossed with disregard. *Whether the demand centered around being loving all the time, being independent of others or being able to do anything in superb fashion, <u>I had to be ready for the next 'challenge'.</u>* Yesterday's victory was forgotten. Self-accusations lay just around the corner.

My real self is emerging unjudged. Innocence requires no court room. The nagging standard for perfection is being removed. I appreciate my genuine interests and my effort applied to those genuine interests. I take joy in new ideas.

The 'qualifying time' has been left behind; the standardized tests, thrown in the trash; minimum requirements, laughed out of existence.
<u>I no longer need prove myself in order to be myself.</u>

I have an interest, I fashion a play, and I take the shot. Sometimes I win; sometimes I lose. *Whatever the outcome, I return to my real self.*

I return to respect.   I return to compassion.   I return to love.

September 16
TALKING ABOUT WHAT MATTERS

I lived life from a rather superficial position, choosing to avoid most significant topics in pursuit of trivia or the 'latest'. ***The payoff was in the distraction.*** I preferred to talk about almost anything, rather than deal with the clinging trauma that had become my life. Avoidance was the key.

Ironically, I could tell complete strangers more 'truth' about my life than I could with friends of many years. ***On the rare occasion that I would talk openly, folks often advised me, lectured me or otherwise, tried to 'help' me.*** I grew weary of being rescued and fixed.

Today, the program has given me all kinds of relationships for all kinds of occasions. ***I have acquaintances. I have friends. I have family. I have intimate friends. I have intimate family relations***.

I talk about what matters with only intimate friends and intimate family relations, those who can validate how I feel and simply listen. I do the same for them. We have a mutual respect for one another's ideas, opinions and activity. ***We are direct.*** I can say when I have a problem with another's behavior and ask for what I need without fear of rejection. I can share a genuine concern without feeling compelled to enforce my solution.

'I can teach a goat to climb a tree, but it's a whole lot cheaper if I simply hire a squirrel in the first place.' In other words, I no longer expect a 'new depth' of conversation from a casual acquaintance.

It's nice when it happens, but I'm not surprised when it doesn't. I don't expect total strangers to be intimate friends. I talk about what is important to me with the people who are most significant to me; ***my trusted friends and relatives.***

September 17
ALLOWING FAILURE

Failure was not an option. Life had become a series of challenges centered around always being the person I should be. *With every step toward self-fulfillment, there seemed to be three steps backward with self-accusation.* I had become my own worst enemy.

The idealized standards by which I fashioned my life proved to be impossible to meet all the time; and yet, I expected nothing short of one hundred percent success. *Even minor mistakes seemed to take on major importance.* Litigating my self-worth was often accompanied with a chorus of self-accusations from the 'committee'; 'You're such a fumble-bunny, you can't do anything right, you're so careless, what an idiot, how stupid was that!'

When others fell short of my demands, *I often blamed them with the same type of denigrating remarks;* 'They're so thoughtless, they only think of themselves, they always get it wrong, they're insane!' Shame and blame ruled the day. Rarely was there a moment's rest from the constant pressure.

I am stepping away from the old ideas that ensued from my once-upon-a-time monster, *my false self.* 'Uncle Adolph', as I like to call him now, has a very small room in the basement where he mumbles to himself, complains, curses under his breath and blames others; sad old chap, really.

I am seeing failure not as a sign of my self-worth, but as an opportunity for new beginnings. I *'practice'* the program. Practice, of its very nature, allows mistakes. I celebrate my progress.

<u>*I let go of the myth of perfection. It doesn't exist; it never did!*</u>
I am content with giving life 'the old college try'. Sometimes I succeed; sometimes I fail. I am neither a 'success', nor a 'failure'.

I am simply, loveable me.

September 18
TRUSTING OTHERS

The component of fear drove just about everything I did. Not only was I afraid of others, I was also afraid of myself; the false self that had taken over the controls. ***Unable to meet the idealized standards of 'Uncle Adolph' (my old false self) I often launched a barrage of accusation onto others in order to deflect my own shame around not 'being enough'.*** Naturally, when it came to trusting others, I was at a total deficit in that department.

On top of all that, I often picked situations that were virtually absent of the conditions upon which trust *could* be built. Unavailable, sometimes both physically and emotionally, these people seemed to be my preferred relations. Some were toxic, as well. I had a penchant for selecting, in many cases, the 'perfect storm' into which I would sail unawares, always astonished that 'things' didn't work out.

Having gone to the considerable trouble of retrieving my abandoned self by taking the Steps, I am far more reluctant to dance with disaster these days. ***'Fools rush in where angels fear to tread.'*** I am no longer cavalier in my approach with others whether it be in the form of institutions or individuals. I am cautious.

No longer addicted to excitement, I prefer a reasonably predictable course. I move toward situations that are safe.

I recognize 'red-flags'. I give myself permission to say no; to change my mind. And what of those new relations toward whom I feel attracted? ***I practice the process. I am an acquaintance first, then a friend; once a friend, perhaps an intimate friend.*** It all depends on the 'availability factor': spiritually sound, emotionally equipped, intellectually compatible, and physically present. I refuse to put my real self at risk for anything or anyone; safety first.

I don't go sky diving with a giraffe,
and I don't play cards with the likes of Jesse James.

See, I AM making progress!

September 19
GIVING VOICE TO MY CONCERNS

There had never been an honest forum for sharing concerns in my family of origin. Avoidance seemed to be the preferred strategy regarding most problems. *And when problems were addressed, it usually meant that the 'strongest' person in the room, the person with authority, would have the final word.* Often, worries would be dismissed, denied or demeaned.

Thus, the habit of not talking was entrenched with the unfolding of my family dynamic. *Everyone seemed to have their separate corners.* Rather than talk it out, we acted it out. I formed secret alliances and hid in the shadows of my distractions: drinking, smoking, eating, watching tv, working, studying. Being real with the people who were closest to me was out of the question.

I am re-connecting with my real self; the self that has a voice; the self that has a voice about what is really going on in real time. I hear my real self, first by feeling; then, by listening to my own 'still small voice'. I act in my own best interest. I take care of me first.

I am more inclined to move toward people who are available emotionally; people who are safe; people who are nurturing. *When circumstances become problematic, I use my voice in order to ask for what I need directly:* 'I have a problem with _____; or I am concerned about_____. And this is what I need.'

Often, this juncture in the relationship proves to be a game-changer; a fork in the road. *Voicing a concern with someone who is not ready for honest dialogue is like asking directions from a parking meter; it does not work.* Sometimes people want to help; sometimes they don't. Sometimes people won't change; sometimes people can't change.

Regardless of the outcome of my direct request for support, I feel better. Using my voice to ask for what I need builds my own integrity.

I remain true to myself.

September 20
STEPPING AWAY

Over the years, my 'attraction' to family events had become a habit. After all, the main event of my life was spent day to day, week to week, month to month, and year to year with the same cast of 'players'. **Regardless of the insanity, I was compelled to show up.** Until I turned eighteen, I had no choice in the matter.

The sheer repetition of ritual created a sense of false security. <u>*'The devil I knew was more appealing than the devil that I didn't know'.*</u>

I would continue to move toward these family events out of loyalty; perhaps out of the mere 'tradition' of it all. Regardless of the motive, I stayed stuck in old roles, old scenes and old endings.

I understand today that I am free to take what I like from my family of origin and leave the rest. *No longer hemmed in by a false self, always demanding outrageous feats of loyalty and 'love', I move away from those who are not safe.* Sometimes I remove myself subtly; other times, I leave little to speculation, regarding my grand exit.

I am connecting with my true self. I am being real. I am getting a life. I realize the importance of saying 'no' to certain members of my family. I am separating. *I am told that separating from my family of origin is a GOOD thing;* that healthy families hope for the day when children and siblings leave the nest and go their separate and autonomous ways.

I create my own home. At the end of the day, I return and rest. <u>*I celebrate my victories.*</u> I grieve my losses. I nurture myself in every way possible, affirming once again, that I am enough.

September 21
SURVIVING THE TERROR

Some dysfunctional family settings are more dangerous than others. And yet, the 'level' of potential threat in my family rarely presented itself in a predictable or measurable fashion. **On the contrary, sudden shifts in mood and action were part of the 'potentially' terrifying equation.**

Whether I was being whipped, cursed out or merely neglected, the hell-on-earth experience was taking its toll. The ambiguity of it all only increased my sense of fear and loathing.

This uncertainty played out with each passing day, week, month and year. I lived as one on high alert, cautious of every move; anxious of the future; my hope being to someday leave, to escape the lunacy. Little did I realize that I would carry the memories, the trauma, the shock, and the horror into the future wherever I would go.

I distracted myself with anything in order to not feel the past. *These distractions, in fact, helped me survive the sheer hopelessness of it all.* I created a false self, hell-bent on molding me into the idealized self that I fantasized of becoming someday. Achieving this would satiate my craving to belong; my craving to be appreciated, loved, admired and respected.

I became 'successful' in most of my idealized endeavors, and yet, *I rarely felt the payoff for which I had hoped…to belong.* Alienated from myself and others, I hit a bottom in my sovereign attempt to survive. I was exhausted. My sole effort to survive had taken a toll. I knew I needed help.

I am supported today by a new extended family that stretches from coast to coast; a family of people just like I am, meeting each week; a family dedicated to the recovery of our abused and abandoned selves; a family committed to celebrating the real deal, life freely lived!

I step from the shadow of the past into the light of day.

September 22
DECIDING HOW TO RESPOND

Throughout the years growing up, many startling events presented themselves; events that demanded a response; and yet, I rarely responded. ***I usually reacted.*** And my reaction was based mostly on unconscious 'strategies' designed to guarantee my survival. I behaved much like an automaton.

Being on guard most all the time limited my opportunity to think 'outside the box'. On the contrary, old 'solutions' to old problems strengthened their grip, even as I approached a life beyond the realm of my dysfunctional family of origin. ***Old solutions ceased working on 'new' problems;*** nevertheless, I applied my old ideas with even more fervor, hoping for a different result. Confusion and frustration lay waiting.

I am composed and collected most of the time now. Thanks to the Fourth and Fifth Steps, I have unearthed the driving dysfunctional design of my so-called moral system. ***My real self is emerging.*** I am connecting with my own voice and I am reasoning things out, accordingly. I have options.

I am aware of my 'hot' topics that trigger emotions similar from the past. I process events that threaten my newfound peace of mind. And with a neutral party, I can usually decide how to move forward in such a way that I enhance my well-being. I affirm that my peace of mind comes first, regardless. I am of little benefit to others if I am distracted with trouble.

I am entirely ready to have God remove all the defects in my old thinking; the ancient, mindless demands of my survival self. Steps Six and Seven come in mighty handy as I move through some of my most disturbing 'real time' events. The process itself becomes a gateway to freedom from the behaviors of the past.

I ask. I seek. And I usually find the answers I am looking for.
I discover new approaches to old problems.

With God's help, I am breaking the cycle.
I respond rather than react.

September 23
STARTING FRESH

Much of what held me down for so long was the endless trail of unhealthy decisions based on my false self; decisions that followed me into and beyond my adolescent life. I felt as though I were on an uphill climb, knowing full well that around the bend there would be yet another uphill climb; and on it would go. I came to see myself as a 'loser'.

Regardless of the success I may have achieved, the 'bar' kept being raised a little higher; the standard always being associated with 'more': being more, having more, doing more. *I eventually came to see myself as 'not enough' no matter what I, in fact, accomplished.*

Fear motivated most everything I did. Some see the glass as half full, some see the glass as half empty. Mine was totally empty, *all the time*.

I see things through the lens of my real self today. *No longer hamstrung with the unrealistic precept of perfection in everything I do, I am free to fail; free to fall; free to come up short.* And thus, my mistakes are not indications of failure at all; rather, they are opportunities for starting over. Each day is a new beginning.

My actual self, that part of me that does the 'heavy lifting', serves at the pleasure of my real self. Becoming who I truly am is a joy as I connect with my genuine interests. A 'perfect' outcome every time is no longer THE measure of my self-worth. Sometimes I get what I want; sometimes I don't.

My real self continues, undaunted on its journey to actualize its passion. **<u>Taking the trip is more important than arriving 'on time'.</u>**

I can smell the roses, pick some grapes, hike a trail, visit with a local, ride a roller coaster, or sample the sinful trappings of a road-side diner. (hot dog, milk shake and fries…yummy!)

Life is good.

September 24
HOPING AGAIN

Due to a series of disappointments, hurts, broken promises, confusing outcomes and sometimes, terrifying abuses, I came to view life as a rather hopeless proposition. ***Despair was the order of the day; denial, my chief coping skill:*** someday things would be different, someday mother would stop, someday father will come back, someday I won't have to put up with all this nonsense!

Over the ensuing years, the chapters changed, but the book was still the same. I merely picked different people to fill the vacant roles of my original family members. In a very cruel way, my hope for a different outcome in new relations would spring to life, only to be suddenly dashed; sometimes in very short order. Toward the end, before I found the rooms of recovery, I seemed to be drawn to dreadful results much like the proverbial moth to the flame.

Upon arriving at my first meeting, the primary thing I noticed was the sheer safety of it all. Nobody seemed to be the boss. No requirements excluded certain people. No demands prevailed. No tall orders were announced. Without realizing it at the time, I felt a twinge of hope; perhaps I could find some real support. Going forward, I began to trust again; make better choices and take care of myself.

Years have passed since that night. ***In the process of it all, I have been given a safe place*** where I can grieve losses, let go of old ideas, recover a lost self, express genuine interests, hope again and be home by nine o'clock, ten at the latest.

All this for a buck! Amazing.

September 25
KNOWING MY LIMITATIONS

Whether it had to do with my capacity to love, my ability to rely on myself or my 'gift' to excel, I rarely felt limited. In fact, I came to see myself as actually being my 'idealized' self; a kind of super-human: always the saint, always the 'stand-alone' kind of person, always a leader. *Of course, there was hell to pay each time I failed*; nevertheless, my pride, my false pride fueled by my demanding false self, always found a way to 'recover' from the set back.

I merely tried harder. *Over and over, I played out the scenario best suited for how I thought I should be all the time.* And when I could no longer tolerate my own self-accusations, having failed at perfection, I turned my accusatory sights on others: they're so selfish; they're so weak and dependent; they're so stupid, they can't do anything right.

Thanks to the program, I consider myself a reasonable person today. I know I am limited and what's more, I *accept* that I am limited. Having fully dismissed the notion that I can perform perfectly all the time under all conditions, I move freely into the world of the living where people address **LIFE ON LIFE'S TERMS.**

Furthermore, my self-worth is not up for debate; it is a given. I function from a place where errors are expected; where no two people perform at the same pace all the time; where mistakes are part of a greater process called learning; where conditions sometimes determine actual outcomes.

I no longer demand the impossible. It serves no logical purpose to hand someone a fishing pole, demanding trout by suppertime if the river is frozen over by three feet of ice.

However, I was raised in a dysfunctional home.
Give me a few days and I'll figure it out!

September 26
VISUALIZING THE NOW

I was quite gifted when it came to daydreams: things I would have, situations I would create, places I would go, people I would meet. I lived in the future, hoping for better days when I could finally leave all my troubles behind; when I could get away from all the dysfunction in my family.

And when the future arrived, I fell into more daydreaming. That illusive concept called 'tomorrow' was always just around the corner. *Ever onward through the fog, I relentlessly pursued the fantasy;* the Someday Sunshine Syndrome: someday I will be loved, or someday I will be truly independent, or someday I will be successful. The present moment was a mere detour; something to be endured, then forgotten.

Having awakened spiritually and emotionally to my true self, I am discovering new ideas and interests. I am revisiting old interests long abandoned. *I embrace the concept of living in the moment, ONE DAY AT A TIME.* I realize that I have everything I need right now in order to be who I am. I have the capacity to use what I have in order to create what I need.

I dream of things to come; and yet, today is the day; now is the time.
This day I envision how I will express myself. This day I meditate on the outcome I hope for. This day I visualize the morning, noon and evening stages of life's unfolding. This day I act on my genuine interests.
I meet the people I need to meet. I find the things I need to find.
I do the things I need to do.

Sometimes I get all that I want; sometimes I don't. *I hold fast to the true vision; the vision of myself;* the vision of my interests; the vision of my ultimate well-being.

Thank you God, for another day.

September 27
SUPPORTING OTHERS

One of the identifying characteristics resulting from my having been raised in an alcoholic home was the skewed concept of self. ***Without really knowing it, I had become very 'self' centered.*** This trait allowed my survival. The level of narcissism to which I rose is a mystery to me. I understand that, to some degree, we are all narcissists.

Part of the problem I faced each day was not knowing where the lines were drawn separating me from others. I knew nothing of establishing boundaries. I was enmeshed with those around me.***I took my 'ques' from the environment and naturally placed myself at the center of my reality.*** This strategy served me well. In fact, I made it through some very dark and confusing times. As I said before, this trait allowed my survival.

I am creating a safe place for the unveiling of my true self; and as a result, I have 'room' for others. I have moved beyond survival and thanks to the Steps, I am thriving. ***I have much to give.*** I am still narcissistic to some degree. And yes, at the end of the day, it is still all about me; however, I can invite others in for 'tea and cake' from time to time.

During these visits, I can give another the opportunity for autonomy. I can allow their integrity. ***In other words, I can politely listen.*** I resist the temptation to rescue, caretake or otherwise, fix their situation. Oftentimes, I can merely reflect what I think they have said in order to 'check out' what I think I have heard. I can even offer an interpretation of an emotion expressed; 'you were disappointed, you were angry, you were excited'.

Four empowering things happen with this form of support: ***boundaries are maintained, autonomy is encouraged, problems are defined, and real solutions appear.***

Five things, if you count the delicious cake.

September 28
CREATING MY OWN MORAL SYSTEM (part one)

With my arrival in the world, I was presented with a variety of 'moral systems'; a variety of ideas from which I could and would eventually choose for my 'own'. Some systems affected me directly, some affected me indirectly and some did not affect me in the least.

For example: my going to church at an early age affected me directly; my watching an American sports event, indirectly; the praying of a Tibetan monk in Asia, not in the least. *Some events were more significant than others in shaping what would become my deeply held beliefs.*

Most of my 'moral structure' had been formed quite unconsciously.
I liked to eat popcorn at the movies because that's what people did.
I did not work on Sundays because that's how I was 'taught'.
My country was always 'right'.

The accompanying factor to this belief system, diabolical as it was, proved to be the 'should always' concept; the idea that not only myself, but everyone else *should always* like popcorn at the movies, *should always* not work on Sundays and *should always* support my country.

I am responding to a Fourth Step invitation: *'You are hereby welcome to inventory what you believe, so that you can eventually let go of the old ideas that keep setting you up.'* In response, I do four things:

I review significant relationships.
I review the events attached to those relationships.
I review old emotions attached to specific events.
I review old ideas attached to those events.

I am trying to get the 'big picture' of who I am.

September 29
CREATING MY OWN MORAL SYSTEM (part two)

Being raised in a dysfunctional family reinforced a myriad of false ideas related to who I was and what I ***should always*** do. I had strong ideas about who others were and what others ***should always*** do, as well.

By the time I found the rooms, I was entirely conflicted with unconscious demands surrounding how I should be all the time and how others should be all the time. In short, I was a mess.

I am looking at my history and feeling what I need to feel.

Finally, I determine what beliefs were ***born of*** and ***reinforced by*** those events and old emotions, respectively. ***I am taking all the time I need.*** I am being as thorough as I possibly can.

I am preparing myself to share these findings with God, myself and another human being in a Fifth Step. I have the option of taking the Fifth Step in stages or I can take the Step all at once.
The choice is entirely mine.

Following the Sixth and Seventh Steps, ***I am free to create MY OWN belief system*** based on my emerging genuine self.

I am vacating a space in order to create a new space…
a new space called ***home.***

September 30
LETTING GO OF DEMANDS

I needed to feel secure in an environment that often proved unsupportive; even hostile. I created a strategic system which I hoped would keep me alive. ***Eventually, this false sense of security dominated almost everything I did.*** I was driven by a false self which had only one consideration, survival. I obeyed.

Naturally, this 'strategic system' grew over time like a clinging vine, out of control, choking the life out of its host. What had started as a few 'rules to obey' turned into an entire structure of laws and by-laws. To make matters worse, these demands applied sometimes under certain conditions, but did not apply all the time under all conditions.

The balancing act required a lot of energy. Exhausted, I finally submitted to the set of demands related to my 'idealized' self. I prided myself and others in our collective attitude toward life; how we ***should always*** think and behave. I justified my failures and rationalized my unpleasant actions. Secretly, I hated myself. When convenient, I blamed others. Resentment rode roughshod over much of what I did.

<u>Steps Six gives me a way to get past the bullshit.</u> *Step Seven gives me the power to do so.* 'Were entirely ready to have God remove all these defects of character.' (Step Six) ***Pain is a great motivator.*** I become willing.

'Humbly ask God to remove our shortcomings.' (Step Seven) ***The glaring error behind all my shortcomings lies in one thing: my old false demand for perfection; otherwise known as false pride.*** I must let go, but I can't. And yet, a power greater than myself can help.
My simple task now?

LET HIM.

OCTOBER

October 1
WALKING IN THE DARK

There were times when the only 'thing' keeping me together while living in a dysfunctional environment was my heartfelt strength in remaining 'true' to myself. I took great pride when I could fulfill the orders of 'strategic command'; orders of my false self. I needed to belong. I *desperately* needed to belong. The more urgent the need, the 'louder' the demand.

Everything I believed I should always do was geared around one thing: to be included. ***Whether it meant being attached to many people or only one, I wanted to be appreciated and respected.*** Staying in line with 'strategic command' assured that outcome; or so, I mistakenly thought. The only requirement? Perfection, of course.

God is removing this twisted demand for perfection. I find in current situations people who 'trigger' old emotions; in some cases, ***VERY*** old emotions; usually centered around fear. Reality is my friend today. I use these emotional events to process the residual issues which remain; the issues uncovered in a thorough Fourth and Fifth Step.

My willingness to change (Steps Six and Seven) naturally carries me to a Tenth Step. I readily admit the error of my old thinking. ***I own my behavior.***

Step Eleven further invites my return to reason. I pause when agitated, disappointed, hurt, angry, disgusted. I pray. Or I meditate. Or I call someone with whom I can process. Perhaps I do all three; and then…***I MOVE ON.*** I accept LIFE ON LIFE'S TERMS. Sometimes I behave as I 'should'; sometimes I don't. Sometimes others behave as they 'should'; sometimes THEY don't.

There are dark days ahead. ***Life is difficult whether I have a program or not.*** And yet, I have a way out of the dark; a way out upon which I can absolutely rely. I no longer curse the darkness.

I simply light a candle. (then I call my attorney)

October 2
MAINTAINING A REASONABLY SAFE WORLD

Part of the false self's appeal, to which I aspired, proved to be the promise of a payoff; the guarantee that all would be well if I merely followed orders: avoid the monster and you'll be OK; or, defend yourself against the monster and it will leave you alone; or, 'love' the monster and there will be peace. The 'payoff was hit and miss. ***I rarely felt safe and supported for long.*** Eventually, I would pick one approach as my primary method. The 'solution' only seemed to work.

Protecting myself became a top priority. ***I had to defend against an otherwise unsupportive and sometimes toxic environment.*** Eventually, the conflict on the outside would move inside; inside my head. When I failed to measure up to my own demands, I hated myself; when others failed, I hated them.

I know today that everyone is limited in some way, including me. I am stepping into a new light; the light of compassion toward myself and others. No longer convinced that I, alone, can create an entirely safe world by maintaining a 'perfect' strategy, I embrace the genuine support of the program; my extended family. ***Within the rooms, I can re-feel and talk openly about events from the past without fear of criticism or interruption.*** Healthy boundaries are maintained. I extend to others in recovery the kindness and understanding I would wish for myself.

Outside the rooms, I choose who I want to see, how long I want to see them and on what terms; especially members of my original family. Some subjects are off limits. ***I can directly ask for what I need with the people I meet.*** Sometimes I stand up for myself (moving against), sometimes I comply with others' expectations (moving toward) and sometimes I seek privacy (moving away from).

I can practice all three approaches without feeling guilty for having included one or excluded another. Creating a healthy environment ***inside and outside*** my head is my number one priority. ***I lower my demands and I set healthy boundaries.*** I practice this in the rooms of recovery.

October 3
TREATING OTHERS WITH RESPECT

The principal driving force in my world of dysfunction was the concept of authority. In other words, the person in charge ruled the day. ***Consequently, the primary source of authority was to be either obeyed, resisted or avoided.*** The idea that each person in the family brought an equal amount of 'power' was never entertained.

To be sure, certain needs of some were portrayed as more important than the needs of others. ***Problems were rarely addressed with the goal being to consider everyone's needs.*** Autonomy was not encouraged. At the end of the day, it was 'every man for himself'. And it was understood that some had more 'power' than others. They were to be feared.

At the core of recovery lies the seed of mutual respect; that no one person or group has more power than the other. ***'Our leaders are but trusted servants, they do not govern.'*** And thus, I have an equal share in the interest of my group; my group has an equal share in the collective interest of all the groups.

I respect the right of each person to act in accordance with their own best interest. I sincerely appreciate each person's journey. I allow them to have their own struggle that comes with being who they are. Whether I agree with their 'solutions' or not, I can detach with courtesy and wish them well.

Sometimes I can work with others in a way that all can win; sometimes I cannot. ***Negotiating a situation that preserves the dignity of all is a difficult business; and yet, the result proves far more productive than the alternative; authoritarian rule.*** 'Our common welfare comes first. Personal recovery depends upon program unity.'

I have no more power than anyone else. I do have needs. ***I am free to negotiate those needs.*** Sometimes I get what I want; sometimes I don't. I walk away a happy man when I employ common courtesy and genuine respect.

October 4
GETTING OFF 'THE STORY'

I had grown accustomed to a set of circumstances beyond my control; the circumstances of my neurotic family; circumstances that had given birth to an emerging set of beliefs designed to protect me. In my effort to defend myself, I created a story about what, in fact, had happened and what was happening. I relied on 'the story'. I counted on 'the story'. **_I believed 'the story'._**

Most parts were true; admittedly, some were embellished. The truth of 'the story' was not the point; it was the telling of 'the story'; the telling of 'the story' not only to others, but to myself, as well. It went something like this: 'the reason I am the way I am is because this happened; the reason I do what I do is because of what 'they' did; if only things had been different, I would be different'. All true. *And yet, 'the story' had ceased working. It probably never had.*

I am presented with a way to reconnect with my genuine self; that part of me that is alive and curious; able and awake; active and spontaneous. *I take responsibility for who I am today: my beliefs, my interests; my feelings, my actions.* I have the power to change a lifetime of energy mis-spent, chasing an unworkable 'solution'. Remaining true to 'the story' is no longer that important. I am not a slave to 'the story'. I am no longer a victim.

Sometimes I choose to move toward people, sometimes I choose to move away. And yes, I even choose to move against some people. Sometimes I comply in order to get along, sometimes I retreat for some privacy and sometimes I stand up for myself. All three are OK; all three are healthy. I am the only person ultimately in 'charge' of acting on my decisions in whatever way I choose. **_Thank God for Step Eleven._**

I let go of 'the story', little by little, every time I talk about three things: what life was like, what happened and what life is like now. **_I have experience. I have strength. I have hope._** Who could ask for anything more? (actually, a little slice of cheesecake would be very nice, right about now)

October 5
BECOMING SPONTANEOUS

Second guessing myself had become a way of life by the time I was seven or eight. *I felt as though I had to 'get it right' and so, I traded 'childish impulsivity' for cautious calculation.* I lived in a war zone. I learned quickly. I 'grew up'. I did what I had to do in order to keep the survival thing going my way. I was very successful. I survived!

Much like one who goes to the movies wearing a blind fold; I was participating in my life, but I wasn't entirely present. Something was missing. Something wasn't right. Over the years, I had lost the capacity to truly feel much of anything. *<u>I had 'numbed down'.</u>*

Life had become rather 'flat' save for the times when something went terribly wrong or jubilantly right; a roller coaster ride of sorts. I grew addicted to excitement. Any 'distraction' would do.

By applying a thorough effort in the search for my real self, I have come to fully rely on a Twelve Step process of trust; in other words, *I have a program and I use it.* At the end of the day, I believe the Steps are designed to bring me into a healthy relationship with God, myself and others.

I give myself permission to feel; usually, it's as simple as mad, sad or glad. I talk about how I feel with a trusted friend or a professional therapist. I come to trust my own voice, my own perception, my own interests, my own decisions and my own actions.

Trusting this new process as I do and returning to my true self as I have, I delight in stepping out of the box; *I like trying new things on the spur of the moment;* I relish a great adventure to the grocery store, a trip to a distant city, a walk about in the woods, a rollicking turn on the dance floor; I embrace the risk of it all; and, *I AM FEELING EVERYTHING*.

Whether I am crying a river, ranting like a lunatic or laughing uncontrollably, I am unmistakably alive! *Whatever goes with being the real me is what I want to fully experience, fully feel and fully talk about.* Ten minutes until the next feature starts and I really don't know what it's about; but it sounds good? Hell yes! I'm going to the *MOVIES*!

October 6
SORTING OUT EMOTIONS

When confronted with loss in my early years, I often denied the accompanying emotions: anger, fear, sadness, embarrassment, humiliation, resentment and the like. As a result, I grew quite proficient at 'stuffing'; that is, controlling my emotions. *I was a stuffer.* I stuffed and stuffed and stuffed until I could stuff no more. As the old saying goes, 'You can cram six pounds of sugar into a five-pound sack, but eventually, somethin's gotta give.'

As I grew older, my 'reaction time' to loss turned into proverbial seconds rather than the usual days, months and years. Unlike the old days when the 'little train' of events slowly chugged up the hill, *the time had come when I was conducting a freight train, hurling downhill at ninety miles per hour,* where anything on the tracks appeared larger than it truly was. I spent a lot of time either depressed about the past, upset about the present or worried about the future.

I am encouraged by others in the program to feel my feelings; that 'feelings are neither good nor bad, they are simply a part of who I am'. *I am emerging from a false life driven by old ideas, sustained by old fears and fueled by excessive demands.* My real self is no longer terrified of abandonment. I feel and act differently compared to the old days and the old ways.

I know the difference today between *F*alse *E*motions *A*ppearing *R*eal (FEAR) and *F*actual *E*motions *A*ccompanying *R*eality. *In short, I have 'fake' feelings and I have genuine feelings;* fake is about the old self, genuine is about the real self.

I know today that any harsh 'feeling' that lasts longer than a few hours (at tops) is about collateral damage from the past; any feeling lasting shorter than a couple of hours is usually about my immediate environment; an indication that I need to do something in the 'here and now' to take care of myself. *Today, I know the difference between fake feelings and genuine emotion.*

October 7
RECOGNIZING RESOURCES

Due to the hours upon hours spent, trying to maintain my composure while living in a dysfunctional family, ***I often overlooked opportunities that were staring me in the face.*** I even told myself that I somehow didn't deserve a break; didn't merit special consideration; didn't justify the proper resources; in short, I told myself that I didn't rate. I sometimes felt like an imposter.

To carry things a step further, I often sabotaged my own effort in trying to get what I wanted. Distracted by a multi-tiered system of ***old emotional needs and false demands, I missed capitalizing on events which might have otherwise served <u>my best interest.</u>***

More times than not, 'the boat had just left the harbor, the train had just pulled out of the station, the last horse had been sold'. Whether it was a boat, a train or a horse, 'the story' remained essentially the same: 'I'm a victim'.

Today, I am unconditionally supported in my effort to establish genuine beliefs and maintain true-to-myself motives. ***The program, like no other, <u>encourages full participation in my own life.</u>*** I find the whole purpose of recovery, in fact, is to reconnect with my **real** life based on a **real** self with **real** interests, in **real** time. In short, I am being reinvigorated to 'get a life'.

In the process of acting on my interests, I am presented with items which support those interests; 'props', if you will. When I commit to the process of ***being*** who I am, ***<u>I usually get what I need, when I need it</u>*** while fully ***expressing*** who I am. *'To be or not to be; that is the question.'*

<u>**The choice to act is mine; and in the acting is where the miracles happen.**</u>
Ask any entertainer who steps from rehearsal onto center stage; something magical happens. Or not.

October 8
HAVING MY OWN PERCEPTION

Being dismissed, discounted and diminished came to be common practice, accompanying the frustration that went along with living in a dysfunctional family. Rarely were my observations validated. *Seldom, if ever, were my feelings supported regarding the world around me.* Little by little, I came to doubt my own reality. I closed myself off. I 'protected' my secret interpretations. I trusted few.

Much like one who is exiled, I began fashioning my assessments in terms of how best I could survive and get back 'home'. I hoped for the day when I would be released. I pressed on with my 'strategy'; hear nothing, see nothing, say nothing. *My true self, over the years, kept slipping away.* Sadly, my chances of returning 'home' diminished with each passing year. My survival self would take me other places; compulsive places I would not have freely chosen.

I have returned to my real self. I am, by miracle, home again. The rooms of recovery invite the search for my own truth; my own reality; my own perception; my own voice.

No longer locked away, I am confident in the way I experience and interpret the world around me. I am free to explore my true self without interruption from the 'discounters and diminishers'. I no longer dismiss my spontaneous impressions. I embrace them! 'I intuitively know how to handle situations that used to baffle me.'

Sometimes I am right; sometimes I am wrong. I have others with whom I can talk about my 'take' on things; my 'feel' on situations. *I 'check out' my ideas with others who keep an open mind and often give me the emotional space I need in order to arrive at my own understanding of events.*

I fear no longer the reprisal of others. I give myself permission to challenge anything. Everything is open to interpretation.
I am free. I am home. I am me.

October 9
DEALING WITH SEXUAL AND PHYSICAL ABUSE

I was subjected to situations and conditions unlikely to have been viewed on *'The Brady Bunch,'* a television situation-comedy in the 1970's portraying two families brought together as a result of a second marriage.

My family practices were more in line with a popular series in the 1960's called *'The Twilight Zone,'* a dramatic portrayal of bizarre twists and turns that cast a shadowy haze of mystery on the hapless protagonist.

All kidding aside, physical abuse was part of the 'family routine', right up until the day I left for college. My need for emotional distraction led me to places where I was sexually abused by neighbors. **The events of physical and sexual abuse left me feeling confused and ashamed.**

The belief that emerged over the years sounded a lot like, 'There is something wrong with me. I am not like the others.' The demand that followed this belief: 'Therefore, I should always keep 'this' secret; lest I not be included.' And I kept the secrets for years.

In order to 'resolve' these past offences, I sought out others with whom I could 'act out' a solution, rather than 'talk out' a solution. **_I picked toxic, unavailable people._** Some were more toxic and unavailable than others; nevertheless, I usually stayed in the hope that **_'things would be different this time'._** I was extremely loyal and had grown addicted to excitement, as well; the good kind *AND* the bad.

I am talking now about being sexually and physically abused. **_I am separating, even if it's only temporary, from those who would enable and trigger my continued acting out._** I am willing to do things differently in relationship. I am committed to keeping myself unequivocally safe; free of harm; free of sexual abuse; free of physical abuse. I readily admit that I am powerless over the effects of this disease.

I rely on the group for support during this fragile time. I am coming to believe that a power greater than myself can restore me to sanity; can restore me to making healthy decisions.

October 10
DEALING WITH VERBAL ABUSE

My mother called me a 'son of a bitch' on several occasions. Later, I couldn't help but chuckle as I considered that she was, in fact, slandering herself! *However, the mean-spirited onslaught of four-letter words never seemed funny at the time. In fact, I felt demeaned and ashamed.* In the beginning, I tried to avoid these humiliating episodes by complying with her tyrannical demands. Later, I would merely hide in my room, watch television, leave the house (sometimes by stealth)
or otherwise, move away from her altogether.

I know today that erratic, excited comments laced with four-letter words can go in three directions: toward me or toward others or toward situations in general. I absolutely forbid the first. I tolerate the second and third. The second and third types of expression are merely that: types of expression. Used in the common vernacular of everyday life, these words usually communicate sentiments of anger, disappointment, outrage and the like.
I allow another person to merely vent.

I emotionally detach with courtesy (most of the time) remain available and eventually, move on to more pleasant pasture.

I forbid slanders, insults, and fits of rage directed at me. There is **ABSOLUTELY NO SETTING** where this kind of behavior is OK. *I immediately attempt to set a firm boundary:* 'What you are doing right now does not work for me. I know you are very upset,
but I cannot hear you when you act like this.' It is indeed my lucky day when a civil tongue is redeployed. Rarely does this occur.
Therefore, I act in a way that takes care of me.

I simply retreat, informing the person that I will return. I merely restate what I have already said, *'This isn't working for me; you're angry, I get it. But I can't hear you right now.'*

Chronic verbal abuse on the part of someone else is not about me. It has *everything* to do with them; how they express themselves when feeling as though things are desperately urgent; a form of manipulation, really.
I do not participate today. I can practice the three R's:
*R*etreat, *R*egroup and *R*eturn (possibly).

October 11
BLASTING OFF

I was not an angry person; or so, I thought. I 'managed' my emotions so that I could stay 'under the radar'. I feared drawing the wrath of those in charge. Any indication of rejection set in motion my old terror around being abandoned; being abandoned meant death.

I rarely talked to anyone about what was truly going on. Shame and embarrassment coupled with blame and humiliation ruled the day.

On occasion, when a circumstance seemed 'safe' enough, I would have uncontrollable fits of emotion; outrageous displays of rage or expressions of deep sorrow. *Most of the time, I explained that the reaction was about something that had just happened,* unaware that the exaggerated feeling had possibly come from a reservoir of emotions attached to old events; old events which I had kept buried, locked away, out of sight.

I am allowing my rage. I am allowing my sorrow. I am moving beyond years of denial. *Admitting my powerlessness over this disease, and the accompanying unmanageability that it brings, often sets up moments where I finally __START FEELING SOMETHING.__* And that feeling is usually anger. Whether I am screaming with clinched fists of rage or sobbing with endless tears of sorrow, I am launching into the great unknown. No longer satisfied to live life on the sidelines of my own life, I embark on the great journey toward the recovery of my true self.

Along the way, people and places can trigger old emotions attached to old events. I know not when or where 'grief pockets' will appear on my path. I accept completely that strong, sometimes overwhelming emotions are part of this process. **_The rooms are safe._** I talk before and after the meetings with those who can listen; with those who can allow my venting of strong emotion; with those who are not compelled to 'calm me down' or 'fix me'. In order to launch, I must blast off. It's OK.
'Houston, we are go for lift off.'

October 12
STRENGTHENING MY OWN RECOVERY SYSTEM

I spent a lot of time developing a strategy designed to keep me alive through all the noise and confusion that came with growing up in an alcoholic home. *This 'development' was an entirely unconscious process and while my approach did, in fact, work in terms of sheer survival, it did nothing for the growth and well-being of my real self.*
Quite the contrary, my real self was weakened, isolated and afraid.

My actual self, that part of me that carried out the 'orders' of this developing strategy, seemed to be very strong. There seemed to be a developing pride in the approach I was creating. *In fact, an idealized image of who I should always be emerged.* Everything was geared to supporting this idealization. There were times when all things dictated by my false self were truly happening.

I was thrilled with the dream; for a while. Upon failing at anything, reality would intrude, fantasy would be destroyed, and any mis-perceived strength would melt away like butter sizzling in a hot skillet.

I have abandoned the old ways for the new. I no longer chase the 'dream' of actualizing my idealized self, driven by false claims and exaggerated demands. I am who I am. *I am free to use my actual energy to pursue my genuine interests.*

My beliefs are *my* beliefs. Having taken Steps Four through Seven, I am in a place to 'strengthen my hand'. I act according to how I truly think and feel. I create health: physically and spiritually; emotionally and psychologically.

With the help of God, I am designing a new belief system based on a new consciousness. I am awakening to the simple message at the core of my *REAL* self. <u>*I am enough, just as I am; always have been.*</u>
I celebrate my strength. I take joy in being. I take pleasure in who I am.

October 13
RECOGNIZING TWELFTH STEP OPPORTUNITIES

Although I was consumed with worry and fear, I still maintained a few relationships with those I could relate. Admittedly, I was more interested in what they could ultimately do for me rather than the other way around. *At the end of the day, it was usually ALL about me.* Perhaps some reciprocal activity, unconscious as it was, played out, as well; in other words, 'you scratch my back and I'll scratch yours'. This arrangement worked just fine, so long as the 'scratching' wasn't too inconvenient.

The practice of the Twelve Steps takes me to a place where I have a kind of 'new freedom and a new happiness'. Thankfully, I am experiencing a life where I have more energy. *I feel emotionally connected with true interests that are developing.* I remain true to myself as I move through the day. I am awake to new possibilities. I can hear my own dialogue.
I am available to myself.

Having had a spiritual awakening of sorts, I am way more available to others. By attending meetings on a regular basis, I am discovering my common ground with others who were raised in dysfunctional homes. It's still all about me, but I am learning to listen more.

<u>*I am allowing others the dignity of owning and dealing with their own issues.*</u> I respect their separate journey. Sometimes I share my experience, strength and hope. I carry the message.

Outside the rooms, I meet people all the time who were and are affected by this disease. I meet them right where they are. *Some are ready to try something new; some are deep in denial, unwilling to look at anything; and some are uncertain.* I can practice the principles of the program: 'patience, tolerance, kindness and love'. I allow their autonomy.
I wish them well.

<u>*'I am not in the world to assure the outcome of the crop. I am here to merely plant the seed.'*</u>

October 14
REMEMBERING MY PRIMARY PURPOSE

I had become so enmeshed in my family that I literally lost myself in all the chaos. I had removed my real self (for security reasons) and employed the services of my false self; a false self, eager and willing to 'run the show'. ***My actual self was enlisted to follow orders:*** *'you should always, they should always, we should always!'*

With these relentless demands, came the exhaustion of trying to always live up to the image of this 'idealized self'.

As difficult as it was, I managed to maintain the façade for a long time. I even came to believe that I was, in fact, the embodiment of this 'self' I had created. I took a great deal of pride in 'who I was'.

I spent an inordinate amount of time trying to convince myself and others that I was superior. Whether I prided myself in saintly qualities, masterful methods or stand-alone tactics, I had something to prove. Failure to become this superior self was not an option. I must succeed.

I am on a different path today. I live in order to be who I am; my real self. And because I don't have to 'live up to' being who and what I am, naturally I have more energy to express myself. ***My actual self is employed to perform the will of my genuine wishes.***

No longer afraid of being abandoned or abused, I act in accordance with what I truly believe most of the time. And when I do, I feel great! In this effort to reclaim and maintain a genuine self, my primary purpose is to stay sober; in other words, to stay awake and connected.

'To thine own self be true and thou canst be false to no other.'

I realize that distractions will come and go. ***<u>Somedays I will be more awake than others.</u>*** When I find myself up to my neck in alligators, I can always return to the primary reason for my schlepping around in the woods to begin with; ***TO DRAIN THE SWAMP***. Has anyone seen my mosquito repellent?

October 15
DISCOVERING NEW INTERESTS

I tried a lot of things in order to distract myself from the chaos and confusion in my dysfunctional family; some were healthy, others not so much. *To be sure, the interest was often short-lived.*
I lacked the 'follow through'. I grew bored easily.

The 'interest' wasn't really an interest. In other words, it rarely came from a place of genuine curiosity. *Most of the activity with which I engaged was generated from a need for approval, not inquisitiveness.* Thus, I played baseball for approval. I played football for approval. I played guitar for approval. I studied for approval. The ingredient of true passion was missing in most everything I tried.

By taking a Fourth and Fifth Step, I am vacating a space in order to create a space; a new space in which *I get to choose the colors, the furniture, the curtains, the lamps and art.* I abandon old ideas no longer serving my best interest in exchange for new ideas that encourage my growth and enhance my well-being. With new ideas come new interests; and past interests are born anew.

I play baseball today. I play football. I play the guitar and sing. I read like a maniac. *I do all these things not for approval, but because I sincerely enjoy doing them.* I am returning to the greatest gift of all: the gift of my real self; 'the gift that keeps on giving'.

Expressing myself is part of the greater process of recovery; the 'giving back' part of the process. *I don't give back because I must. I give back because I can.* Absent of the fear of rejection, free of the demand to 'do it perfectly', I connect with my genuine interests and from these interests, I act. I have fun.

Having fun?! Now, **THERE'S** a concept!

October 16
GIVING MY SELF PERMISSION

As events in my life unfolded, I learned very quickly to take my cue from others. ***Being able to 'read the signals' was, in fact, my primary survival skill.*** 'Is this permitted? Is this OK? Is this acceptable?' I grew so proficient in this practice that I rarely had to even ask. I knew what was 'right' and I knew what was 'wrong'. And so, ***my moral structure began.***

Pretty normal, one would think. And yet, thirty years later I was still 'watching for the signs' in order to determine whether or not my behavior was OK, especially with those in authority; especially with those toward whom I had grown 'affectionately' dependent. ***I believed that their approval could make or break me.***

I feel a subliminal sense of freedom the first night I attend a meeting. Something says, 'You are home. You need look no further.' ***I relax into what seems to be a world of honesty, respect and genuine support.*** I am encouraged to 'explore the old tapes'; the old ideas that keep driving me. What unrealistic demand is out of control? Who, in fact, is driving the bus? Me or the false self.

I am permitting an investigation of sorts; an inquiry. What DO I believe? Where did the belief come from? And, more importantly, ***do I want to continue to believe as I always have?***

The choice is mine. I am in the process of deciding what I want to keep and what I want to discard. I am, in truth, making a searching and fearless moral inventory.

With the guidance of a higher power, I will ultimately call all the shots; I will make all the plays. ***<u>My response to life's events will be up to me.</u>***

How I will emerge from Steps Four through Seven is between me and my higher power whom I choose to call God. I am already beginning to know a new freedom and a new happiness as I…reconnect with my real self.

October 17
WAITING FOR THE RIGHT TIME

There seemed to be a sense of urgency at the core of most everything I did. ***Anxiety drove me to do things at speeds unrealistic to the human condition.***

I felt desperate most of the time. I preferred to distract myself rather than focus on my feelings or what my feelings might be trying to tell me. I would simply deny it all and rush off to my next destination or move on to my next item on the 'things-to-do' list.

When an idea popped into my head and the opportunity presented itself, I usually did it. ***So impulsive was this pressing urge to act, that I spent an inordinate amount of time cleaning up the latest mess caused by my reactions.*** Rare were the moments when I reasoned things out with someone and THEN, took the action. I usually took the unreasonable action and ***LATER*** tried to sort through the rubble.
'Look before you leap' did ***NOT*** apply.

Part of the payoff with having a program includes utilizing an awakened state of mind. ***No longer driven by dozens of conflicting demands and expectations, I am growing more and more conscious of my own process.*** I am aware of the discomfort when I am doing something that really isn't part of me. I can choose to retreat, regroup and return. I can talk to a friend. I can reason things out, THEN take the action.

A cowboy in Texas, so the story goes, took off all his clothes one day and jumped in a 'mess' of cactus. The next day when asked, why? His response: *'It seemed like a good idea at the time.'*

As the old saying goes, ***TIMING IS EVERYTHING***. I take it slow. I reason things out. ***I don't have a problem waiting for the right moment.***
And when I do act, I act with confidence.

AND I AVOID CACTUS!

October 18
CREATING SUPPORTIVE SETTINGS

My family could be described in one word; unavailable. *The subtle toxicity that accompanied the diminishing of ideas, discounting of feelings and dismissal of concerns wove a solid strand throughout the fabric of my home life.* Overt toxic displays of rage lowered the threshold of trust even more. It's a miracle that I survived this torment with even a small portion of my sanity still in tack.

The unavoidable reality that factored into this distorted equation was my inability to leave. I remained in the home until I turned eighteen. *I had been victimized my entire life.* The only 'supportive' family setting I knew was the kind that played out on television. This portrayal was distorted, as well. **EVERYONE** seemed so happy, **ALL THE TIME.**
There was no such thing as a 'bad' ending.

I have been given a model of what 'safe' looks like; the rooms of recovery. *I share my thoughts and feelings without fear of being interrupted, put down or ridiculed.*

People show up at regular time each week. Folks are reasonably available.
I have never been the recipient of toxic wrath in a meeting.
The rooms are among the safest places on earth.

These reliable friends seldom disappoint in their ability to show up and listen without fixing me. I create space outside the rooms for myself where I can meet with others whom I trust; people with whom I can genuinely share my ups and downs of the week. They remain long enough to allow my gathering of a new perspective.

Talking to somebody who can't listen is like eating a bowl of tomato soup with a fork; you can do it, but you'll probably go hungry.

For the love of Pete, may I please have a spoon?!

October 19
LETTING DOWN MY GUARD

Initially, there were only an immediate few toward whom I kept my guard up; my family. Later the circle would widen as I encountered other authoritarian players who were prideful and abusive.

This uninviting, sometimes hostile world gave birth to my false self;
that instinctual entity that knew how to survive,
knew how to take a punch, knew how to throw a punch
and knew how to get through a tough round.

I came to rely on the 'coaching' of my false self in order to get through the hazards of being alive. ***The subtle coaching in the locker room grew to maniacal yelling from the sideline.*** I would play harder, try harder. I prided myself in fulfilling these idealized strategies. I even came to see myself as having become my 'idealized self'. Constant vigilance was the price to be paid in order to sustain my growing fantasy of being superior to all.

The rooms have set me free from the need to perform perfectly all the time. ***I have nothing to prove.*** My real self and my true worth are not up for assessment. Period. End of conversation.

I set appropriate boundaries when it comes to unsolicited advice from those who would impose the 'yes, but; you should' syndrome of control and manipulation. For example: '***Yes** you feel sad,* ***but*** *it's only a feeling. You **should** think happy thoughts.*' I avoid the 'yes, buts' and I don't allow others to 'should on me.'

Happy thoughts, indeed! 'Thank you for playing. I have some lovely parting gifts for you. Goodbye.' I say no to people and places that foster fear and intimidation. 'There's the door. Get the hell out.' I am better able to connect with who I am and what I want.

I act with confidence, employing my pure energy in pursuit of my genuine interests. I make no room for false internal demands about how I 'should' perform all the time. No longer inundated with the barbaric yelling from the sidelines, I hear my own voice with clarity and distinction.
I am relaxed. I am at ease. I am myself.

October 20
CREATING OPPORTUNITY

Fear crushed my ability to think 'outside the box' when I was growing up. *As time went on, my anxiety level grew at an exponential rate.* It seemed that the only relief lay in the distractions which I could create in order to not feel. When the distractions no longer worked, the anxiety would return. My internal demands grew even louder. Shame and embarrassment drove a deep seeded depression.

Whether I regretted the past or feared the future, I rarely found myself in the here and now. I seldom had the opportunity to consider what I truly wanted. *I reacted to life.* These reactions would often lead to troubles far worse than the initial event which triggered the reaction. I spent an extravagant amount of time cleaning up 'the mess'.

Overwhelmed and confused, I ventured forth as one marching onward into a fog, uncertain of any exact destination; functioning on autopilot, as it were.

Having had a spiritual awakening as a result of these Steps, *I am reconnecting with my true self.* I employ the full faculty of my actual self; the part of myself that takes the action, does the heavy lifting. The two, in fact, are becoming one. In other words, I am acting according to how I genuinely think and feel. I am productive.

I consider a possible outcome, take the action necessary to create opportunity and leave the results up to a power greater than myself. *My value as a human being is not defined by a 'perfect' result, nor a 'timely' accomplishment.* The joy is in the journey.

DEFINITON: 'luck' (noun); when hard work meets opportunity.

October 21
BREAKING FREE OF THE LIE

As the result of living life from a survival self's perspective; that is, the perspective of doing what I had to do in order to stay alive, ***I created a self which I believed to be ideal; a false self.*** Initially, I developed general strategies which seemed to bring stability to an otherwise unstable world. Over time, I would hone specific skills. I had a menu of three basic approaches from which to choose: to comply, to avoid or to resist.

I would pick compliance in the beginning. On the surface, I seemed to be a well-behaved and courteous young man who would do little things for the adults in his life to let them know that he loved them. Later, I would choose to secretly resist. ***I grew to see myself as a gifted manipulator.*** This approach proved to be my number one 'solution' to any problems in the environment. I believed I could master any situation regardless how challenging.

As time went on, I took pride in my silent 'rebellion'; even gloried in my ability to break the rules and get away with it. In my imagination, I saw myself as a great 'behind the scenes' leader.

I began to idealize this self to the point where my real self was abandoned in exchange for the pursuit of a phantom idealized self. The older I grew, the greater my deceptions became. I lived in a nightmarish fantasy.

Walking into my first meeting, I connect with something deep within. The truth beckons to my real self. ***On some level, I respond, knowing that I am in the right place; knowing that hope is still a possibility.*** I go home optimistic. I have a group of people with whom I can truly relate.

They know of my struggle. Returning to the meetings, I hear others sharing honestly of their anger, their sadness and their joy on this journey.

I am stepping out of the shadows of make-believe and into the light of reality. No longer hounded by false demands, insisting that I should always be my idealized self, I search to recover my real self.
I search for the truth and let go of the lie.

ONE DAY AT A TIME

October 22
LIVING WITH THIS DISEASE

During the years leading up to the program, I coped with a debilitating disease and called it 'living'. I moved through my days as one tethered to a small elephant in a traveling circus. ***The towns and clowns came and went, but the elephant grew bigger and bigger.*** My distorted thinking, once used as a temporary fix, had morphed into a separate creature with a life all its own; my false self.

I attempted to live up to the demands of my false self, thus creating an unrealistic, idealized image of who and what I thought I should be all the time. ***<u>I got dragged around A LOT.</u>*** The underlying payoff, however, seemed to be the notion that I could earn and maintain the respect of all, if only I could stay on my feet; in other words, perform well enough.

With the help of God and the Fellowship, ***<u>I am off 'the hook'.</u>*** Tethered no more, I am free from the incessant unrelenting demands of the past.
I let go of my elephant. I walk away from the circus.

Some of my family members and friends remain in dire straits due to this insidious disease of dysfunction. I live with it. Especially at holiday time, the challenge seems to be simple: go to the circus when it's in town, pet the elephant, laugh at the clowns and be back home by five o'clock.
I am no longer compelled to run away with the circus.
I have a life independent of all the circus 'excitement'.

And so, the story goes: *One friend said to another who worked in the circus cleaning up after the elephants (a messy job), 'Why do you keep doing this same old dirty job, year after year? Why not try something new?' To which the elephant keeper replied, 'And **what**, give up **SHOW BUSINESS?!!!**'*

<u>I visit the circus, but I don't live at the circus.</u> And when I do visit, they tell me you're ***SUPPOSED*** to laugh at the clowns. Here come the holidays!

October 23
CALLING SOMEONE

I had begun to consciously move away from my family at a young age due in large part to a growing awareness that the adults 'in the room' were not really in the room. *In short, their respective distractions rendered them unavailable; checked out.* I preferred to isolate rather than be with people I could no longer count on.

I acted out my need for attention, held my true feelings inside and tried to present a united front. I was anything but united. In fact, the conflict with myself and others had just begun. I selected a specific way to deal with life and spent all my time attempting to carry out my demands. *I was building an internal wall without really knowing it.* The battle had begun: my real self vs. my false self. At the height of the 'war', I trusted no one.

The safe rooms of recovery offer me a chance to trust again. *A familiar group that meets once a week presents something consistent; something upon which I can rely.* I begin to let my guard down. I realize that the overall process is greater than any one person. I embrace the hope of recovering my abandoned self.

During the week, I connect with people in the meeting with whom I relate. In other words, I call someone. *I ask directly for what I need; something like: I just need you to listen, I need to check in, I need to know you are OK, I need your input on something, I need to just talk for a minute or two.* Sometimes the person I call picks up on the first ring. Sometimes not so much. Sometimes the person is emotionally available; sometimes not. Perhaps I call someone else. I smile and dial.

Whatever the outcome, *I am building a bridge* that I once burned; the bridge to trusting myself and others.

October 24
CONTINUING TO TAKE A PERSONAL INVENTORY

I spent very little time before the program analyzing my distorted thinking. I had no clue as to what was truly driving my behavior. ***Anxious most of the time, I merely relied on my automatic 'guidance system' to get me through the tough times.*** I entirely blocked out strong emotions like embarrassment, humiliation and resentment. I was 'asleep at the wheel' most of my life.
My philosophy?   *F*orget *E*verything *A*nd *R*un. *(FEAR)*

Reality was not my friend. Few were the days when I could relax and simply be myself. ***Avoidance of conflict had become a way of life rather than an occasional inconvenience.*** The struggle started on the outside, but always ended up on the inside; the inside of my head. Torn between opposing coping strategies and tossed about with uncertainty,
I moved through each event with dwindling confidence.

I have a strategy today that ***always*** yields more confidence; the skill of facing reality. In fact, ***reality is my friend.*** I discover through Steps Four and Five that my actions and reactions are predicated on ideas; some ideas work, some don't. The ones that don't are usually the ones where I am insisting that myself and others behave in a certain way, all the time.
I am entirely ready to have these exaggerated stressors removed.

I further discover the Tenth Step. Events in the present trigger strong emotions from the past. Reality presents me with an opportunity to
*F*ace *E*verything *A*nd *R*ecover. 'Courage ***IS*** fear, ***that has said its prayers.***'

<u>***I continue to let go of the old ideas that no longer serve me.***</u> I have been given the privilege of reviewing my moral structure in order to remain awake to new ideas; new ideas better suited to living life based on my real self. The closer I move toward ***being who I truly am***, the more confident I become in ***acting as I truly am.*** And when I act in accordance with my genuine self, I usually feel terrific.

And when I feel terrific, gosh-darn-it, people like me.

October 25
STAYING IN FOCUS

I was easily distracted prior to finding the rooms. In fact, I searched out distractions in order to avoid my emotional conflicts. **_Some of these detours became major compulsions in and of themselves_**: smoking, sexually acting out, drinking, using mood altering chemicals, surfing the web, working, studying, exercising, helping others, shopping, watching television, travelling.

All of these, in one combined form or another, led adequate interference; thus, disengaging my capacity to feel what I was feeling at the time I was feeling it.

The driving force behind these distractive symptoms was the utter frustration, accompanying the effort to become my idealized self; that part of me which believed that I could, would and should become everything I demanded. *With each mistake, set-back or error, I plunged deeper and deeper into despair; the despair of being a 'failure'.* I would try harder, blame others or give up altogether. Anything but feel the shame.

The shelter I find in the rooms of recovery affords me the chance to regroup; to take inventory of what is left, following the storm called 'my life'. _I emerge from the rubble with a real self still alive;_ barely breathing, but still alive. I abandon the lies of a false self. I embrace the well-being of my true self.

Caring for myself is my number one priority; my major focus. *I stay focused by allowing my emotions to point me in the right direction.* By feeling what I am feeling, I can either identify old ideas that keep setting me up and let them go; or I can identify what I need in the moment and act on it. No longer satisfied with 'fuzzy', I seek clarity in both past and present events.
I nurture myself accordingly.

October 26
NURTURING MYSELF

The pressure to perform, whether it came from inside or outside myself, eventually wore me down. I was exhausted. ***The 'off' switch had been removed from my internal program that raged out of control with hysterical expectations.*** Desperately needing to feel safe, included and accepted, I marched on; regardless of the torment.

I relied on my 'superior' moral strength to carry me through. I prided myself in sacrifices made, victories achieved, and liberties established. At times, I saw myself as a saint; other times, a courageous captain; and still other times, a free-spirited wild child.

I bought the false notion that I could make myself into the 'ideal' self which I romanticized. Maintaining this façade took a lot of work. I felt like a phony most of the time.

I have let my guard down in the rooms of recovery. I have turned off the machine in my head. ***I am free to simply be who I am.*** I have more time to pursue interests, more time to connect with friends and more time to explore new ideas. I go forward with the confidence that comes with acting in a way which reflects how I think and feel. I have ***nothing*** to prove.

Following a lengthy attempt at solving a tough problem, I can take a break. ***I can do something that will nurture my mind, body and soul:*** take a walk, call a friend, go to the movies, read a book, workout, meditate, take a hot bath, fix a good meal, go out for a special coffee, take a nap, make love, go for a drive, go to the beach, hike a trail, play my guitar. Whether I do one thing or a combination of several things to nurture myself, I usually come away feeling refreshed.

One final suggestion: I recommend hiking the trail first; and ***then***, taking the hot bath.

October 27
BELIEVING IN THE GROUP

I seemed to be the outsider most of my life. I rarely felt as though
I belonged. In some circumstances, I even felt like an imposter.
***Hyper-vigilant in my attempt to be what I should be,
I spent a lot of energy denying my own interests.*** I sought the approval
of others, often to the exclusion of being true to myself. I misread
situations, sometimes taking what someone had said or done
in the wrong way. My self-confidence dwindled.
I felt awkward in most social circumstances.

Without really knowing it, I picked a role; a role that represented the ideal of
what I thought I needed to be in order to get what I wanted. I fashioned a
mask of sorts. I grew 'comfortable' in my pursuit of perfecting my lines and
delivery. ***At some point, I believed that I had, in fact, achieved becoming
my idealized self.*** True intimacy with others came to a halt.
I felt compelled to protect the image.

I am invited each week at meetings to take off the mask; to become
transparent in my struggle toward finding my real self. Old habits die hard.
I hold onto my old ideas.

I am ready to stop going to meetings.
I wonder if the whole thing is worth it.
And then something slightly magical happens.

I start ***really hearing*** others tell of their experience: their fears; their
embarrassments, their setbacks. On some level, I relate. I feel sad for some;
contempt for others. I am confused. ***Someone says something with which I
undeniably relate and then the <u>absolute magic</u> happens:***

 <u>I share my own experience for the first time.</u> Nobody shuts me down.
Nobody cuts me off. Nobody presses their opinion. Nobody tries to fix me.
I am simply allowed to speak my mind.

I am thanked for sharing. I am encouraged to 'keep coming back'.
And, I do.

October 28
HEALING IN THE LONG-TERM

It took years to develop a strategy designed to get me through the dysfunction and trauma that came with growing up in my family. These 'coping skills' followed me into adult life.

This evolving mechanism which I had used in order to make sense of my world, in fact, never worked. It only seemed to work.
And yet, I would continue unheeded in my effort for years.

As the days grew more unmanageable, I virtually doubled down on my bet that all would be well if only I 'stick to the script', stay with the plan and maintain more control over myself and others. ***Old ideas (the shoulds) grew hard-wired,*** reinforcing behaviors that had become habitual in nature; no thought required. Just do it!

I realize that the process of recovery, the retrieval of my lost self, is not an overnight matter. ***What took years to create (a false idealized self) is not undone in several weeks.*** On the contrary, the longer I have 'hiked the old canyon trail', the longer it will take to, in fact, get out of the canyon.
I am prepared for a long haul.

I visit and revisit old 'lessons' in dismantling a belief system which continues to drive unproductive behavior. This process takes time and lots of it. ***I am powerless to speed up the process. I am powerless to slow down the process.*** <u>***It moves of its own accord.***</u> I can bring to the setting a willingness to go to any lengths to recover my genuine self: go to meetings, read the literature, and take the Steps. And if that doesn't work, I can always take the Steps, read the literature,
and go to meetings.

My confidence in the long-term healing of the program grows with each passing *year* wherein I **PRACTICE** the program. Will I ever graduate? Doubt it. *'Repetition strengthens and affirms habit; faith, then becomes natural.'*

Play it again, Sam.

October 29
MAINTAINING MY BALANCE

Throughout the years before I found the program, I had difficulty finding and establishing a balance in my loyalties and activities. ***In other words, I often did things that I didn't want to do with people I really didn't like.*** I spent time working on projects for which I had little or no interest. As a result, I felt disconnected with my own life. I was off balance a lot of the time.

Most of the effort put forth in my world was applied to pleasing others. Rare was the time when I functioned from a place of genuine interest. <u>*I was torn in several directions at the same time.*</u> Managing the relationships, the events and the attached outcomes (or the lack thereof) grew to be an impossible challenge. And yet, I thrashed about, ever hopeful of finding the right 'situation' that would finally 'fix' me.

I am on new footing. I am in search of my real self. I let go of old ideas associated with surviving, in exchange for new ideas linked to who I am. *No longer obsessed with being perfect,* <u>*I have extra energy*</u> *to explore a safe world around me; a world virtually unavailable to me as a child.* I take care of myself. I stand on solid ground, confident that I will not abandon myself in order to gain the approval of others.

I move with certainty throughout the day. Having prayed for the knowledge of His will and the power to carry that out, I co-create the events I genuinely want to include in my day; the day God has given me.

I say 'no' to the people and events that no longer serve my interest. <u>*I say 'yes' to those that do.*</u> My thoughts and actions complement one another. No longer driven by conflicting loyalties, I stand firm; loyal to one; myself. Today is the day. Now is the time.

This is not a dress rehearsal. ***This is my life.***

October 30
RE-ESTABLISHING MY SENSE OF CURIOSITY

I had to defend my world at a young age. This pre-occupation with surviving the insanity that comes with living in a dysfunctional family took me away from what might otherwise have been a series of events linked to my natural curiosity with life. *I was deprived the privilege of exploring my world in a reasonably safe and natural way.* My 'real' self was dead on arrival (DOA).

Far from having the time or inclination to discover this thing called 'my life', I had to remain hyper-vigilant lest the adults in my world neglect, abuse or abandon me. This full-time job left me depressed about the past and anxious about the future; and it only got worse.

As time went on, my entire interest lay in the gaining of others' approval. What mattered most was the world on the outside; not the world on the inside.

I am exercising my God-given right to be who I am. I do this by keeping me safe. I do this by letting go of the old exaggerated ideas associated with a false 'survival' self: 'I should always do this; I should always do that'. *Step Seven encourages my enlistment of God's help.* Set free from an unrelenting 'pride system' laced with exaggerated claims and demands, I explore my world unhindered by distraction and 'false' emotion.

Establishing my true interest makes all the difference in the world when it comes to 'spending' my time. I search out my curiosities. I linger at times with a true interest. I am as one who is on a vast expedition. My life is laid out before me like a wide, ever-expanding river canyon.
Whether I am at the library, on the web, in my yard, across town or out of state, *<u>I am open to new ideas;</u>* willing to consider avenues of genuine desire.
The possibilities are endless.
My time is now.

October 31
HOLDING A CONVERSATION

Events leading up to the beginning of school had been very rough. I had already begun harboring secrets without really knowing it. I had already begun to feel ashamed of my circumstances. ***Being in the company of others was very awkward.*** I resorted to taking my cues from those who were obviously in authority. I would say the right things and act the right way; all would be well.

I was a person within a person. I had my 'outside' façade and my inside reality. I fell into the trap of comparing my 'insides' to other's 'outsides'. ***I felt terribly inadequate most of the time***, *not really knowing what to say in the off chance that I might have to talk to someone.*

Fast forward the film to a year before I found the rooms. My anxiety, while around other people, was so intense that I stayed distracted most of the time; in other words, I stayed intoxicated in one form or another: eating, drinking, working, obsessing and the like. I had checked out.

I am discovering a new way to interact with others. By attending meetings over the years, I am learning to listen. ***Usually, when approached openly, most people LOVE to talk about their favorite topic: themselves.***
When feeling awkward about what to say at a party, a wedding, a funeral, a break in between classes, I can merely ask a 'leading question' and listen. I maintain the momentum of conversation by offering
short verbal and non-verbal cues.

When I take the focus off myself, I feel at ease most of the time.

This approach has not only the advantage of increasing my confidence in conversation; it has the added convenience of inviting others to speak freely, as well. ***As a result, I feel more connected.*** And when the time comes to tell of my own life's tale, I have a rather good idea of where to go.

You can inform a cowboy of Manhattan's fascinating opera season, but it would be far more captivating to talk about the time you saw a cow while visiting Texas. Moo.

NOVEMBER

November 1
BEING TRANSPARENT

I worked overtime in grade school trying to fashion a perfect alibi for my father's absence. Finally, I landed on the perfect tale: 'he died in the war'. A few years later, learning that **had** my father 'died in the war' (WWII), I would have never been born. Ooooops; a slight miscalculation. Ironically, nobody ever asked me about my father the whole time I was in school.

As my experiences grew in number, so grew my 'story'. Upon meeting someone for the first time, I talked of a well-rehearsed account of my life. *I would embellish the strong points and avoid the weak ones.*

This effort was a mere symptom. I was really hiding me. I was really protecting me. The belief: if you really knew me, you would never call; you would avoid; you would judge; you would leave. I know the difference between fair weather friends and trustworthy friends; and I have both. I talk to my 'surfacy' friends about sports, new restaurants, old movies, my stamp collection (not really, I have no stamps). *I talk to my substantive friends about everything:* traumatic events past and present, feelings linked to those events, considerations about how to solve problems.

I know the difference between a friend and an intimate friend. I spend time developing the latter. During the transition period of going from one to the other, I am observing how I am received when sharing anything of substance, especially when I talk of how I feel. Is the person receptive? Are they easily distracted, wanting to change the topic? Do they discount and diminish how I feel? Do they try to fix me?

The answers to these simple considerations usually determine the trajectory of the relationship. *__With those whom I trust, my life is an open book.__* Talking honestly with another person is the cornerstone of my healing strategy.

Wilderness Wisdom: It serves no good purpose to go hunting with a fishing pole. It only makes the other hunters talk about you maliciously back at camp.

November 2
MOVING BEYOND DOUBT

By the time I found the rooms of recovery, my confidence level was at an all-time low. The various 'solutions' I had been trying over the years to solve the problem of not having a 'real' self were not working. *In fact, the pursuit of a phantom 'idealized self' set in motion an impossible state of affairs:* quicker, nicer, smarter, slimmer, tougher; more loving, more masterful, more independent; all these demands pushed me and pulled me in ten different directions at one time. I felt exhausted.

I had little or no desire to move 'forward' with much of anything. It seemed my whole life had been structured around making 'something' right that had gone wrong years before. *And to add insult to injury, the making 'something' right was not working. It was only making matters worse.*
I came to not only doubt myself, but I stopped trusting life, as well.
I had given up.

My finally admitting the unmanageability of my life naturally sets in motion a chain of events; one thing leads to another and another. *I discover my first meeting.* And the next thing I know, I am entertaining the idea that perhaps there is hope after all: 'Came to believe that a power greater than myself could restore me to sanity.' Well, there it is. I see others moving beyond being 'stuck'. I reason that if *they* can do it, so can I.

A few Steps later, I am unstuck. I am off the victim story. I embrace my remaining 'real' self. I pursue genuine interests. I let go of the quicker, nicer, smarter demands of my false self and I rest; assured of my innate worth and dignity. *<u>I am a survivor.</u>* I emerge with a life. I get a second chance.

When I act in tandem with my true self, I feel happy; I feel confident. *Sometimes I win; sometimes I lose. That's OK.* The joy is in the journey. The destination is here. *<u>The time is now.</u>*

November 3
HEALING ORGANICALLY

The process by which I survived my dysfunctional family was not natural. *I had to create a false self in order to be what I thought I had to be in order to survive.* The many demands which I created and applied to my condition were over the top; unrealistic. I was perfectly healthy and yet, these 'coping' mechanisms disabled my growth. As one trying to breathe through a pillow, I was suffocating; and I didn't even know it.

'Normal' was not normal. I rehearsed the notion that being 'super-human' was a basic requirement for belonging. *These exaggerated demands set me up for frustration, confusion, indecision and grief.* I expected too much from others, as well. My claims concerning how others ought to behave towards me kept me isolated and sometimes afraid.

Re-connecting with my true self is like seeing an old friend on a crowded street. I tug at the stranger's sleeve, hoping for recognition. Suddenly, we are having coffee at a local shop. *Love is timeless.*

The program invites me to take the focus off others and simply love myself. *<u>I am responsible for keeping myself safe.</u>* I am responsible for supporting myself. I am responsible for nurturing myself.By placing my recovery first in my life for my life, *I position myself in such a way that I can naturally grow.* I say 'no' to old ideas. I say 'yes' to new ideas:

*It's **OK*** to care for myself.
*It's **OK*** to compliment myself.
*It's **OK*** to make sure my needs are met.
*It's **OK*** to keep the focus on me.
*It's **OK*** to treat myself with respect.

I step from the shadows into the light. I am growing, ***naturally***.
Please pass the bean sprouts and tofu.

November 4
MOVING BEYOND THE DISTRACTIONS

The one thing I counted on the most to get me through the tough times was the ability to distract myself when unwanted emotions disrupted my world. In the beginning, the distractions appeared to be those like any other child's preoccupations: playing with toys, playing with others, watching cartoons. ***As time marched on, the distractions grew more and more obsessive.***

By my early teenage years, I had moved from mere obsessions like television, baseball and chocolate to early addictions like cigarettes, girls and booze. At age seventeen, I would have already created a pack a day habit with cigarettes, 'dated' at least two dozen girls and been arrested twice while driving under the influence of alcohol.

I would return time and again to the big three: alcohol, sex and cigarettes. ***Dependency in some form would ultimately dominate my entire life.*** Later, I would add geographic cures, mastery of religion, a 'way-too' ambitious attempt at a college degree and an insanely rigorous career path. I layered one distraction upon another. I felt little or nothing except anxiety and depression.

I am no longer held entirely hostage by obsession. ***The program gives me a daily reprieve from the incessant demands that drove my old ideas;*** old ideas that led to my distorted behavior; distorted behavior that created my anxiety; anxiety that launched my depression; depression that brought on my shame; all of which, ultimately kept me separated from myself and others.

Fixated behavior is not OK. An early pioneer in this recovery process once observed, *'Many of us have tried to hold on to our old ideas, and the result was nil until we let go absolutely.'*

God makes the 'letting go' possible. Thank you, God, for a program. Thank you for the Twelve Steps.

November 5
OWNING THE COLLATERAL DAMAGE

The neurotic world of dependency, whether on display inside or outside my family, left an indelible mark. ***Without question, many distorted beliefs were passed from one generation to the next.*** Many disruptive behaviors were carried over without challenge. I came into the world as one having a 'clean slate' and by early adulthood, the script had been, to a large degree, already written.

As a 'responsible adult', I met and engaged with many people before finding the rooms of recovery. Naturally, I carried a multitude of old ideas and behaviors into these relationships. Some ended well; some, not so much. As one who had been victimized, I acted out many of my old conflicts unconsciously.

'Man takes the act. Then, the act takes the act. And finally, the act takes the man.' ***I was unaware of the process behind what I was doing; nevertheless, I caused harm.*** I perpetrated some of the very same acts that were visited upon me. In some instances, I acted like a monster. I admit it; guilty as charged.

I know today that I am NOT a monster. I am merely a person who was severely affected by someone else's disease. The Eighth Step affords me the opportunity to review those relationships wherein I harmed other people. I realize that most of my hurtful acts resulted from a prolonged unconscious effort to deal with my own emotional pain. In some cases, the collateral damage was egregious. The Ninth Step offers a clear opportunity to own my part in past disturbances. ***I take this Step so that I can recover.*** I may want to re-establish relations; I may not. Whether my amends is accepted or not is immaterial. ***I DO THIS FOR ME.*** My purpose is clear: to move toward a better relationship with God, myself and others.

I DO NOT OWE ANY PERPETRATOR OF ABUSE AN APOLOGY FOR THE SO-CALLED, 'MY PART'.

I place myself at the top of the list. ***At the end of the day, this is a selfish program; I am number one.*** I deserve a life free from tyrannical shame and self-loathing. 'God knows the hurt I suffered; the pain I rise above.' I deserve a life. I deserve a life ***that works.***

November 6
SAYING GOODBYE TO SELF DESTRUCTION

Whether I was trying to avoid feelings of shame and depression or simply trying to 'escape' the frustrations that go with living in dysfunction, I sought out ways in which I could 'check out'.

I needed a constant supply of distractions in order to get through the day. I grew addicted to excitement, fear and to some extent, pain itself. Expanding my potential as a growing, living human being was greatly hindered due to the ever- increasing demands I placed on myself to be what I should be all the time. ***I employed a constant vigilance toward becoming my 'idealized' self.*** My 'real' self, I abandoned.

With the loss of operating from my true self came the loss of growing naturally. To the degree that I denied my own genuine interests in pursuit of demands made by a false self, I became more and more destructive with my 'distractions'. It seemed my entire life had been thwarted in pursuit of solutions designed for problems I had not created. My spontaneous capacity for expressing my thoughts and feelings had decomposed. I hated myself. Self-destruction, in one form or another, would become a silent obsession; covert, even to me.

I celebrate my true self today. I have examined my old ideas thoroughly, admitting the obsessive-compulsive nature of their false demands. ***I am no longer a miserable prisoner in my own house.*** I release the diabolical dictates, not only on myself, but on others, as well.
I enjoy a growing ease with daily events.

Far from attempting to avoid my thoughts and feelings, I awaken to a burgeoning world of new intellectual and emotional dimension. ***I connect with this unfolding world of possibility.*** I keep myself safe.
Reality is my friend. I have interests. I ***WANT*** to live.

If a behavior stunts my growth, I change it immediately with the help of God. If a behavior promotes my growth, I embrace it
with all the strength I have.

I say 'no' to destruction.   I say 'yes' to life.

November 7
LEARNING FROM LIFE'S INTERACTIONS

One of the core beliefs coming out of my old life sounded like this: 'Painful events are to be avoided; therefore, you should always move on; you should always put them out of your mind'. *This policy of never looking back did not serve me.* In fact, I kept applying this same old solution to new problems, hoping for different results.

One of the ways I chose to 'move on' came in the form of alcohol. I could 'move on' without ever leaving my driveway. After finding the rooms of recovery, I switched from my primary addictions, drugs and alcohol; to my secondary addictions: geographical cures and co-dependent relationships.

Ironically, I began learning about how *NOT* to do life. In other words, my emotional pain (because I was allowing myself to feel) grew with such an undeniable force that I became 'teachable'. Pain is a great motivator. The Steps seemed to be the 'easier, softer' way to go.

Eventually, I would 'humbly asked him to remove' my shortcomings. *Looking back, I realize now that God was doing for me what I could not or would not do for myself long before I formally took the Seventh Step.* The recovery process, at some point unbeknownst to me, had already begun; a process so precise, so calculated, so mysterious that the ensuing result, the removal of a shortcoming, rarely presented itself until long after the pursuant events were over. Rather than my having taken the Steps, it seemed as though the Steps had been taking me. Willingness was the key, unlocking the door of 'grace' all along.

I am usually the last to know of my own progress in the program. I practice, nevertheless. When old feelings surface as a result of new events (when I am 'triggered'), I promptly submit the incident for *THOROUGH* consideration in a Tenth Step. This is where I learn. This is where I get better. As a result, I recognize old emotions, raging in current conditions a lot sooner. I resist the urge to 'blame'. I go to the Tenth Step. *I gain more and more 'clarity' into the errors of my past thinking that continue to set me up for disappointment in the here and now.* Painful events become the schoolroom wherein I truly learn how to move beyond the grief, embarrassment and shame of the past. I no longer regret my former life.
I do not wish to shut the doors to the past.
It is from these corridors that I learn the most.

November 8
PAYING ATTENTION TO MY INTUITIVE SELF

Growing up in a distorted environment, I had to deny my true feelings. This enabled me to be laser-focused on the outside world. *The old survival tactic went something like: My world is unsafe and unpredictable; therefore, I should always be on alert for trouble.* This old idea served me well. I survived. However, channeling out my emotions left me with very little confidence, if any, in myself. I took most of my cues from others.

By placing my attention on external forces, usually those in authority, I severely limited the growth of an emerging genuine self. In fact, I had to squelch the 'voice' of my true self, lest it interfere with the more important business at hand; that of 'surviving'. I would eventually bury my 'real' self, alive; adopting a false self, more qualified for the job of 'environmental control'.

With the help of the program, I am unearthing my true self. The Steps are resuscitating an otherwise, dead self. *As one brought back to consciousness, following a lengthy coma, I am uncertain of how to respond to this 'new' world.* Feelings are returning. I am encouraged to talk about them. Old events, once never addressed, are appearing. I am encouraged to talk about them.
I am angry. I am sad. I am grieved.

I struggle with recalling the events of the past, the people involved, and the fallout of emotions still lingering. *Nevertheless, I muddle through with the taking of Steps Four and Five.*

I am crying more. I am laughing more. I am talking more. I am connecting with myself and those around me who are safe. I am coming out. I am trusting my own internal perception regarding current external events.

I intuitively know how to handle situations that used to baffle me. *__I am alive, and well__*. Thank God.

November 9
REUJUVINATING MY SOUL

In terms of 'old school' description, I virtually 'sold my soul' in order to survive growing up in a dysfunctional family. It seemed like a good idea at the time. It seemed like the only idea at the time.Hey! Wait a minute. It WAS the only idea at the time. ***I did what I had to do in order to stay alive.*** 'Desperate times call for desperate measures.'

What started as a mere strategy developed into an entire moral structure. False though it was, I nevertheless, marched to its orders. I obeyed its commands. I even prided myself on how well I acted out its 'requirements' for myself and others. *A mounting drive possessed my every waking hour to become this imagined, idealized self.* And what was the grand prize? Anxiety, depression, self-hate and false security. And what was the cost? The abandonment of my own soul.

The program reaches out. The program says, 'Enter here, all you who labor with no reward. Enter here, all you who have no hope.' Having the good fortune of reconnecting with my true self by taking most of the Steps (one thru nine), *I am willing to go a few Steps further.* Yes, the truly hard work is behind me; and yes, I have recovered my lost self; but I cannot afford to stop now. In my effort to nurture myself back to life, Steps Ten, Eleven and Twelve (the maintenance Steps) summon my full attention.

This 'fine tuning' of the program removes the remaining 'static due to poor reception' (an old reference to radio days). ***I want to be 'dialed in' to my real self.*** I *want* to act according to my genuine interests and desires. I *want* to be true to who I am.

I AM RESPONSIBLE for rejuvenating the growth and development of my recovered self; my real self. Step Ten: I am honest in owning my still twisted thinking. Step Eleven:

I am open to enlisting God's help to guide me through these current days.

Step Twelve: With this new-found spiritual awakening, I am *supremely privileged* to carry the message to those who still suffer.

November 10
STAYING WITH MY EMOTIONS

The one thing that measured my 'progress' the most was my behavior. Whether operating in my family or working outside the home, ***I judged myself by how well I performed.*** I associated staying alive with acting perfectly. I lived in a state of high anxiety most of the time without really knowing it. ***I became very skilled at 'turning off' my emotions.*** I shut down my feelings, hoping to tune out 'unnecessary' distractions. My emotions simply got in the way.

Going entirely numb requires time. As the years unfolded, I became a walking robot fixated on my ideal 'role' and how I should always behave in that role. Conforming to what I thought to be an 'idealized' self, I disregarded all emotion. ***I was cut off from life.*** The only thing that mattered was my performance; my ability to deliver. When I did allow feelings, they were rarely experienced in the moment. I usually had to wait until after the event to feel anything associated with being there.

The First Step challenges me to admit that my 'life' has become unmanageable. I realize today that I can no longer maintain a policy of emotional management. I am powerless to 'control' my feelings; always was. ***Now I know the unmitigated TRUTH: 'I live in as much as I feel; no more, no less'.***

The Second Step states a fact: the hope of sanity is possible. ***Sanity is simply defined as 'one's having the capacity to consciously think and feel, thus, prompting a genuinely reasonable act.*** My feelings have always been a part of me. The notion that I can turn my emotions on and off like I would a water spicket is insane.

With the help of the group, I am growing more aware of how I feel. I am checking in with myself throughout the day; mad, sad or glad. ***I am sitting with my emotions.*** I am talking about how I feel. This, for me, is **GREAT** progress. This, for me, is the sheer essence of Steps One and Two.

'I want to feel what I am feeling, at the time that I am feeling it, about what I am feeling it about.'

November 11
CHANGING OBSESSIVE THOUGHTS

I was entirely unaware of the one capacity unique to all human beings; foreign to the rest of all God's creatures, great and small: the 'magical' ability to change one's mind. ***I single-handedly pioneered a trail, uniquely designed to guarantee my survival as a child.**† The trail became a clear-cut path. This path, well-worn over the years, would be forever etched in my mind. It would become the only way I knew how to live.

I grew 'comfortable' in my day's routine. Limited though it was, the 'rut' leading to the lane was familiar. I met another with whom I would venture forth into the broader road; another with whom I could relate. Old fears were shared; old ideas validated. I made a promise: I will do whatever you tell me to do so that I can feel safe and respected. ***Loyalty reigned supreme.*** And so, that is how my long relationship with and total submission to my 'false-self' began. I was obsessed with obeying its rules. Its demands would become hard-wired in my thinking.

A false self's moral system, comprised of nagging habitual ideas, literally has a mind of its own. This twisted belief system, used to fortify the creation and support of a driven 'idealized' self, is virtually **IMPOSSIBLE** to deconstruct. ***The unaided 'human will' is rendered powerless.***
That's where the Third Step comes in. That's where God comes in.

I stand at a turning point. I ask for protection and care with complete abandon. I make a decision to turn my will and my life over to the care of God as I understand Him (or Her; or It). I realize that the task which lies ahead, the **ACTION** to take the rest of the Steps, is **IMPOSSIBLE** without the help of God *in one form or another*.

This will be a life-long endeavor. Proceeding one day at a time, *I look at my past:* the relationships, the events, the feelings and the beliefs which shape who I am. Whether I am looking at an incident that happened twenty minutes ago or twenty years ago, I can challenge the old demands behind the old ideas that are no longer serving my best interest. I am willing. I am able. I am ready. ***BRING IT ON!***

November 12
RECEIVING THE ANSWER (part one)

Due, in large part, to the unavailability of responsible adults in my life, I was left to figure things out on my own. I guessed at what 'normal' was. I faked it. **<u>When I did ask for help, I was often dismissed;</u>** the insinuation being that my needs were not important. I felt as though I was an inconvenience; a nuisance.

I would come to rely on practically no one else in order to get the answers I needed. I gave up using my voice to ask for help. I was embarrassed to admit that I didn't know. On the rare occasion when I *would* work up the courage to request something, if the appeal was denied or postponed, I felt humiliated. *I moved through life much like one walking a high wire by candlelight; uncertain and frustrated with every step.*

I am no longer disabled with the old idea that 'truly worthwhile' people always act independently; that I *should*, therefore, never ask for help. Valuable people enlist others' assistance all the time.
<u>It's OK to use my voice to ask for what I need.</u> Period. End of conversation.

There is only one more little problem; timing. Another old idea sets me up: I should always get what I need when I need it. *When I ask others for support, sometimes they come through; sometimes they don't.*
I can embrace that, but what about the times in prayer when I ask God for support? The answer may reveal itself within the hour or the 'answer' may seem to never appear. What then?

I am a mere mortal reconciled to a life of trust; trust in a power greater than myself that sometimes presents itself in the form of other people; sometimes presents itself in the form of conditions and circumstances. In *practicing* Step Eleven, I often come to an intuitive thought regarding a baffling, reoccurring situation. Eureka! I get what I need. Or sometimes, I slowly realize that God is doing for me, *at this moment*, what I *cannot or will not* do for myself. Some call this acceptance.

I call it an *AFGE…A*nother *F*rustrating *G*rowth *E*xperience.
In any event, I can *always* ask for what I need.
No shame, no blame. No fuss, no muss

November 13
RECEIVING THE ANSWER (part two)

I rarely had the chance to simply talk things over with the responsible adults in my life. And when I was given some time to talk, my disclosure was often met with authoritarian 'solutions' that really did not work.

In other words, my sharing was met with approaches like the following: directing me, warning me, preaching to me, distracting me, giving me logical arguments, judging me, interrogating me or advising me. Although I nodded in agreement, my heart *rarely* got the answer I needed.

Today, I move toward people who are available; people who can listen; people who can support me right where I am without trying to fix me. *When I am given ample time to talk about a problem without interruption, I usually discover a genuine solution that really works for me.*
The answer I need comes from within.

When an answer is not immediately forthcoming, I can always ask for someone else's 'input'. *I take what I like, and I leave the rest.* Sometimes another person's 'experience, strength and hope' lends an entire new perspective to an old problem; sometimes another person's suggestions only confuse me more.

I am no longer compelled to follow any 'suggestions' that do not feel right for me. I allow time to take its due course. I am realistic. I know that certain problems are not solved in a day or even a week. Time takes time. *I am willing to practice Step Eleven, remaining in the day, hoping for a solution to present itself; a solution that genuinely works for me.*

'When the student is ready, the teacher will appear'; and I get the answer I need. Has anyone seen my writing tablet and pencil?

November 14
MAINTAINING OPTIONS

By the time I turned fourteen, I had created a belief system that virtually locked me in. I was committed to a specific approach when it came to handling conflict and uncertainty. Rarely did I deviate. *I felt proud when I remained true to this survival 'morality'.* I romanticized a time when I would perfect this ideal way of life.

Like most people raised in dysfunctional settings, I was hyper-intelligent; almost too smart. I waged my own secret war against those I perceived to be a threat. I was 'locked and loaded', laser focused on my mission. <u>*Nothing would stop me from becoming my triumphant, idealized self.*</u> Functioning much like an unfeeling machine, I maintained my course, regardless. I often took counter-productive action out of habit, spending an inordinate amount of time 'cleaning up the mess' *...later*.

The 'tyranny of shoulds' no longer dominates my every waking moment. The 'itty-bitty-shitty committee' in my head is in recess. *I have a reprieve, of sorts, now that I have taken the Fourth and Fifth Steps.* Rather than locking myself into a course of action with any one person, group or institution, I develop several possibilities: plan A, plan B; even a plan C, if need be. I am free to change course at any time.

The nurture of my true self is priority one. I am loyal to myself, first. Regarding others, I place loyalty where loyalty is deserved. *Being able to move freely in a world unfettered by exaggerated expectations for myself and others is like having an all-day pass at the county fair.* I pet the ducks, I ride the roller coaster, I have some cotton candy, maybe a hot dog; or I have a hot dog, ride the roller coaster, then pet the ducks.
The choice is all mine.

Hey! Maybe Aunt Peggy would like to go. On second thought, maybe not. She hates ducks.

November 15
TAKING THE ACTION; LETTING GO OF THE RESULTS

By the time I found the rooms, I had come to see myself as a failure, although I rarely admitted it; even to myself. ***In short, I hated myself.*** I had become an egomaniac with an inferiority complex. I had accomplished a lot. I had failed a little. I focused on the 'failed a little' aspects of my life. I had come to demand nothing short of perfection. Any shortcoming was further 'proof' my inadequacy.

To make matters worse, I thought and acted mostly out of habit; doing the same thing again and again, expecting different results. It was all I really knew *how* to do. This way of life was ingrained. ***My false 'survival' self was calling all the shots.*** I performed its bidding. The right 'results' were an absolute must. My identity depended on it.

I am on new footing. I operate most of the time from a sense of loyalty to my *genuine* self. I act spontaneously. I meet new challenges with a fresh approach. Winning is still important. I like getting the results I hope to achieve. And yet, I am letting go of the 'all or nothing' approach to solving problems. ***Sometimes I get what I want; sometimes I don't.*** Nobody wins *all* the time. I accept life on life's terms.

Here is the grandest thing of all. Feeling productive is no longer dependent on getting the outcome I demand. I feel productive when I simply act according to how I genuinely think and feel. ***When my actions match my true interests and desires, I feel gratified in the process.*** I hope for certain results and yet, I can let go of the need for 'perfect' performances.

A famous failing bull-rider when asked why he kept riding bulls, only to be thrown off time after time, responded: 'I just love the freedom of feeling airborne right before I hit the ground'.

Hmmmm. OK. Ride 'em, cowboy!

November 16
BECOMING MORE REALISTIC

Because my dysfunctional world had no 'off' switch, *I had to create a future in my mind that would carry me far away from all the trouble.* Someday I would find that person who would truly love and appreciate me. Someday I would become so independent that I would need no one. Someday I would become so successful that everyone would feel compelled to respect and adore me.

When the future finally arrived, the exaggerated expectations launched toward others and the unrealistic demands placed on myself proved to be too great for reality. 'Reality' had not been my friend for some time. *I lived in a perpetual state of disappointment and skepticism.* As the years rolled by, I became more and more withdrawn; isolated in a world of what could've, would've or should've been.

I am processing events that occurred during my formative years. I am owning how I felt at the time. I am uncovering the beliefs that were formed. At the center lies the **UNRELENTING DEMAND** which dictates not only how *I should always* act, but how *others should always* act, as well. This old notion; this old idea continues to set me up for shame, blame and resentment.

The Fifth Step invites me to own this fundamental flaw in my thinking; this 'all or nothing' claim which leads to all kinds of unproductive behavior; all kinds of 'wrongs', if you prefer. *This juggernaut; this tangled mass of prideful delusion IS the epicenter; IS the 'exact nature' of my wrongs.* It is **EASILY** undone.

I, quite simply, accommodate **THE TRUTH: I am not God.** Steps Six and Seven await my arrival. Human nature *itself* is, in fact, the 'exact' nature of my earthly wrongs. Humility suggests that *I have no more control over myself all the time than I have control over anybody else.* Realistically speaking, sometimes I behave the way I want and sometimes I don't. I am a mere mortal; a mere mortal amongst billions of other mere mortals. *Does this fact dismiss my moral responsibility to myself and others? Absolutely not.* My well-being (my peace of mind) is directly related to the *willingness* I bring to bear on lowering my prideful demands; and all the while, *remaining true to who I am*.

November 17
RESPECTING THE DISEASE

My family members were victims of an invisible and insidious genetic disease passed on by generations of exchange. I had no idea. *No one else did either* up until the early 1900's. Before that, the disease was interpreted as a moral issue. *The disease certainly FELT like a moral issue for me;* Mother's leaving me unattended for the night, Dad's unwillingness to send child-support payments, Mother's rants and inappropriate behavior, her drunken episodes.

I was ashamed of my mother and father; and thus, I was ashamed of myself. This disease felt dirty. Immoral acts were committed. Verbal and physical acts of abuse were practiced. I believed that other children's parents were normal like the ones I saw on television. *I thought we were the only ones that acted the way we did.* People who behaved as my parents were viewed as 'no damned good, sorry, low-life and evil'.

I know today that my parents were not 'evil'. They were no more 'low-life' than the other children's parents on the block. They were human beings; mere mortals; creatures susceptible to pain and suffering; illness and death. *I know today that my parents, IN THEIR OWN WAY, battled this silent disease;* a disease, the nature of which, still dodges the best effort to develop a 'cure'.

I have the disease. Am I immoral? *My children have the disease. Are they 'evil'?* Are we 'defective characters'? Are we riddled with wicked 'shortcomings'? If being a mere mortal constitutes guilt, I guess the answer is 'yes' to all the above. *TRUTH:* There is no shame in being, feeling and acting like a human being on planet earth.
Last time I checked; I *AM* a human being!

You can put a cowboy hat on a pig, dress it up, take it to the dance; but at the end of the night, it's still a pig. I just *LOVE* little cowboy piggies. Oink, oink.

November 18
CREATING HEALTHY BELIEFS

At the core of my dysfunction lay an overwhelming moral structure that served to 'protect' me. I had very little to do with creating this system. It had a mind of its own. I selected and adopted strategies in a most unconscious manner. The idea that I had choices never occurred to me.

Whether the tactic played out as always being compliant, always being independent or always being masterful, *I rarely experienced myself as being reasonably confident in who I was.* I was 'an identity crisis having an identity crisis'.

To make matters more difficult to navigate, the developing beliefs themselves often contradicted one another. *How could I 'detach' from my family* and remain loving and 'loyal'? How could I be a 'giving' person and, at the same time, be competitively 'ambitious'?
How could I succeed and not feel guilty?

I felt like two people pulling in opposite directions.

With the help of the program, I am awakening to choices. I take Steps Four and Five in order to vacate a space, once clouded with contradiction, so that I can create a new space; a new space more reflective of my conscious self; my real self. *I keep the beliefs I want to keep. I let the others go.*
Steps Six and Seven make this process possible.

With each new day, I encounter new experiences; and with those new experiences, I am feeling the emotions associated with those new experiences.

*No longer burdened with the fear of abandonment,
I am free to connect real-time events with real-time feelings.*
I create new beliefs around my actual well-being. I create new beliefs around what is, in fact, **WORKING** for me today.
I feel to be real and I get real to heal.

November 19
COLLECTING MY SUCCESSES

There was a time when I could not accept a compliment. My pride system was so intense that I rarely experienced any accomplishment without feeling the nagging secret message of shame; 'you could have done better, you should have done it the other way, it would have been perfect if you had just…'; *__I felt like an imposter.__* I focused on what I had done wrong. I was, by far, my own worst critic. I came to see myself as a perpetual failure.

This neurotic demand for perfection resonated from my very human need to be included; especially to be included by my family, upon which I was utterly dependent.

__The reasoning went something like this: the better I perform according to what I should be, the greater my chances for not being rejected; the greater my chances for survival.__

I am a survivor. I am no longer in danger. I create a safe place where I can live. I am included by healthy people. I belong. I experience my real self against the backdrop of the total human condition. Sometimes I accomplish exactly what I hope for. *I compliment myself.*

When I choose to act in a way that is complimentary to what I think, what I feel and what I hope for, I usually walk away gratified; regardless of the 'result'. *__It is simply enough to be who I am.__*

And, upon occasion, when I do get the exact outcome I want, wow! What a feeling! I take note of these moments. *I cherish the times when I express my true nature in a way that is tangible; notable.*

I embrace the thrill of success. And when others pay me a compliment, I have discovered an amazing fact: 'Thank you' *IS* a complete sentence. *__Thank you__*. See?

November 20
MAKING MY NEEDS KNOWN

Requesting help, in my mind, was a sign of weakness. I secretly feared being 'left behind' should I fall short. I came to see myself as an inconvenience. **<u>Minor mistakes loomed large.</u>** I often felt the brunt of my mother's impatience when events proved difficult. Somehow, I was to blame. Verbal abuse accompanied her frustration, as well as, occasional physical episodes.

I came to believe that my best strategy was to avoid asking for help at all if I were to survive. **<u>I would soon withdraw into my own world,</u>** avoiding trouble with Mother at all costs. I attempted to gain her approval by being who I thought I should be in order to not be rejected.

I denied my own genuine need for love and support, placing my emphasis rather on how I could mold myself into the 'ideal'. This shift in my young mind proved to be *the turning point of no return.* I applied this approach far into my adult life, especially as it related to people from whom I needed approval.

Today, I have reconnected with my real self; that part of me that needs to love and be loved; that part of me that needs to feel genuinely respected. I make healthy choices about the people with whom I honestly relate. **<u>The process of a caring relationship allows for transparency:</u>** 'this is what I see happening, this is how I feel *when* I see it, and this is what I need'.

I am interdependent with others. I advocate for my needs, requesting what I prefer. Sometimes people further my growth; sometimes they hinder my growth. I am the only person that can know the difference. **<u>I can always negotiate a new deal when the old deal isn't working.</u>** I am prepared to walk away from any deal that is spiritually, emotionally or physically harmful to me.

I am true to myself. I risk making my needs known. **<u>The risk is worth it.</u>** I emerge knowing myself a little better each time. Sometimes I get what I want; sometimes I don't. And, gosh-darnit, that's OK.

November 21
BELIEVING IN 'MY WAY'

I spent all my young life and most of my adult life trying to figure out who I was supposed to be. I took my cues from the environment. I wanted to feel included. I wanted to feel appreciated. ***I did what I had to do in order to gain approval.*** In the process, I lost myself. I judged myself harshly according to how well I acted out who I thought I should be all the time.

I carried into most situations an image, an illusion, of how I should behave under every condition. ***I 'beat myself up' when I failed to live up to this idealized self.*** My demands were unrelenting. The worst thing of all; the demands were usually unrelated to my genuine interests. In fact, I had buried my real self for years; one shovel full of demands at a time. I performed mostly out of habit.

I am unique. No other person on earth is quite like I am. I like that idea. I have the capacity to remember the people and events that have shaped my thoughts and feelings. I also have the freedom to choose what beliefs I want to keep from those relationships *and* which ones I want to release. In this process of give and take, I establish myself. I create new ideas, new beliefs, and new interests. I create a fresh approach to my identity with each passing day.

Being who I am, and risking action involves, in and of itself, a universal concept common to man from the beginning: winning and losing. I am reasonably free to express my true self that lives inside. Sometimes I get the outcome I want; sometimes I don't.

I *own* who I am. I *own* how I think. I *own* how I feel. I *own* how I act. The action I take, at any given moment, is 'my way', regardless of outside 'inspiration or influence'. ***I celebrate who I am.***

I *believe* in my way. And, win or lose, I act with confidence.

November 22
RENEWING MY INNER STRENGTH

Because survival carried a full-time priority status, I rarely allowed myself to take a break. *It seemed there was always something that required my attention.* Whether I was looking to some future event or reviewing some past action, I was preoccupied with gaining the approval of another.
I was exhausted.

A pervasive anxiety mounted over the years, as the resounding demand to always act as I should dominated much of my thinking. *I came to identify with an ideal way of dealing with life.*
And when I failed, there was hell to pay.

To further complicate matters, my false beliefs associated with this 'ideal' self were often at odds. *In other words, I was damned if I took a certain path and damned if I didn't.* I spent an inordinate amount of emotional energy just getting through the day as the battle raged on.

For the most part, I have let go of the intrusive nature of a life dominated by unrealistic expectations for myself and others. I review old ideas attached to extravagant anxieties by taking a Fourth and Fifth Step.
I am entirely ready to be free of these unrealistic notions.

As one awaiting the arrival of a long-lost friend, I am making room for the return of my 'real' self. I am connecting with how I *really* feel.
I create a safe place inwardly. I return to that place often. *I rest.*

I explore new ideas. I act in accord with my genuine interests. My sense of self **IS** my strength. With each passing day, I practice the art of nurturing who I am. Being who I am is fun and easy because it's so natural. Relating to an inner core of curiosity and wonder releases a sense of being truly alive. I explore my world with the wide-open eyes of a child.
I embrace my well-being. *I embrace my true self.*

November 23
GETTING THROUGH THE HOLIDAYS

Holidays of the past seemed like a reoccurring staged play wherein every actor stepped into their familiar role and, as if on cue, performed in accord with the unfolding events just as they had for years. ***The predictability of the 'show' itself gave rise to anxious feelings.*** Of necessity, there would be certain topics to be avoided, certain people to be placated and certain distractions to be embraced like food and drink and televised sports.

At the end of a good day, everyone would retreat to their respective quarters with their respective issues neatly tucked away, respectively having had a 'good time', and respectively having avoided any conscious emotions attached to the 'festive' event.

At the end of a bad day, there would have been those for whom no amount of distraction could conceal their seething resentment, no topic too 'off-limits' and no person so respected as to be free from attack, covert or otherwise. ***In short, the holidays were a crap shoot.*** Rather like sampling an assorted box of chocolates; one never knew what one might bite into. One had to bite to find out.

I establish myself. And with that establishment, I am no longer compelled to bite. ***I have boundaries.*** I don't take the bait. I am part of an alcoholic family. I am easily entertained, as I detach from my old compulsive role and connect as an amused spectator. The holiday setting can be fun.

I am free to take what I like and leave the rest. All my family and friends are on their separate journeys during this holiday season. ***I celebrate the spontaneity and beauty of the unfolding human drama called life.***

Deck the halls, carve the turkey, hang a stocking, steal a kiss, have a second helping; but whatever I do, wherever I go, I always have an exit plan. Now, where ***did*** I put those car keys?

November 24
KEEPING IT SIMPLE (part one)

Relationships in my adult life resembled to a large extent what my relationships had been like in my family. I had been totally enmeshed with my parents. In my young mind, rejection felt like neglect. *And, on some primal level, neglect seemed like death itself.* I was entirely dependent on my parents for support. Survival trumped everything.

The solution seemed simple: behave and all will be well. Only, all was not well. All could never be well with parents who were *chronically* unavailable. As the old saying goes, 'love me, hate me, but for God's sake, don't ignore me'. Rejection I could deal with, neglect was a whole different game. Thus, I changed my solution. *I would go beyond mere conformity and PROVE my worth to the family;* thus, I would be an asset; my survival essentially guaranteed.

Over the years, I tested new ideas about how I should always act. These new ways of thinking centered around three basic approaches to relationships: moving toward others, moving away from others and moving against others. Through trial and error, I eventually selected my primary 'solution'. <u>I doubled down my bet on always behaving a certain way.</u>
This, it seemed, would solve the isolation issue. I took great pride in my chosen course. This 'moral' system would dictate my every waking moment for years to come. I was terrified of abandonment.

A common denominator in my ensuing relations after family seemed to be the *dependency* factor. 'Alone' was not OK. Whether I saw myself as a rescuer, a victim or a perpetrator, I brought specific strategies to bear on all my significant relationships. *And all these tactics were designed to do one thing; remove the agonizing feeling of death itself by proving my worth.* Here is the simple part: *I AM A SURVIVOR.* Regardless of my 'progress' in recovery or lack thereof, I am a living, breathing human being capable of staying alive. I am strong.

<u>I need prove nothing to anyone, including myself.</u>
Just for today, I celebrate the touch, taste and smell of life.
I see and hear the world around me.
I am alive, after all.

November 25
KEEPING IT SIMPLE (part two)

One of the agonizing subliminal messages in my family seemed to be: you're never going to be good enough. And yet, I tried with all my heart to be the person I thought I should be. ***Of necessity, I would go through stages of what the 'should be' looked like.*** Somedays a saint, somedays a loner, somedays a Billy-bad-ass; but, everyday looking to prove something to myself and others.

Eventually, I would pick one primary way to deal with my flagging self-esteem. I romanticized how becoming that idealized self would truly look: perhaps a doctor, a minister, a teacher, a gunslinger, a cop, a monk, a wilderness junkie, a wise philosopher, a football player, a movie star, a rock n' roll legend, a foreign correspondent, a secret agent.
The list could go on ad infinitum.

I am grounding myself in the here and now. Sometimes reality sucks. Nevertheless, I am alive. I have an opportunity to recover my lost self; the one that got buried alive as I pursued the demands of my idealized self. ***This real self is at the core of who I am.*** I search through the rubble.
I reach out, embracing this long-lost friend; no demands, nothing to prove.

Today is the day. Now is the time. I explore my genuine self.
No longer driven by the need to become something more,
I am free to think and feel just as I am.

When I act according to how I genuinely think and feel,
I usually stay reasonably grounded. I stay connected to my real self.
In other words, I stay sober. I am keeping it real…

ONE DAY, ONE HOUR, ONE MINUTE AT A TIME.

November 26
FINDING NEW FRIENDS

Going outside the 'comfort zone' of my established setting with family and friends seemed impossible. Indeed, 'birds of a feather flock together'; and when they're not flocking, they're planning for the next time when they CAN flock; thus, the holidays. ***Holidays are a time of flocking.***
(except for the unfortunate turkey)

I usually felt obligated to attend family gatherings. I was loyal to friends, as well. ***And, quite naturally, I played my 'role'. (hero, scapegoat, lost child, mascot) I knew my lines.*** I knew the script. And I was intimately familiar with the story. For the most part, these parties lent a certain accustomed levity to life; a distraction with a twist of fun.

At least, that was the hope. ***More often, the occasions would take a turn for the worse:*** harsh words spoken, boundaries stepped on, subtle inferences scattered here and there; even drunken brawls. Are we having fun yet?

I have a difficult time during the holidays. ***I feel anxious about the days leading up to and during the holiday season.*** These are times rife with memories; some good, some bad. These are times when my emotions are attached to a 'hair trigger'. I can react at any time for any reason.

I keep myself safe when I go to holiday parties. ***I usually have an entry plan and an exit strategy.*** I know how long I can 'tolerate' the behavior of others. I can detach with courtesy. I give myself permission to leave, as well.

Sometimes I include a meeting in my holiday rounds. ***I have come to count on my faithful friends in the program to bring me back to center.*** In any party setting, holiday or otherwise, I can *R*etreat, *R*egroup and *R*eturn. ***I have friends*** upon whom I can absolutely rely.

November 27
TRUSTING THE TRUSTWORTHY

Part of the big problem, before and after finding recovery, was my uncanny ability to pick people who were so narcissistic that they had little or no capacity to think of anyone else but themselves.

<u>I was, in fact, one of those people.</u> I was so preoccupied with arranging and re-arranging my 'insides', that the 'outsides' completely past me by. Opportunities to connect with others on a genuine level were impossible. I was 'unavailable'.

I was attracted to others who, like myself, took themselves very seriously. I had great difficulty trusting others with 'sensitive' information. *I avoided true intimacy; the kind where I tell another person how I really feel about what is indeed going on.* I relied on emotional 'honesty' only as a last resort. I preferred to make stuff up when to tell the truth would have worked just as well.

I am becoming more transparent as I select people who are safe; people who see emotional honesty as a good thing; people who can make off their mask long enough to let me take off my mask.

<u>This mutual 'unmasking' requires trust.</u> Much like one approaching a swimming pool on a cool summer's day, I dip my toe in the water to test the temperature **BEFORE** diving in head-first. I am outgrowing my addiction to excitement.

When connecting with another, *I offer small samples of emotionally charged events* when talking about the past. I wait. The response can go one of two ways; supportive or non-supportive. When supportive, I may choose to proceed. When non-supportive, I can assess that today may not be the best day to go for a swim.

Now. Where **DID** I put my sun-tan lotion?

November 28
LOVING OTHERS

Early in the 'dance' with my family, I rehearsed the idea of compliance as a solution to 'getting along'. The simple logic: if I do what is expected of me, I will be approved and included. I will not be abandoned. ***And so, I acted out my need to survive.*** I called it 'love'. I honored my mother and father.

As time went on, gaining the approval of my parents proved to be a difficult endeavor. The 'bar' seemed to be getting higher and higher. It seemed like the more I tried to 'love' my parents, the further and further apart we grew. ***Aspects of physical and verbal abuse coupled with sheer neglect left me cynical and cautious.*** The element of ***emotional absence*** played a big factor. And yet, I remained unduly optimistic and loyal.

I am learning in the rooms how to love others without losing myself in the process. It seems to me that the cornerstone upon which the program rests is the concept of autonomy; the right to be who I am.

I respond to my own journey, in my own way, in my own time.
I am supported by those in the rooms. I am respected
in my effort to recover my lost self.

Regardless of how I may judge another's progress, I am learning to truly value their sovereign struggle. I support others by primarily listening, thus giving them the gift of human 'presence'. ***Sometimes I need say only a little as I provide a safe emotional space where others can explore their own problems, in their own way.***

I give others the opportunity to discover their own solutions. I genuinely appreciate each person's attempt at becoming who they are; free and independent.

November 29
BEING LOVED

Growing up, I believed that my worth and value was entirely dependent on how well I performed. I don't remember a time when any adult directly established this expectation, but it seemed crystal clear by age six. ***I began rehearsing the notion that I should always behave in a specific way in order to be loved.*** I would pursue this obsession for the better part of my life.

Whether I needed the approval of an entire group or just one person, I was entirely ready to 'sell my soul' in order to be included. ***I feared rejection.*** I was terrified of abandonment.

The program gives me a clear way whereby I can recover and discover my real self; the self I had to leave behind in my compulsive drive to be loved and accepted. ***I am potentially free to love myself,*** however, I still face battles with my false self; that demanding, dominating part of me that insists on my undivided attention; that insists on my unadulterated loyalty; that insists on doing life the old way. ***I struggle.***

I respect my own process in the letting go of old ideas that keep setting me up for a lifetime of hatred and disdain toward my actual self. ***I am lowering the demands. I am becoming more realistic toward myself in what I can and cannot do. I allow for mistakes.*** I make room for setbacks.

I realize that being loved is an 'inside' job. When I genuinely love and accept myself, I am naturally attracted to those who can genuinely love and accept me, as well.

In short, I enhance a more tolerant position toward my 'real' self; and thereby, I enhance the possibility of first recognizing, then receiving genuine love from others. ***Loving people attract loving people.***

November 30
EMBRACING MY LOST SELF

The constant trouble in my home led to my abandoning who I really was. Survival required top priority. *Like one hiding below deck until the storm passed, <u>my real self was overlooked for years.</u>* I rarely checked on its welfare. And when I did check, I was usually distracted by yet another storm.

Storms would become my entire life; my preoccupation. I was either recovering from their devastation or preparing for their next intrusion. I came to believe that crisis prevention was my sole mission. In all of this, *I came to view the interests of my real self as the tiresome curiosities of a pesky little brother;* the nuisance to be avoided.

During this disconnected phase, I would spend frantic amounts of time, going places I really didn't want to go; doing things I really didn't want to do; being with people I really didn't want to do be with. *I acted out my insatiable need for approval, never settling for simply being myself.* My real self was lost in the madness.

I discover the program; a program designed to accomplish one thing: recover my abandoned self. *Step One validates what I have known all along; <u>my life is unmanageable.</u>* I can barely hear my real voice and yet, with the advent of Step Two, I hope for a reunion of sorts with who I truly am; some semblance of sanity; some capacity to act according to my genuine interests; my true nature.

I remain in safe harbor where my real self may emerge; safe harbor where old events can be reviewed; safe harbor where feelings can be expressed; *safe harbor where old ideas can be confronted; safe harbor where new ideas can be incorporated;* safe harbor where the language of nurture is spoken. I embrace who I am. I am not alone. I am in recovery. I am home.

DECEMBER

December 1
REALIZING STEPS SIX AND SEVEN

Reality was not my favorite thing. In fact, I took great measures to avoid it whenever possible. ***The 'grown ups' had proven themselves undependable; and at times, 'down-right' mean.*** I avoided them. I even grew to sometimes hate them; although I didn't realize it.

As a result of their neglect, I alone reasoned my way through all the trouble. ***I would survive no matter what.*** I developed methods and strategies to deal with the unpredictability of it all. I managed reasonably well…
for a five-year-old.

These 'coping' skills would eventually take root as so-called moral principles; basic beliefs upon which I would absolutely rely; basic beliefs that demanded perfect responses; basic beliefs hard wired into my approach to life's conditions. ***Managing these self-inflicted expectations proved impossible.*** I hated myself for not living up to who I thought I should be all the time. Thanks to Steps Four and Five, I have inventoried my old moral system and the *exact nature* of its unrealistic proposition; perfection. ***I want these old, unproductive ideas to be removed.*** And so, I enlist the help of God himself or herself or itself. Whatever self, I enlist it.

Reality is my friend. I ask myself in morning meditation, who am I to meet? What am I to learn today? Events *in the now* trigger old emotions from the past. ***Old ideas are consciously revisited, honestly challenged and with the help of God, abandoned for good if need be.*** My 'shortcomings', the behaviors attached to my old thinking, are being removed. I trust this process, realizing that this task of changing my antiquated thinking and behavior would be impossible, but for the 'grace of God'.

The most detestable people in the universe potentially become my greatest teachers; the beautiful people become my 'angels'. ***This process of interchange and growth is a mystery.*** The *when* and *where* and *how* of all this is none of my business. All that is required is a ***simple willingness*** to embrace the awakening of my truth; my real self.

Now. Let me see. Do I ***REALLY*** want to go to that family reunion this weekend?

December 2
KEEPING MY DREAMS ALIVE

I had plenty of dreams. Some were realistic; some were not. Nevertheless, I had them. Amidst the noise and confusion that was my family, lay my broken dreams. *I didn't realize the loss at the time because of my preoccupation with trying to get through another day, alive.*
Fear eventually misplaced faith.

What I *could* become was replaced with what I *should* become. I spent a lot of time forming and reforming ideas connected with gaining the approval of others. *I gave preference to the development of this 'false' self, abandoning the desires of my 'real' self.*

As time went on, I substituted achievement for genuine passion; success for heart-felt desires; approval of others for true self interest.

I am returning to an uninterrupted relationship with my real self. *No longer plagued with the nagging demands of how I should be all the time in order to be validated, I am free to explore my <u>sovereign true interests.</u>*
I am connecting with my God-given creative nature. I am tuned into who I am and what I want to do. I try new ways in asking for the support I need in order to keep my dreams alive.

Whether my passion lies in cooking, writing, playing tennis, painting, swimming, surfing, sky diving, stamp collecting, bowling, dancing, singing, or attending the opera; no matter what the interest…

<u>*I am free in my pursuit.*</u> I am free to say, hello world!
What's happening here?

December 3
RETAINING MY CAPACITY TO PROMISE

I made a lot of promises over the years, spoken and unspoken. I kept a few.
I needed the approval of others in order to get my own identity needs met.
I was absolutely convinced of my good intentions. *I tried with all my might to be the person all would respect.* During most of my waking hours,
I rehearsed subliminally what an 'end game' would look like;
how I would appear.

Having ditched my real self in exchange for an idealized self, my essential energies were drained. I was obsessed with fulfilling who I should always be; and what I should always do. To complicate matters, these expectations often contradicted one another, often leaving me further 'off balance'.

My effort distracted, my attention diverted, I felt like one caught up in the middle of a tug of war. *I had no confidence in my capacity 'to deliver';* no confidence in my effort to please the important people in my life.

In my recovery process, I am discovering a core self; that part of me that is authentic; that part of me that is genuine. I am verifying my faith in who I am. I am re-establishing myself.

Faith in myself is a precondition for my ability to promise anything.
In other words, I must be available to myself before I can truly
be available to anyone else.

I want and need friends. *Part of being a friend involves trust.* Trust requires making good on certain agreements; certain promises. Whether I promise to meet someone for lunch on Tuesday at one o'clock or loan a friend $400 until payday or always be faithful 'til death do us part', the fundamental requirement of the process is the same: genuine faith in a genuine self; me believing in me.

Now. About that $400.

December 4
SITTING WITH MY CURIOUS SELF

There was little time for reflection in my family. It seemed we were constantly doing, doing, doing; going, going, going. **<u>One crisis bled into another.</u>** Don't look back. Keep moving. Hurry up. Let's go!

I remember those days as the 'onward-through-the-fog' days. Very little was clear, roles were confused; who was the parent in the equation? **<u>Hyper-vigilance seemed to be the order of the day.</u>** Always on guard, I rarely had the opportunity to let down; to simply relax.

I am returning to an emotional space which I once *intuitively* knew; *a space where I consider my 'real' self; my true feelings, my genuine interests.* No longer driven by the push and pull of a dysfunctional need for approval, I am free to rest; free to regroup; free to meditate on new ideas and new paths.

I discover a natural curiosity that comes with being relieved of unnecessary distractions. ***<u>Life unfolds as a series of possibilities;</u>*** *possibilities connected with the core of my being; a core to which I can spontaneously return over and over.* I am my own best friend.

I know me better than anyone. I am not afraid to sit alone. In fact, I rather appreciate the sound of silence.

I creatively visualize where I want to go, who I want to be with and what I want to do. *The time I spend alone, exploring my passion, lays the foundation for becoming who I am.*

I step into each new day with fresh vision and renewed purpose.

December 5
SPOTTING 'IT'

Much of my young life was spent blaming others. ***There were certain 'types' for whom I held no appreciation.*** I even hated them. The 'things' I observed were often detestable. I loathed the very thought of what these people represented.

As I grew older, 'these people' seemed more and more pronounced. I was bolder in expressing my outrage. I believed that I was *justified* in my observations. The list of violations went something like this: weak, sentimental, phony, 'goody-goody', mama's boy; aloof, weird, loner, strange, freaky, nerdy; mean, egotistical, demanding, controlling, selfish.

Whatever the label, I was quick to judge. Although I was unaware of it at the time, my 'righteous' claims on others seemed to go hand in hand with the relentless demands on myself. ***The more I failed, the more I hated myself; the more they failed, the more I hated them.***
Envy and jealousy prevailed.

I am aware of the outrageous demands I place on myself thanks to Steps Four and Five. When events take place and I have strong emotions connected to the behavior of others, *I need look no further than the 'man in the mirror' for the cause of my discontent.* Usually, the very thing I find so abhorrent in others is the very thing I am *unconsciously* rejecting about myself.

When I 'spot it', I usually 'got it'. When overwhelming feelings of disgrace and humiliation about someone else's behavior breaches the wall of my own denial, ***all I need do is employ the practice of Step Ten.*** Programming returns to a 'normal' volume when I can lower the demands on myself, first; and then others.

Sometimes I behave 'right'; sometimes I don't. Sometimes they behave 'right'; sometimes they don't. It's called 'life'. ***People do stupid things all the time. So, do I…(sometimes). People do selfish things all the time. So, do I…(sometimes).***

SPOT IT, YOU GOT IT

December 6
LIVING LIFE FROM THE INSIDE OUT

I felt lost, anxious, and inferior when it came to most situations. Without really knowing it, I had begun to rehearse a solution to this problem. I selected over time what I believed to be an ideal type of person. ***I would mold myself into this ideal, I would become this ideal and I would be fulfilled in this ideal.***

That was the plan. Instead of growing into my genuine self, naturally; ***I would call into service all my core energies to satisfy the relentless demands of a false self.*** By sheer will power, I would become who I should always be in order to always 'belong'.

This idealization gave me a false feeling of significance; even superiority over others. ***This idealized image reigned supreme in my effort to 'fit in'.*** My unique experiences, earlier fantasies, and human abilities all came together to create this custom designed self. I did this for one reason; to be accepted and loved; even revered, ***first by others***; then by myself.

I would live life from the outside in.
Appearance to and performance for others dictated my reality.
This was the ***beginning of the end*** for my 'real' self.

I am changing course in my journey toward 'belonging'. The program gives me options to old ideas. I am moving through the grief associated with 'life' thus far; the losses, the disappointments, the hurts. ***I am looking at the past.*** I am reviewing relationships and the experiences connected to those relationships. I am letting go of old demands brought on by a driven false self.

I reconnect with my real self. I own my feelings from the past.
I gently step into who I am. I own my journey. I am acting according to who I am; how I genuinely think and how I really feel. I am accepted and loved, ***first by myself***; then possibly by others. My insides are matching my outsides. I remain...true to myself.

I am living life; from the inside out.

December 7
RETURNING TO MY DEEP SOURCE (part one)

Of necessity, I abandoned my real self in order to survive. I conformed to the erratic demands of those in authority instead of exploring the genuine curiosities of my young self. ***Maintaining a surface appearance of <u>who I should be</u> was more important than discovering the core depth of who I was.*** My energies, normally spent toward realizing my true interests, were mis-applied in my effort to gain the approval of others; specifically, those upon whom I had to rely.

And thus, my co-dependency was born. Over the years, I would develop an entire 'moral structure' based on what I thought I should always be in order 'make it'. ***I would spend inordinate amounts of time trying to gain the approval of another; sometimes, in abject opposition to becoming my true self.*** This tragic shift in the unfolding of my personal energies proved to be my undoing. I lost myself in the process.

I am making choices not only in relationship with myself, but in relationship with others, as well. ***<u>I create a space wherein I can reconnect unconditionally with my core self; my real self.</u>*** I let go of any expectations surrounding others who are not safe; who are chronically unpredictable. In some cases, I let go entirely of these relationships. Sometimes I walk away. Sometimes I run like hell.

I am preparing for the most important part of my life's journey: the road less travelled; the road to my deep energy; the road to my 'real' self. ***<u>This requires my complete dedication.</u>*** I am uncertain of the perils which lie ahead. I am afraid to look back and yet, look back I must.

The Fourth and Fifth Steps assure the extension of the bridge I am building; the bridge, reconnecting me with the greatest source of strength I have; my true self.

December 8
RETURNING TO MY DEEP SOURCE (part two)

Looking back, I realize that most of the events that shaped my strategy toward becoming my idealized self were comparatively harmless; subtle insinuations, unspoken slights, broken promises, mean spirited comments.

And then, there were those monstrous events: the whippings, the vulgar verbal abuses, the threats, the unwanted sexual advances. ***The sadistic climate to which I was exposed, whether mild or harsh, took its toll over time.*** I lost the connection to me.

I am searching for and returning to my real self. ***I am feeling again.***
I consider the emotions attached to old events; the pleasant times and the terrible times. I am literally re-membering the pieces to the puzzle which is me. I am facing the old structure which kept me alive; the belief system that saved my life. Dysfunctional as this structure is, I now realize and appreciate the horrific degree of urgency that gave birth to this false sense of self. 'Desperate times require desperate measures.' I grieve.

I get angry. I reason things out. I get sad. I accept. ***I take all the time I need.***

I *embrace* all the elements in my current journey in order to face all the associated events of my past. I *recognize* my present relationships as shadow relationships from a time gone by. I *awaken* to the lessons I am to learn; the old ideas I am to release; the new ideas I am to create.
I *trust* the process.
I let it be.

I enter a new phase. I live in the here and now. I am connecting with my genuine desires, my real hopes; my deep passion.
I employ a new faith…in me. I act according to how I truly think and feel.

I know the play and with God's help, I *confidently* take the shot.

December 9
OPENING MY MIND TO NEW BEGINNINGS

I was born into a world defined by death, disease and destruction; the sixties. I maintained a survival mentality as I grew uncomfortably aware of the conflict and upheaval in my own home; due in large part, to my parents' insufferable preoccupation with themselves. ***Naturally, my emotional development was thwarted.*** Rather than developing a solid sense of belonging in the world, I grew to see myself as isolated and helpless in a potentially hostile environment.

As time went on, I honed my survival skills; skills designed to acquire and maintain the approval of another more powerful than I. ***Whether my loyalty was placed with an individual, my family, a group or institution, I was fixated on performing the role which I believed would guarantee my survival.*** And this is where I stayed; anxious and afraid most of the time.

The world is still the same. And yet, the program offers a reasonably safe space where I can return each week. ***I rest in its solid structure of unconditional support.*** The group is my constant 'north'; my guiding compass.

I share freely, knowing that the boundaries of the group prevent anyone from interrupting, judging, fixing or otherwise, nullifying my own experience in dealing with this disease. ***I feel my feelings.***
I am at ease most of the time.

My fear of being all alone in a cold and unreceptive world no longer hounds my every waking moment. Little by little, I am trusting others in the group. ***I take comfort in knowing that there is a solid way out of all the trouble into which I was born.***

Every time I attend a meeting, I am subtly reminded of the new beginnings represented in my extended family seated all around the room; my extended family that I am growing to trust and appreciate.

December 10
TRUTSTING A HIGHER FULFILLMENT

Growing up in a dysfunctional family restricted my emotional growth.
I had only three essential ways to deal with the conflict.
I could give into the those in 'control'. I could resist. I could avoid.
Sometimes the prevailing circumstances required that I do
all three which further complicated my world.

In short, I was emotionally conflicted. Eventually, I would select one main
way; and so, 'resolve' the internal battle.

The more intense my anxiety, the greater I blindly obeyed the demands
of the emerging 'one main way'. I hated myself when I failed to fulfill the
'one main way'. Failure was not an option. Whether I chose a standard of
complying or rebelling or remaining aloof, there was always hell to pay
when I failed to meet the standard. *This IRRATIONAL HATE stemmed from an emerging self, false in nature, hell bent to survive.*
I grew to not only hate myself; I grew to resent others, as well.

I am on new footing. I function from a place inside where I am *celebrating*
my real self. With God's help, I am actively involved in changing the old
demands emanating from my false self. *No longer driven by hidden fears of not surviving, I am free to lighten up.* I am growing more tolerant of myself
and others. The hard-wired, neurotic notions are being removed.

Is this happening overnight? I wish! *My process of recovery has a course of its own and moves at its own pace.* However, there are many payoffs along
the way: a return to my real self, an awareness of my true feelings, a genuine
interest in the prospect of simply being me,
a shot at becoming who I am.

I trust a higher fulfillment; win, lose or draw. I trust the process.

December 11
GROWING

The environment into which I was born was unhealthy. As a result, I got sick. And stayed sick. I denied it for a long time. I looked OK from the outside and for the most part, performed very well. Like a lively young oak, I grew as best I could; all things considered. From the very beginning, a vine of clinging ivy restrained my every move. ***Encumbered with the weight of dysfunctional family distractions, I had little chance of becoming my real self.*** Healthy conditions essential for becoming my real self were sadly compromised. Real growth had no meaning.

The capacity to become a healthy young oak was in the seed and yet, a tree only flourishes if it is placed in conditions *necessary* for growth. ***In other words, I became an oak tree alright; but I had been robbed of my full potential.*** I had to settle for being covered in ivy half my life.

The clinging ivy is dying; the old ideas and unrealistic claims, fading away. The main root has been cut; the 'exact nature of my wrongs', my demand for perfection, removed. ***I am free to grow.*** I need good soil, plenty of fresh water and a lot of natural sunlight. ***I go to meetings.*** I rely on the Gardener to keep the ivy from coming back. I am nurtured to my very core.
I am supported mentally, physically, spiritually, and emotionally.

The meetings, by their very nature, are named among some of the safest places on earth. 'Safe' is a *good* thing. ***I need to feel safe in order to keep growing.*** In order to keep growing,
I need other people.

With God's help, ***I am becoming my own best advocate.*** I make choices that will *in no way* harm my own growth. I am becoming my own best friend.

Birds of a feather flock together…ooops, wrong idiom.
The fruit doesn't fall too far from the tree. There, all better.
Now, where ***DID*** I put those pruning shears?

December 12
NURTURING MY EMOTIONAL LIFE

Life in my family was stormy. Somedays were more 'exciting' than others. At some point, my life ceased being fun. I grew more and more anxious as time passed. ***I obsessed about events over which I had no control, believing that somehow my behavior determined the outcome of everything.***
I seemed to be nervous all the time; worried about what might go wrong.

Nobody had informed me that the unavailable, sometimes sadistic, behavior of my family had nothing to do with me. It had everything to do with the disease. I would shut down my emotions in order to get through the erratic days. ***I closed myself off from myself.*** I distracted myself with mood altering substances, compulsive behaviors and co-dependent relationships in order to establish a 'false' serenity.

Today, I am connecting with my true self. I avoid storms and yet, the storms still seem to find me. I genuinely want to know how I am feeling in the middle of it all. I want to fully experience my life and all the emotions that go with it. ***<u>I want to feel what I am feeling at the time that I am feeling it;</u>*** happy, sad, angry, joyful, hurt, outraged, puzzled, curious, romantic; all of it!

Remaining 'friendly' toward my genuine experience is a challenge. ***Nurturing my emotional life requires a willingness to remain awake even while riding out the storms of my life.*** I no longer settle for one 'fix-all' emotion, ***serenity***. No longer closed off from myself, no longer terrified; ***I embrace all that is me.***

Chasing serenity is like trying to catch a butterfly in the middle of a hurricane. ***You can do it, but it's a LOT easier to just wait for the storm to pass.*** Now. Where *did* I put my butterfly net?

December 13
BEING HAPPY

Without really knowing it, I traded freedom for 'security' at a very young age. The conditions into which I was born demanded it. I believed that I could control the world around me and to some extent, I could for a while; ***but the time came when no amount of 'control' could make my parents available and genuinely nurturing.***

Apparently, I didn't get the memo that this 'control' strategy was doomed from the start. I would continue for years believing that by controlling events on the outside, I could fix my feelings on the inside. That is, I could one day find 'happiness'. ***I shifted all my natural energies.*** Instead of allowing my real self to unfold naturally, I had to assert the demands of an emerging false self; a self that dictated who I should always be in order to get what I desperately wanted; approval, validation and love.

The program is leading me back to my core self. I realize that my God-given ability to act, this power unto itself, creates a natural desire to *use* this power. The failure to use this power results in dysfunction and unhappiness. In other words, I have legs; but, if I were not allowed to use my legs, I would feel limited and frustrated. ***By acting in unison with my legitimate interests, I grow to realize my true self.*** I don't do 'limited' and 'frustrated' anymore.

I am using my legs. I am stepping from the shadow of a tyrannical survival self into the light of my real self. I embrace my genuine interests. I act on my own behalf. I naturally validate who I am. ***I approve the gift of my own energies; energies employed for the express purpose of being me.*** When I act according to my genuine beliefs and my true passions, I usually feel productive. Regardless of the outcome, I find joy in simply remaining true to myself.

Being me IS being happy. Being me is what I do best.

December 14
STAYING IN 'MY LANE'

One of the illusions I carried prior to finding the rooms went something like this: ***I should always be able to read a situation and behave accordingly.*** I put a lot of stock in this old idea because it had worked for me as a child. I needed to feel safe and so, I quickly adjusted to the circumstances around me; the conditions outside myself. I grew very skilled at manipulating my environment.

Whether that looked like helping around the house, standing up to a bully or just disappearing somewhere, ***one factor played a key role in it all: my reaction was always 'others' driven.*** Over time, loyalties would become divided. Conflicts would arise. Pleasing everybody all the time seemed impossible. Things got 'complicated'. I was figuratively 'all over the road'; darting here, stopping there, speeding ahead, slowing down, checking the rearview, swerving into oncoming traffic. I was overwhelmed.

I am retiring from the life management business; the business of managing other people's affairs. I am keeping the focus on myself. I am not in this world to save, protect and govern. In the process of becoming who I am, do I sometimes help others? Do I sometimes fight for what I believe in? Do I sometimes keep to myself to avoid conflict? Yes, on all counts. I do what I do because it is who I am.
<u>I am in this world to be who I am, naturally.</u>

I am free to fully concentrate on my own journey. I afford others the privilege ***<u>and the right</u>*** to be on their own journey, as well. ***No longer attached to the idea that my survival depends on the approval of another, I move with grace and spontaneity down the backroads and highways of my life.*** I go where I want to go. I do what I want to do. The autonomy I give myself, I give to others. ***I LIVE AND LET LIVE.***
Now. Where the-dickens did I put that map?

December 15
ENGAGING MY OWN AUTONOMY

I was convinced that something was terribly wrong with me and my family. On the surface, I had no idea of the core problem and yet, deep inside, I knew. I felt isolated. I felt afraid. ***I needed 'them' in order to be me.*** Emotional dependency seemed to feed on itself. I needed approval in order to exist. In order to exist, I needed approval. In order to stay alive, I had to perform well. I had to not wake the dragon.

Avoiding conflict became the primary purpose in my young life. I literally sacrificed myself, employing all my human faculties in order to do what I thought I had to do. ***One way or another, I would gain their 'love'; or at the very least, their 'respect'.*** One way or another, I would survive.

And so, I did survive; but there remained a problem even after I left home. I would come to see others just as I had seen my parents; the ones with all the power. ***Being rejected is a fearful thing.*** Whether as the one in 'control' or the one being 'controlled', I lived in silent terror that I would somehow be left behind. Afraid of losing 'everything', I became morbidly dependent on people, places and things.

The Steps guide me toward a life of interdependency. I need to love and be loved. I need to be included. ***I need to relate to others and, at the same time, retain my own integrity.*** I re-establish a core self by taking the Twelve Steps. I move beyond survival, into creative expression. I am naturally autonomous, free and independent; capable of directing my own thoughts, feelings and actions.

I respond to life in accord with my genuine interests. I am no longer dependent on one person or institution for the fulfillment of all my needs. ***I am solving problems; acting on the solutions; and becoming who I truly am,*** one minute, one hour…

ONE DAY AT A TIME.

December 16
RELYING ON GOD

In my formative years, the 'adults in the room' were like 'gods'. Having no understanding of my environment, I was at their mercy. *It seemed simple; follow the 'rules' and all would be well.* Trying to follow the rules in an alcoholic family was like trying to roller skate in a buffalo herd; frustrating and sometimes dangerous.

The erratic behavior, the broken promises, the verbal abuses, the physical abuses, the acts of neglect; all these dysfunctional elements took their toll. <u>*I came to despise the gods.*</u> I even vowed that I would
never be like the gods.

I find the rooms of recovery. There are no gods; only mere mortals like I am, trying to make sense of what the hell happened back there; no one to obey, no one to follow and no one to worship. *I am free to take as much or as little as I like in our weekly discussions.* Admittedly, the group itself is a power greater than I am; and yet, I am not compelled to accept anything coming out of the group; *even the literature.*

Step Three states, 'Made a decision to turn our will and our lives over to the care of God, *as we understood Him'*. I reluctantly approach Step Three. *Some say, Step Three is a mere indication of my willingness to take the rest of the Steps.* The Step itself requires no action at all;
only a simple prayer: 'God help me.'
I begin my journey through the Steps.

I complete the Steps. *I ask myself, 'Am I better off now than I was before I found recovery?'* The response is a resounding YES.

God, as I understand God, is exactly that; *AS I UNDERSTAND GOD.*

I come to rely on a God of MY understanding; in my own time, in my own way.

December 17
BATTLING FOR HIGHER GROUND

As 'war' unfolded in my family, I 'buddied up' with a survival self. This
'friend' was like a big brother in the beginning, showing me 'the ropes',
laying out strategies, making plans, establishing solid approaches.
I followed willingly. We navigated many battles. And finally,
one day, I left home. I had survived the war!

Funny thing; my 'friend', my 'big brother'? He hadn't been informed that
the war was, in fact, over. I was stuck with my 'buddy'. Everything and
everybody appeared as they had seemed in war. Losing my real perspective,
I continued to act and react to the dictates of this shadow self.

I created a whole belief system around how myself and others should always
behave. *I obeyed the commands of this false self with unquestioned
loyalty.* My every move judged by its false standards, my every action
rooted in its unrealistic demands, I abandoned my real self on this internal
'battlefield'.

Of necessity, the recovery of my genuine self, left behind, involves a true
fight; *the fight for my very life.* I know that the fight is between my real self
and the imposter, my false self. I know that the fight *is and will be* ongoing.
*All the common characteristics outlined in the Laundry List are outward
symptoms of an inward dis-ease.* These symptoms are the manifest
expressions of the fight; the fight which my healthy self puts up
against the crippling influences of my old 'buddy'; now dictator.

I am bivouacked at Fort Function; my weekly recovery group. I am,
once again, preparing for war. This time I have a true plan, the Steps.
I have genuine support, my brothers and sisters in recovery.
There will be many battles waged for the higher ground;
for the reclaiming of my true self. I can face them all,

Some fights I will win; some I will lose. I ask myself, is it truly worth all
the trouble? The answer: what is life's profit, were I to gain the whole world
and lose my own soul?

December 18
EXPERIENCING PLEASURE

The tension in my family would sometimes build to the point of radical explosion; sometimes the tension simmered just underneath the surface. *Some measurable level of anxiety permeated our family's every waking moment.* Naturally, there were moments of relief. It usually centered around some form of distraction: eating, watching television, playing board games, going to the mall, giving parties and the like. We called it pleasure.

Some of these forms of distraction evolved into full dependency. *The need to relieve ongoing stress literally grew at an insatiable rate.* I became an alcoholic. To further complicate matters, these efforts at distraction were grounded in emerging emotional needs, as well.

These emotional 'desires' dominated most everything I tried to do. *On occasion, I would get the outcome I hoped for; and yet, the satisfaction was often short-lived.* I was chronically dissatisfied with myself. I yearned for escape. And so, these passionate cravings and unconscious reactions persisted.

I am returning to the true satisfaction of simply being who I am. The Steps have given me a life. *I am responding in ways that compliment my best interest.* I actively lower my stress level. I am slowing down. I consciously experience my five senses: touch, taste, smell; seeing and hearing. I recognize false distractions for what they are; false.
I am willing to change.

True pleasure is a result of; not a reaction to. *I think and feel and desire. I act accordingly.* I am present. I have plans and yet, I stay in the moment. I am at ease. I am productive. *I connect with others who are safe.*

I am hungry. I eat. I am thirsty. I drink. I am tired. I rest.
I create and trust my own rhythm.
I take joy in being who I am.

December 19
LEARNING TO LOVE AGAIN

I came into this world loving. I remember loving. It was a natural thing. My world soon darkened, and I had to defend myself. **Love took a back seat to survival.** And so, the years progressed along the lines of a sometimes cold and calculating need to stay alive. The demands of the day in my dysfunctional family drowned out my natural ability to love.

The program invites me into a world of unconditional support. The program says I am unique in my own genuine way. ***The program helps me find my true self.*** The program celebrates my discovery all along the way. The program is available.

I am returning to love. I know my journey and in knowing my journey, I respect my history. I honor my effort in recovery; my *struggle* to realize my genuine self. I truly care for myself, naturally. I respond honestly to my own life. I am productive.

I am allowing others to love me, as well. I tell a close friend of my struggles. They get to know me. And in knowing me, they naturally respect how far I have come. <u>**They care.**</u> And it shows in their eyes. They encourage my autonomy. They invite my transparency.
I trust them.

I express love in many combinations of thought, word and deed: *a lingering ear, a gentle touch, a thoughtful question;* a hug, a handshake, a gift, a dinner; a cool drink to quench the thirst on a hot summer's day, a warm coat to ward off the bleak mid-winter's chill, a fleeting smile to a passer-by on a crowded city sidewalk.

The program, in its own mysterious way, brings me full circle to what I have known from the beginning: <u>**there is hope, there is faith and there is love.**</u>

The greatest of these is love.

December 20
MEETING NEW OPPORTUNITIES FEARLESSLY

Almost from the onset, my young life was governed by fear. I adjusted accordingly. What other choice did I have? There seemed to be a lurking sense of caution as each day unfolded. ***Uncertain of a solid source of support, I rarely felt 'comforted' in returning home.*** In fact, my family was the epicenter of my worries. Trusting my family was like jumping out of plane with no back up parachute…*every day.*

It seemed that with each new endeavor came a subset of anxiety. I grew to see myself as all alone in the world and rarely felt confident enough to ask for help. *I was afraid of appearing defective.* I had to guess at what 'normal' looked like. My talent and ability compromised; I faked my way through most situations. I functioned with *no self-assurance* for fear of being rejected.

Under the circumstances, I performed amazingly well most of the time. However, little failures were big deals. ***I judged myself harshly.*** *I would try harder next time.* And I did; until one day, I ceased trying altogether. I went from being super responsible to being super irresponsible, and then back again, over and over.

I am now on new footing. I am taking the Steps. The Fourth Step invites me to look at the fundamental ideas that drive me to do what I do. ***The Fifth Step identifies the exact nature of my ongoing dysfunctional behavior that sets me up;*** the behavior that perpetuates constant disappointment and anguish toward myself and others; that 'exact nature' of my 'wrongs' being, ***the unbridled need for perfection based on irrational fear.***

Yes, my unbridled need for perfection based on irrational fear is the CORE of all my problems. I am willing to have God remove all these exaggerated demands in Steps Six and Seven.

In short, I am accepting the inescapable truth. I am only human. ***NEWS FLASH: I make mistakes.*** Sometimes I perform perfectly; sometimes I don't. And when I don't, I can usually ask for a 'do over' without fear of rejection. I am unlearning the old ideas that hold me back. I can face the future unafraid as the *fully capable* person that I am. Now. Where the *dickens* did I put that back up parachute?

December 21
AWAKENING TO A LIFE BEYOND PLEASURE

During all the trouble in my dysfunctional family, there were moments of pleasure designed to distract us from the clamoring symptoms associated with the disease; the blaming, the shaming, the resentment. ***Anything was a welcome relief:*** eating, going to the movies, going out on the town, working on a project, playing music, reading, exercising, going on vacations.

All were pleasurable and yet, one fundamental element was missing; a genuine sense of being happy. As George Washington once said: As entertaining as it might be to attend a firing squad,
it's hard to be especially happy when you're a potential target.

Today is different. I see myself as a fully functioning human being; no shame, no blame. ***I see myself as a person surrounded by support; the essential support I need in order to be who I truly am.***
God makes this possible. Having completed the first nine Steps, I enter a new phase wherein life is more than satisfying a mere hunger. It is about acquiring an appetite.

I return to my unrestricted self. I embrace abundance. I awaken to my own thoughts, my own dreams, my own feelings. ***I apply all my energies in one concerted effort toward realizing my true self.*** I am productive.
I anticipate a visualized outcome of my true interests.
I act in accordance with the vision.

I am free to celebrate my effort. I savor the moment of a 'job well done'. I am alive. I move through the day with ease and confidence, meeting the people I need to meet in order to learn what I need to learn. My life unfolds, as one growth experience leads to another and another.

I feel my freedom and productiveness with joy; pure energy; pure light.
I awaken to a life beyond pleasure. I awaken to my own happiness.

I awaken to my own joy.

December 22
DIGGING OUT

Without knowing it, I had buried myself alive while growing up in a dysfunctional family. Of necessity, I had to cover up and protect that vulnerable part of myself that would have otherwise developed naturally. **<u>I was disabled in the pursuit and realization of my true self.</u>** Due to these outrageous conditions, I labored non-stop to avoid rejection.
My survival depended on it. I lived on high alert.

During this 'developmental' time, I felt conflicted when it came to forming relationships. **Whether compliant, defiant or aloof, I rarely relaxed into who I was becoming.** On the contrary, I grew extremely anxious about being myself with other people. I saw people as either utterly superior or grossly inferior to who I was. My sense of belonging deteriorated.

Somehow, I needed a way to lift myself above feeling estranged. And thus, I created a false self. *The transfer of power shifted from my real self with its inner most thoughts and emotions to an imagined idealized self;* a self that incorporated a system of absolutes; absolutes which would give me a hold on life, an identity.

As one trapped underground following the collapse of a tunnel, I am digging my way out of the rubble which is my life. *I can see light up above on good days; other days, total darkness.* I light a candle and keep digging.
Somedays it seems I am making no progress.
I discover others trapped as I am.
We dig together.

Steps One, Two and Three provide a sense of reality, hope and direction.
The reality: I am stuck.   *The hope: I can make it.*
The direction: I can ask for help.   I am not alone.

The Fourth Step is my shovel. This is where the work begins.
<u>I embrace the mission which lies before me, as only the dying can.</u>

This is my life. This is my time. This is my choice.

December 23
LETTING IT SNOW

Part of the problem with my growing up with alcoholic parents was the constant shift of boundaries. The capricious revision of roles led to uncertainty and this uncertainty led to a blind enmeshment.

As a result, **<u>I had no solid identity.</u>** I placed loyalty where loyalty was undeserved, hoping to gain favor. I looked to others in order to define myself. The outside world determined my fate.

My best interest hinged on the not-so-small task of trying to control this 'outside' world. ***At the very least, I could manipulate the actions of others so that I would survive another day.*** This would become my great obsession; control.

The program gives me an alternative; ***the concept of detachment***; the concept of letting others be ***who they are*** and ***where they are*** without my interfering. I find this to be a rather novel idea; an idea which, at first glance, appears impossible to carry out. And yet, I am finding that this is, in fact, the easier, softer way when it comes to relating to others. ***I can let others manage their own lives and in turn, I have more energy to manage mine.***

I can establish boundaries. I can write my own rules. I own my thoughts and emotions. ***I 'need' the validation of no one person.*** I will survive. I have a healthy respect for the world outside myself. I allow the world to be the world. I am loyal to myself, first and foremost.

It snows in my part of the country. This is an annual fact. I cannot control this force of nature. I cannot manipulate the wiles of winter. However, ***I CAN take care of myself.*** I buy a good snow shovel.
I let it snow. And then, I start shoveling.

'God grant me the serenity to accept the things I cannot change; the courage to change the things I can; and the wisdom to know the difference.'

December 24
RELEASING THE STRESS

There lingered a level of incomprehensible stress for hours, sometimes days, following family fights. And yet, we seldom talked about what had happened. ***We rarely took the time to talk things over.*** We didn't 'resolve' the problem; we denied the problem. As a result, I compressed my fear and anxiety. I pretended that all was well. I moved on.

I stacked anger on top of anger. For years, I said nothing. I 'checked out' by distracting myself with a combination of activity which usually netted the intended result; to 'forget' about what had happened; to put it out of my mind. ***Over the years, I tried not to think about a lot of things that had happened in my family.*** Any event that remotely resembled the tension of the past, I tried to avoid. And what I couldn't avoid, I endured; pretending again, that all was well.

Closed off from myself and afraid most of the time, I created a world with limited options; but a world, nevertheless, into which I could always retreat; a world where I could imagine that, in fact, all was well; despite the evidence to the contrary. ***I lived in this tug of war with fantasy for years.*** I was exhausted.

The program gives me a safe place to talk things over; a safe place to express my anger; a safe place to resolve problems. ***I am free to express my concerns, my worries and conflicts.*** I let go of the unhealthy distractions that keep me isolated. I move toward people who are safe; people who are available; people who understand my struggle. I ask for help.

Anger can be an early indication that I need to set healthier boundaries. Anger is my friend. It tells me when something in my world is not OK. I can respond to what I need honestly. What do I need to do right now to take care of me? And then, I do it. ***Whether I call a friend, go to a meeting, take a break, go for a run, take the day off; whatever I choose to do, I put MY welfare first.***

I take care of my emotional needs. I take care of me.

December 25
TIDINGS OF COMFORT

Christmas had finally arrived, but not in the way that a twelve-year-old might have hoped. *Awakened at two o'clock in the morning to the horrific sound of adults screaming at one another, I slipped out of bed and crept to the end of my grandparents' long dark hall.* I listened intently, crouching at the foot of a closed door, where a thin ribbon of light from the other side etched the growing division between their world and mine.

Worried and afraid, I returned to my bed, closed my eyes and tried to not think about it. What could have happened? Why all the uproar? I fell back asleep, awakening later to what was a virtually empty house. My mother, my uncles, my aunts, my cousins; all gone. Only my grandparents remained.

Merry f@#$*&^ Christmas! *I was pissed.* We had breakfast, opened presents and carried on as though nothing had happened.
Mother returned later that night only to leave again.

The program gives me a 'do-over' of my life. I am awakening to a new Christmas Day. My sense of awe and wonder is back. As I maintain a safe world, I grow closer to myself and others. *My sense of trust is enhanced as I say 'no' to the old; and 'yes' to the new.* There is no long dark hallway.
There are no people screaming in the night.
My life is worth more than settling for that.
It always was.

I embrace new loyalties to those who are, in fact, loving and supportive. *I am, in turn, capable of giving back that which I have freely received; unconditional positive regard;* unconditional positive regard for all mankind. Everybody hurts. Everybody is challenged in some way.

There is a bright red Cardinal perched at my feeder.
      Laden with snow are the boughs of a tall cedar.
A cup of tea at my elbow and a fire burning bright.
      Merry Christmas to all and to all, a goodnight!

(I stole that last line) Bad Santa.

December 26
REVIEWING ALL THE OPTIONS

By the time I found the rooms of recovery, I felt utterly restricted.
My options had run out. Without really knowing it, I had locked myself
into an extreme approach in dealing with life's inevitable conflicts.

***The greater the tension, the more rigid my expectations for myself
and others had become.*** Little mistakes had the potential of
igniting a powder keg of thunderous emotions.

To make matters worse, I had grown skeptical of ever finding a way out of
all the mess. Life had become one big unfolding problem for which there
seemed no solution. ***The distractions upon which I had relied for comfort
appeared to be losing their effectiveness.*** In fact, some had become toxic.
Some had become chronic. I knew I had reached the end of the line.
How much longer could I go on?

Upon arriving at my first meeting, I felt an immediate release from the
persistent worry that had grown to dominate most of my waking thoughts.
At least for the one hour, I felt hopeful that there was, in fact, a way out.
The more meetings I attended, the more confident I grew.

I am months into the program. The Steps are still a mystery; and yet, there is
no mystery in my feeling better. ***I find comfort and reassurance by getting
to know others in recovery.*** They, too, have faced and are facing some of
the same problems with which I struggle. There is strength in numbers. I can
use all the strength I can muster.

I am years into the program. Most of the Steps are behind me now. I am
experiencing a new freedom; a new happiness. ***I still have problems and
yet, <u>I have all kinds of options, all kinds of ideas and all kinds of support.</u>***
I am no longer stuck. Step Eleven works every time…every time I use it.
I have the power to review all my options today and today,
all the options are on the table.

Now. Let me see. Shall I go to the bakery first or the gym?

December 27
CHOOSING MY CHOICES

I had few actual 'choices' growing up in an alcoholic home. I was a victim of the disease from the 'git go'. *My parents' attitude toward me was determined in large part by their own neurotic needs and reactions.* Whether they were dominating, overprotective, intimidating, irritable, over-exacting, over-indulgent, erratic, partial to others, hypocritical, absent or indifferent (just to name a few), *they were always emotionally unavailable on some level.* I felt as though I were all alone in the world. Not a good place to be for a child.

For the better part of life, my early childhood experiences determined practically everything I did. I believe my fate was predetermined. And by that, I simply mean this: *most of my so-called 'choices' were mere reactions* which I had developed as a 'hard-wired' approach to surviving life in an unlivable world.

In the beginning, I chose the 'choice'.
Then, the 'choice' chose the 'choice'.
And finally, the 'choice' chose me.

Thankfully, I am returning to my true self in a conscious way. I feel my feelings spontaneously. I can talk about my deepest emotions. I can make decisions based on how I genuinely think. *I respond to who I truly am and what I really need without fear of rejection; without the lurking terror of being abandoned.* I am, after all, a survivor; a champion.
I *CAN* take care of myself. The worst is behind me now.

I am no longer a volunteer victim. That role simply doesn't work anymore. Remaining true to myself, I move toward those who are available, nurturing and reasonably sane. *And if circumstances will not allow a healthy distance away from those who ARE unavailable, toxic and insane, I detach in any way I can; by any means possible.* Better choices lead to better outcomes; and better outcomes lead to a happier life.

At the end of the day, I am the 'sum total' of all my choices.

December 28
VALIDATING THE AUTONOMY OF MYSELF AND OTHERS

I moved through several strategies when it came time to consciously deal with my family. Initially, I had to 'hurry up' to grow up. In other words, *I usurped the role of 'adult' because the adults in my world were often physically absent or emotionally unavailable.* Family problems became 'my' problems. We were enmeshed. I believed that I could 'fix it'.

Further on, I grew disenchanted with my main solution and I moved on to another approach. *<u>I would avoid the family altogether; withdraw.</u>* This only seemed to work. I still carried the idea that my parents' behavior was an indication of who I was. I couldn't get far enough away to 'fix' how I felt about me; ashamed and humiliated.

My final attempt at 'resolving' my self-esteem issues resided in the idea that I could perform in such a way that I would command the respect of all, family included. I would, therefore, be 'loved' and included; a simple hope I had carried since childhood. *At the height of my 'success', I still felt insignificant, alone and afraid.* Gaining the approval of others in order to establish a genuine sense of belonging was clearly not working. But what else was I to do?

The Steps enable reconnection; the recovery of my true self. I am making peace with my history. The challenges I have faced and surmounted over the course of this life make me a champion. I recognize the unique struggles of others also. *I am who I am, due in large part to a unique constellation of events, most of which at their very core, are common to all.*

I appreciate my sovereign journey and the independent journey of others. I reverence life's unifying struggles. I recognize my singular human travail, as well. *<u>I establish my own identity.</u> I allow others the dignity of establishing theirs.*

December 29
TAKING IN THE BIG PICTURE

Dashing from one crisis to the next left me with little perspective on 'reality'. *The sheer exhaustion of trying to keep up with all the demands of a 'situation' made <u>dealing</u> with the 'situation' impossible.*

I had a short-term plan and a long-term plan. Often, the two were in direct conflict, complicating matters even further. And what of the past?
The past was something to be forgotten and avoided.

Avoiding the past and living for the future left me unable to live in the moment, the day or sometimes, even the week. *There were times when a small mistake rendered me utterly disabled.* In my mind, I hadn't simply made a mistake, I *WAS* a mistake. It seemed that I was a failure and all the mistakes simply validated what I already mistakenly believed;
I was a loser, a phony, an imposter.

Today, I know that I am none of those things. I am revising my exaggerated expectations regarding what I can do in order to achieve what I want to accomplish. With the unfolding of each day, I review the 'high points' and 'low points' of the day. I can own the 'wins' *AND* the 'losses'.

<u>*Who I am is no longer dependent on how well I perform all the time.*</u>
Sometimes I get rave reviews; sometimes not so much.

I take the time to rate my day. Very simply, on a scale of one to ten, I grade the day according to the lows and the highs. 'One' signifies a day reflecting a 'hell on earth' and 'ten' indicates a day more akin to a 'little slice of heaven'. *All things considered, my rating usually falls somewhere between a 'one' and a 'ten'.* I am gaining a more realistic feel for how things are going.

I relax and take in the big picture. Rare is the day when I haven't done *SOMETHING* right.

December 30
CHANGING LOCATION

When I was growing up, I had no choice but to remain enmeshed with a family hell bent on destroying itself. Whether it meant sitting through icy cold moments at the dinner table, cleaning up the raucous mess from the night before, waiting by the door in hopes that they would come home or lying awake alone in my room, ruminating about previous disappointments; *I felt utterly alone in a world that was becoming potentially more and more hostile by the day.*

The very fabric of my being was devolving. I was imploding, spiritually and emotionally. *Rather than integrating into a world where I knew that I was loved and supported, I was disintegrating into an existence where I believed myself to be freakish and all alone.*
I was stuck.

Having found the rooms of recovery, I am stepping into a new world of mutual help and support. I say no to people and institutions that insist on abusing others.

My moving toward those who remain toxic and unavailable is like the alcoholic taking the first drink; not a good idea.
<u>*I can longer afford the 'excitement'.*</u>

Like my friend back home who stood for days outside his favorite café, waiting for his favorite burger, refusing to accept the
'CHANGING LOCATION' sign on the front door.
There are people in my life who refuse to accept that
I have, in fact, moved on. <u>*I have changed location.*</u>

I am responsible for my own welfare. I have choices. *I don't have to be enmeshed with anyone hell bent on destroying themselves and the ones around them.*

I move with a new freedom. I move to a new location… *recovery*.

December 31
GOING PLACES

The future, for the most part, seemed bleak as I stumbled through the early years of my life. I feared looking forward and I dared not look back. **<u>My life had become an unending problem.</u>** I muddled through, hoping for something good to happen, but always fearing the worst.

Even during the 'good' years of my life, I had a difficult time seeing the progress that I perhaps *had* made. **There seemed to be a 'not-good-enough' cloud hanging over my head most of the time.**

This final day of the year, I mark the time that I have spent in the rooms of recovery. *Experience* is everything to me. Indeed, my *strength* depends on it. And from this mounting strength, I build *hope*.

Who I am the first week in the rooms is not the same person I am at one year. Who I am in the first year, is not who I am in my second year; nor am I the same person at year three or four or thirty-four.

<u>The PROGRAM is changing me.</u> I am going places: spiritually, physically, mentally and emotionally. This hope leaves me eager for the coming year's adventure and the *certain* growth that will accompany my future, whatever it may bring.

'Truly my soul waits upon God: from Him comes my salvation. He only is my rock and my salvation.'